2925

Frieda
7/9/91

D0936864

Bearing the Unbearable

SUNY Series in Modern Jewish Literature and Culture
Sarah Blacher Cohen, Editor

Bearing the Unbearable

Yiddish and Polish Poetry
in the Ghettos and Concentration Camps

❏❏❏

Frieda W. Aaron

Foreword by David G. Roskies

State University of New York Press

Published by
State University of New York Press, Albany

© 1990 State University of New York

For information, address State University of New York
Press, State University Plaza, Albany, N.Y., 12246

Library of Congress Cataloging-in-Publication Data

Aaron, Frieda W., 1928–
    Bearing the unbearable : Yiddish and Polish poetry in the ghettos
and concentration camps / Frieda W. Aaron.
        p. cm. — (SUNY series in modern Jewish literature and
culture)
    Bibliography : p.
    Includes index.
    ISBN 0–7914–0247–9.
    1. Yiddish poetry—Poland—History and criticism.   2. Polish
poetry—Jewish authors—History and criticism.   3. Holocaust, Jewish
(1939–1945), in literature.   4. Concentration camps in literature.
I. Title.   II. Series.
PJ5141.2.A27   1990
839'.0916209358—dc20   89–11593
                                                        CIP

10 9 8 7 6 5 4 3 2 1

*To the memory
of my father, Symcha Wakszlak, who died in Majdanek,
and to all the fathers killed in the Holocaust.*

❑ ❑ ❑

*To the memory
of my mother, Michla Wakszlak, who survived not only
for herself but for all the mothers who did not.*

Contents

Foreword   ix

Acknowledgments   xi

Introduction   1

Part One
Poetry as Documentation

1. In the Beginning   19

2. The Great Chain of Being   39

Part Two
Morale, Moral Resistance, and the Crisis of Faith

3. Breaking through the Wall of Silence   71

4. The Cultural Ferment and the Moral Mandate   95

Part Three
Issues of Resistance

5. Poetics of Exhortation   133

6. Word into Deed   159

7. S.O.S.   173

Epilogue   189

Notes   213

Selected Bibliography   223

Index   235

Foreword

The message of Frieda Aaron's book is in the order of her presentation. For she has put the poems first, her own life experience at the end. As painful as it is to revisit the nightmares she actually lived, unravelling the hidden meanings of Holocaust poetry is still more difficult. Indeed, the poetry requires a mental curriculum almost as exacting as the study of medieval Hebrew poetry, or of the Talmud.

First one must know the external facts: the precise chronology of mass murder; the names of every occupied town, city, and street, since every ghetto street was a world-in-miniature; the difference between ghetto, labor camp, and death camp; the technology of death and starvation. Then one must know how the people singled out for destruction organized their inner lives: the soup kitchens and schools, the concerts and poetry contests, the underground bunkers and resistance movements. Then one must know the languages spoken and written by Europe's Jews—and since no one can master all of them, one should start with Yiddish, Hebrew, Polish, and German. Then, since artistic expression draws in equal measure from earlier art as from observable reality, one must be thoroughly at home in classical and modern Jewish and European culture. Having done all that, one can begin to evaluate the satiric broadsides, the sentimental lyrics, the lullabyes, the epics, and the hymns written and sometimes performed in the valley of death.

The two representative poets of Frieda Aaron's book are well and carefully chosen: Abraham Sutzkever and Wladyslaw Szlengel are almost extact contemporaries, both schooled in the idioms of modern European poetry and both thrust headlong into the vortex of their people's destruction. Each was cut off by the war from his major source of creative inspiration: Sutzkever from the forests and fields; Szlengel from the bustling cultural life of the Polish metropolis. Each turned that painful separation into a powerful metaphor at once intensely personal and exemplary of the people as a whole. As the scope of the destruction became ever more apparent, each poet pushed his poetic medium to its uttermost limit.

Discussed here in more thorough a fashion than has ever been done in any language, these ghetto poets shed light on the full range of poetic selfexpression during the Holocaust. Because Aaron doesn't limit herself only to the best or most carefully wrought poetic works, the reader can begin to appreciate the multilingual culture of the Jews as defined on its own terms, with its own set of internal symbols, allusions, and illusions. Scattered throughout her informed readings are invaluable data as to how these poems actually came into being: where they were sung and performed and how they were received by their immediate audience. Most memorable is her personal portrait of Gutka, the barracks poet of Skarzysko. Hers were the kind of songs that many readers will recall from their own youth in summer camps. But in these camps, designed for annihilation, the very act of composing an old-new song was a radical affirmation of life.

Separating the old from the new is perhaps the most difficult task that Aaron has set for herself. In her desire to place these poems within a larger cultural framework, she consistently and correctly identifies the historical archetypes, the ancient symbols and medieval verse patterns that the poets—even the non-Jews among them—had recourse to. What is most remarkable about these poems, however, is that they partake of a "tradition" less than a century old. These are not the kind of poems that Jews included in their liturgy or recited on days of collective mourning. The God of these poems is not the biblical God of Abraham, Isaac, and Jacob or the rabbinic God of compassion. The anger, the pleading and the prophecy expressed in these poems are the product of a modern secular Jewish culture. They are centered on a human understanding of inhuman events. Yet in the end, as Aaron demonstrates, they form a new kind of liturgy, a time-bound but timeless document on the ultimate value of life. As such, they rightfully take their place alongside the sacred texts of Judaism that will be studied and read and recited and memorized long after the murderers are ground to dust.

DAVID G. ROSKIES

Acknowledgments

At the end of the arduous task that the writing of this book has often been, I take great pleasure in expressing my gratitude to those persons whose advice and encouragement made my work possible. I am indebted to Daniel Gerould, Irving Howe, and Burton Pike, whose gentle but expert guidance helped to produce this work. I owe a *special* debt of gratitude to David G. Roskies, whose generous and expert criticism, notably of Yiddish poetry, was inestimable. I am also grateful for the advice and encouragement offered by Michał Borwicz, anthologist of *Pieśń ujdzie cało* (The Song Will Pass Unscathed), a work that figures in this study; Abraham Sutzkever, one of the few poets who survived the Holocaust and whose poetry constitutes a large part of this book; Yechiel Szeintuch, Terrence Des Pres, Irving Halperin, Herbert I. Zagor, and Ellen Fine.

For the grants and fellowships that supported this work, I wish to thank the following institutions: The Memorial Foundation for Jewish Culture, The Institute for the Study of Modern Jewish Life of the City College of New York, The Jack P. Eisner Institute for Holocaust Studies at the CUNY Graduate Center. For their assistance, I am indebted to both Dina Abramowicz, librarian of YIVO Institute for Jewish Research, and Miriam Nowicz, writer and curator of the museum at Kibbutz Beit Lohamei Hagettaot, who encouraged me and provided hospitality during my research at the museum. I am also indebted to my editor Carola F. Sautter for her general excellence.

I take special pleasure in expressing my gratitude to my daughter Fern Zagor, son-in-law Barry Glaser, and my friends

Sylviane Baumflek, Thelma Goodman, Lenore Israel, Gloria Kelman, Arlene Levy, and Natalie Zagor for their proofreading the manuscript.

For their patience, and indulgence when my "nerves were frayed," I would like to thank my children Fern and David Zagor and Stephanie and Barry Glaser, my sister Estelle Laughlin, and my friend, Ruth Pagirsky. Each one sustained me with love and empathy during difficult moments. Although they expressed their concern that—as a witness to the events which "inspired" the writing of poetry in the Holocaust—the journey on which I embarked was bound to be fraught with pain, they refrained from attempting to dissuade me from my decision. For their understanding that I undertook this work precisely because I was a witness, I am very grateful.

To my husband, Sol Aaron (Shleymke Aronowicz), a former partisan in the Rudnicka Forests near Vilna, my debt is the greatest. Not only did he discuss with and read to me some of the Yiddish poetry in his impeccable Vilna Yiddish, but he also gave me the courage to undertake this study and the strength to complete it. He was my loving companion throughout this undertaking.

Introduction

While they themselves and their civilization were being destroyed in the crucible of World War II, European Jews—among them those of Poland—were feverishly recording the unfolding events for posterity. Even after waves of mass deportations to death camps, those who managed to live continued to write. This flowering of literature reflects a determination both to leave a testament to future generations and to affirm traditional values in a disintegrating world.

Although this ferment produced a whole spectrum of literary expression, poetry was the dominant form. In fact, "the quickest reaction" to the genocide, as Henryk Grynberg writes, "came in poetry; first of all from the Polish-Jewish poets who wrote while locked in the ghettos and isolated in their hideouts before the annihilation of the ghettos and the so-called final solution."[1] The instantaneous reaction in poetry probably derived from its nature, its greater ability than prose to generate the most exact correlatives for feelings and states of consciousness in response to the unfolding catastrophe. Perhaps also poetry's quick and spontaneous reaction to the assault sprang from its lyrical impulse, one connected with the mystery of religious rites and myths of suffering and endurance, immortality and mortality, continuity and finality.

Studies of Yiddish and Hebrew poetry written in the Holocaust were undertaken by several scholars, notable among whom are David G. Roskies and Yechiel Szeintuch.[2] But the corpus of Polish-Jewish poetry of the same period has remained largely unexamined, perhaps owing to the difficulties of Polish—a language not accessible to most Holocaust scholars. My objective is to continue the discussion of the Yiddish poetry and to bring the largely unexamined Polish-Jewish poetry to light, to examine its relationship to the Yiddish poetry, and to determine the significance of both as literature—a poetics in extremis. Hence, in addition to other concerns, this study is an analytical and critical attempt to explore the impact of the immediacy of Holocaust experience as a formative influence on perception, response, and literary imagination.

It is assumed that literature coeval with unfolding events is different, in some ways, from that presented by eyewitnesses writing after the fact. Literature produced in the ghettos and concentration camps may not reflect the dramatic or tragic irony exemplified in *post factum* writing. Survivor writers have been granted a temporal and spatial perspective their counterparts who did not survive could not have. This perspective is apt to produce a relative point of view. Indeed, as Roskies notes, "a writer automatically changes his perspective as soon as a given stimulus is removed, so that anything written after the fact is colored by the new reality.[3] This is not to suggest that the perception of the new reality is either superior or inferior to the old one. While only total recall can attempt to express the existential *exactness* contextualized in the immediacy of experience, witnesses seeing themselves in past contexts can provide insights that only distance is bound to vouchsafe. One need only mention the work of such writers in the Holocaust as Abraham Sutzkever and Władysław Szlengel on the one hand, and Elie Wiesel and Primo Levi on the other, to make the point.

Nonetheless, memory, by virtue of its intrinsically selective nature, tends to reshape the texture of past experiences. Indeed, as Janusz Korczak observed in his *Ghetto Diary*, "reminiscences hinge on our immediate experience. Reminiscing, we lie unconsciously."[4] Yet the time element that precipitates "unconscious lying" is the aesthetic distance, part of the very artistic process required to distance suffering from the creative mind in order to polish the form.

Perhaps then, to attain a wide-angled perspective on the Holocaust, we are equally enjoined to provide a forum both for *post factum* writers and for those who wrote during the catastrophe. The mission of the poets in the Holocaust was, among other things, to have an audience in generations to come. They wrote so that their poetry, read and reread, could provide testimony to their epoch, bear witness for themselves and for those who perished, for us all: the living eyewitnesses and those who were not there. Of poetry as bearer of witness, the Polish poet and Nobel Laureate, Czesław Miłosz, writes the following:

> The twentieth century, perhaps more protean and multifaceted than any other, changes according to the point from which we view it, a point in the geographic sense as well. My corner of Europe, owing to the extraordinary and lethal events that have been occurring there . . . affords a peculiar perspective. As a result all of us who come from those parts appraise poetry slightly different than do the majority of my audience, for we tend to view it as a witness and participant in one of mankind's major transformations. I have titled this book *The Witness of Poetry* not because we witness it, but because it witnesses us.[5]

Precursors and Successors

Both in concentration camps and the ghettos, most of the poets created poetry less as a means of self-expression than as succor, a vehicle of mitigating daily disasters. This phenomenon reflects the tradition of Jewish literature that responded to over two millennia of Jewish suffering with poetry, threnodies, and liturgy of consolation. Interestingly, as David Roskies writes, consolation was drawn from earlier paradigms of calamity:

> Even when the catastrophe was perceived as being unprecedented, the historical song, with its use of biblical quotations, its liturgical framework and its theodicy, all served to console the listener, to mitigate the disaster, to render the actual, time-bound event into something transtemporal. This is because, in the traditional Jewish view, the greater the scope of the destruction, the more it recalls historical precedent.[6]

Yet between the wars and even in the last decades of the nineteenth century modern Yiddish poetry—Europeanized and secularized as it was by the Enlightenment (Haskalah) as well as by Zionism and socialism—forced an opening in the link to traditional themes and modes of expression. Indeed, several major currents appeared on the heels of each other: each as a reaction to its forerunner and, above all, to unalloyed traditionalism. The first were *Di Yunge*, a poetic movement that appeared simultaneously in Poland, Russia, and the United States at the turn of the century. Brought up on Yiddish literary conventions, these writers resolved to merge their Yiddishkayt with such literary currents as romanticism, expressionism (largely German), symbolism (mostly Russian), and the Polish *Skamander*. This dialectic produced an emphasis on individuality, subjectivity, and unhampered—sometimes audacious—methods of expression, rejecting the rigidity of traditionalism, political propaganda, didacticism, and chauvinism.

The credos of *Di Yunge* were radically modified, if not totally changed, in the 1920s by another group, the *In Zikh* (Introspectivists), a progeny of Americanized immigrants. The Introspectivists stressed intellectual poetry, experimental forms that reflected the natural rhythms of Yiddish speech, and free verse, as well as the equal importance of expressing eloquently feeling and rationality. Their intellectual principles included the primacy of the self (the *zikh*) as the prism through which the outer world was refracted. Champions of Yiddishkayt, their ultimate aim was to establish the Yiddish poet more firmly in the modern world.

In Warsaw, a major center of secular Yiddish culture and literature, a parallel movement called *Di Khaliastre* (The Gang) appeared in the twenties. Like their counterparts on the other side of the Atlantic, these poets made emphatic the primacy of individuality and experimental forms; but they also showed unmistakable expressionistic tendencies, proclaiming a form of anarchy, one that denounced the Haskalah, religion, and politics. Another group established in the 1930s in Vilna—the cradle of Jewish learning referred to as the "Jerusalem of Lithuania" (*Yerushalaim de Lite*)—was known as *Yung Vilna* (Young Vilna). Although highly politicized by poverty and anti-Semitism, as well as by such political movements as Zionism, territorialism, and socialism, *Yung Vilna* did not provide unified poetic principles.

The Holocaust at once subverted and intensified each of these interwar movements and their rhetoric. Overwhelmed by the cataclysm and the indifference of the world, Yiddish poets during and after the war saw the sterility of the humanistic promises and later socialism. Nonetheless, they drew sustenance from major Yiddish and Hebrew as well as European antecedents even if these were perceived to be bankrupt. Even the Polish-Jewish poets, while influenced by the various European literary trends, reclaimed the ancient paradigms, notably that of Lamentations, stressing the continuum of Jewish disasters and suffering. This phenomenon is reflected in the work of such poets in the Holocaust as Władysław Szlengel and Mieczysław Jastruń, who were not only avowed secularists but who were also grounded in Polish literature; Yiddish poets like Abraham Sutzkever, Shmerke Kaczerginski, Isiah Spiegel, and Simkhe-Bunem Shayevitsh, who had their literary roots in both biblical paradigms and modern Yiddish poetics; and Hebrew poets like Yitzhak Katzenelson, who during the war significantly returned to Yiddish, the daily tongue of the Jewish masses. Thus Jastruń, for example, using the idiom of lamentation liturgy, invokes Jerusalem and casts a bridge between the destruction of the temple and that of the Warsaw ghetto, "Here too as in Jerusalem / There is the somber Wailing Wall, / Those who stood near it, / Will see it no more" (see chapter 3). Apparently, Jastruń saw in Lamentations not a reaction to a specific historical event of 587 B.C.E. but an archetypal work that established a model of Jewish catastrophes and suffering.

By the Waters of Babylon, written by Katzenelson in the Warsaw ghetto, invokes, as the title of this play indicates, the memory of historical precedents to recall both disasters and principles of morality and human values. For older examples of Jewish conduct during catastrophes were needed as the Jews in the Warsaw ghetto grappled with physical and spiritual survival. Later in Vittel, a camp in France, from which he was dispatched to Auschwitz to meet the fate of most other Jews, Katzenelson poured out his lament in *The Song of the Murdered Jewish People.* This Yiddish jeremiad abounds in allusions to Ezekiel, Lamentations, Jeremiah, and other biblical references, all of which invoke the memory of communal grief. But while the biblical models, deeply figured and troped as they may be, are structured along logical lines, Katzenelson's threnody combines a neoclassical pattern of external architectonics and symmetries (fifteen cantos, fifteen four-line stanzas each) with a disjunctive internal arrangement. The latter is primarily revealed in the dissolution of time, for the chronological order of events is suspended, and the cantos are held together by the displaced logic of nightmares and grief. The recounting of the sequence of events dissolves in a lament, and the words tumble out in the distraught confusion of uncontrollable weeping.

The poem's disjunctiveness is not only a genuine reflection of grief but also an unobtrusive rejection of all historical paradigms, for none compares to the Holocaust. Thus the poet uses biblically allusive language to undermine archetypal lamentations and to highlight the difference between earlier catastrophes and the Holocaust. As Noah Resenbloom writes:

> Jeremiah and Ezekiel saw the destruction of their land; Katzenelson saw the annihilation of his people. Job was bereft of his children and afflicted with pain, yet even the celestial Satan was admonished to "save his life." Katzenelson lost everything and everybody and the German Satan was now about to take his life too. The voice commanding the poet [to write] is not the voice of the omnipotent and omniscient God of the prophets in whose wisdom and justice they believed. The poet's skies are blind and empty and he is called upon to play and make believe "as if a God were there . . . as if a great joy still shone for us there."[7]

The crisis of faith, whether poetic or theological, adumbrated in Katzenelson's threnody, while not universal, is a pervasive theme in the poetry in the Holocaust. Władysław Szlengel's "It's High Time," discussed at length in chapter 2 of this study, is an example of a bitter diatribe against God. A more subdued accusation, but one that also shows the paradox of recalling and rewriting historical precedents is Abraham Sutzkever's "Under Your White Stars." Here the poet prostrates himself under God's firmament and prays for deliverance. Hiding out in a cellar, he laments that his "cellar-vision" causes the stars and, by implication, his faith to fade. Since "in the cellars and hovels / slaughtering silence weeps,"[8] the poet finds loftier places. Thus he runs across rooftops—another hiding place—seeking his God. This ironic statement is followed by a desperate avowal of faith. "I hang—a shattered chord / and dedicate my song to you."[9]

Yiddish poetry written since the end of the war grapples with similar problems. As Irving Howe and Eliezer Greenberg have stated in the introduction to their anthology, *A Treasury of Yiddish Poetry:*

> About the ultimate preoccupation of Yiddish poetry there can be no doubt. After the Second World War all the schools, groups, and tendencies melt away; disputes as to poetic direction must now seem trivial; every Yiddish writer finds himself under the most crushing and sacred of obligations. The memory of cataclysm is decisive. . . . To an overwhelming extent Yiddish poetry becomes a *Khurbn* or holocaust poetry.[10]

The concerns of these poets are similar to those in the Holocaust—namely, the eternal suffering as a major component in Jewish history and the role of the Jewish God during the greatest tragedy in that history. Thus, Jacob Glatstein comes close to Sutzkever's perception of the extinction of the divine firmament:

> Now the lifeless skulls
> Add up into millions.
> The stars are going out around you.
> The memory of you is dimming,
> Your kingdom will soon be over. . . .
> Jewish God!
> You are almost gone.[11]

Another dialogue with God is Kadia Molodowsky's reversal of Sutzkever's and Glatstein's perception of fading divinity. Hers is a bitter and ironic plea that the ancient bond of the covenant established at Sinai be recanted and imposed on some other people:

> O God of Mercy
> For the time being
> Choose another people.
> We are tired of death, tired of corpses,
> We have no more prayers. . . .
>
> God of Mercy
> Sanctify another land
> Another Sinai. . . .
>
> O God of Mercy
> Grant us one more blessing—
> Take back the gift of our separateness.[12]

Non-Yiddish-speaking Jewish poets like Nelly Sachs and Paul Celan, whether writing about the Holocaust or not, without abandoning them return from German literary conventions to biblical and Hasidic sources. At the same time, they hold the God of the covenant accountable for the processes of history. Thus these poets comment respectively:

> I just have the deep feeling that Jewish artists must begin to listen to the voice of their lineage, so that the old spring may

awaken to new life. With that in mind I have attempted to write a mystery play [*Eli*] of the suffering of Israel.[13]

The landscape from which I come to you—by way of what detours! but are there even such things as detours?—this landscape may be unknown to most of you. It is the landscape that was the home for a not inconsiderable part of those Hasidic tales that Martin Buber recounted to us all in "German."[14]

In her poem, "O The Chimneys," Nelly Sachs transforms the chimney, the final agent of Jewish martyrdom, into an ironic image of eternal Jewish martyrdom preordained ("devised") from the dawn of Jewish history, the time of Jeremiah and Job:

> O the Chimneys
> Freedomway for Jeremiah and Job's dust—
> Who devised you and laid stone upon stone
> The road for refugees of smoke?[15]

A more explicit indictment of the God of the covenant is Paul Celan's "There Was Earth in Them:"

> They dug and dug, and thus
> Their day wore on, and their night.
> And they did not praise God,
> who, they heard, willed all this,
> who, they heard, knew all this.[16]

Language and Image

Although the poets in the Holocaust share with their post-Holocaust counterparts fundamental historical and suprahistorical concerns—"the voice of their lineage," the "landscape ... of Hasidic tales," the invocation of earlier disasters as a vehicle of solace, and the diminished stature of God—the former show much less concern with issues of aestheticism that were to preoccupy the latter. The ongoing debate among postwar writers on the inappropriateness of aesthetic forms to articulate the horror of what David Rousset called *l'univers concentrationnaire* (concentrationary universe), did not trouble the poets in the Holocaust, even if some of them intuitively avoided high rhetoric. Nonetheless, some of their poetry shows unmistakable modernistic tendencies—that is, unusual patterns of both versification and grammatical structures as well as punctuations—while other poetry adheres to principles of classical architectonics and figures.

Warnings that there are inherent dangers in transcribing the horrors of the Holocaust into artistic representations would probably astonish most of the writers in the Holocaust. Was it not Chaim Kaplan who said in the Warsaw ghetto that "more than bread we need poetry at a time when we don't seem to need it at all?" It was certainly Kaplan who wrote in his *Warsaw Diary* that "a poet who clothes adversity in poetic form immortalizes it in an everlasting monument."[17] And it was he who exhorted the poets to write, "Poet of the people where art thou?"[18] It is doubtful that either Kaplan or the poets on whom he called were concerned with problems of aesthetic form.

Hence the other challenge—namely, silence, whose vociferousness has been somewhat subdued recently, rather than serious and responsible discourse and exegesis, would probably also puzzle writers in the Holocaust. For, surely, silence would grant yet another victory to the forces of darkness. Based on the literary ferment in the ghettos and camps, it can be assumed that the poets in the Holocaust would wish posterity to read their poetry and to discuss its implications. Even if language does not suffice, and even if literature is inappropriate to the Holocaust, literature in and of the Holocaust, nonetheless, is a defense against forgetfulness; and redemption, we are told by the Baal Shem Tov, "lies in remembering." Paradoxically, those who in the past called for silence, intuitively wrote and continue to do so. Although, as they insisted, ours may be a time for silence, "silence is impossible; nothing can be said, but everything must be spoken; and from the impermissibility of words comes powerful speech."[19] In the end, inappropriate as art, in general, might be to human suffering, no other vehicle of expression articulates it more convincingly or more enduringly.

Every occasion in the Holocaust—memories of the lost world or exploding events—inspired poetry. If nothing else, this literary activity "repudiates," as Yechiel Szeintuch writes in his essay on Katzenelson, "the assertion that the Jewish response to Nazi terror was spiritual paralysis and submission":

Katzenelson's prolific work in the Warsaw ghetto in no way expresses despair or spiritual disintegration, but rather the very opposite—it is a symbolic act of resolute resistance in a situation in which all other effective forms of resistance were blocked.[20]

Indeed, as Szeintuch further observes, "Katzenelson is a vivid example of the phenomenon whereby literary response is heightened the more direct and immediate the writer's confrontation with death."[21] The same is true of many other poets, Szlengel, for example, whose early ghetto poetry is not of the highest artistic maturity. The poetry that confronts the impending destruction has greater profundity, maturity of feeling, and artistic quality.

Since a concerted effort was made to retain or to invoke a measure of "normal" life, and since such attempts lie within the purview of instinctive human behavior, especially when survival is at stake, not all the poetry addresses the cataclysm. A whole spectrum of other poems was produced, including banal and jocular ones. Although such endeavors helped divert attention from the gloom and despair of daily survival, they invariably reflect the historical context of the occupation as well as patterns of response to it. The dominant theme of these poems, even when they are satiric, is usually life and the primacy of moral resistance, as articulated in the following folk song written by Kasriel Broyde:

> *Moyshe, halt zikh, Moyshe, halt zikh!*
> *Nit tsefal zikh.*
> *Halt zikh Moyshe, fester.*
> *Moyshe, halt oys.*
> *Gedenk—men darf aroys!*

☐ ☐ ☐

> Moyshe, keep going, Moyshe, keep going!
> Don't fall apart.
> Moyshe, keep going even stronger.
> Moyshe, don't give up,
> Remember—we must survive.

Banality, jocularity, and satire are the dominant modes that especially mark the early poetry of both the established and folk poets who proliferated in the ghettos and who were determined to leave a testament for posterity. Both handled the initial period of occupation and its brutality with incredulity, believing that the war would soon end or the outside world or God would intervene on their behalf. This strategy helped them to achieve a semblance of distance from the increasingly intolerable reality. Frequently the mockery was bitter and directed against the neighbors beyond the ghetto walls. One such poem is Władysław Szlengel's "Telephone," discussed in chapter 1.

Other early poetry reflects nostalgia and yearning for freedom, for the lost prewar world. These characteristics inform another of Szlengel's poems, "Windows Facing the Other Side." This poem establishes the extent to which the Jew is degraded and separated from the world outside the ghetto. The window of the poet's ghetto apartment faces not only the "Aryan" side of Warsaw but also the lovely Krasinski Park. Yet looking out the window and feasting his eyes on "Aryan" trees is strictly forbidden. He is "a Jewish worm and a Jewish mole," and it is "right and just" that like all the other Jews he "should and must be blind."[22] However, at night the poet rushes to his window, "ravenously gazing and stealing snatches of darkened Warsaw."[23] Szlengel's longing for his beloved city is intensified and spiritualized by the anguish of loss and by memory. The poem ends on a cadence of ironic resignation; Warsaw beyond the window and, therefore, the world, the culture, the life that were once his own are lost forever.

Later poetry, Szlengel's or that of other poets, rejects concerns of cultural truncation because of the inverse relationship between the increasing atrocities and the intensified sense of Jewish identity. This poetry reflects the growing awareness of the conflagration—an epiphany that provoked many poets to use their poetry as a call to armed resistance. Poets who carried the poetic banner of Jewish revolt and heroism include Sutzkever, Szlengel, Kaczerginski, and Glik. The last is known for the famous partisan hymn "Never Say You Walk the Final Road." The work of these poets, as well as that of those with humbler reputations, is a testament to and an example of the evocative power and political function of poetry in the Holocaust. Such poets as Katzenelson were a source of inspiration not only of the uprising in the Warsaw ghetto, where he lived, but also of the rebellion in the Bialystok ghetto. Hence, like the poetry that provided spiritual succor, the martial poems, too, refute the assumption that the Jews were passive.

Poems put to music were especially popular in the Holocaust. This phenomenon reflects the Yiddish folk tradition, for as

Shmerke Kaczerginski writes in his introduction to *Lider fun Ghettos und Lagern* (Songs in the Ghettos and Concentration Camps), "*Dos lid, dos glaykhvertl, dem sharfn vits—hobn bagleyt dem Yiddn shtendik un umetum: ven er iz gegangen tsu der arbet, ven er iz geshtanen in rey nokh a shisele zup, ven men hot im gefirt tsu der shkhite, un ven er iz gegangen in kamf.*"[24] (The song, the proverb, the witty joke, have always and everywhere accompanied the Jew: when he went to work, when he waited on a soupline, when he was driven to the slaughter, and when he marched in combat.) Whether written by established poets or amateurs, their work was feverishly saved from destruction by such institutions as YIVO in Vilna (to mention but one of the most prominent ones) and deposited in hermetically sealed containers, which were stealthily buried.

A popular forum especially for the poetry written in the early period of the occupation was the literary café, the cabaret, and some of the theaters that proliferated in the ghettos. In the Warsaw ghetto, for example, before the commencement of mass deportations in July 1942, there were four Polish language establishments: the cabaret *Sztuka* (Art), whose central figure and motivating force was Władysław Szlengel, and the theaters *Femina, Melody Palace,* and *Na Piętrku* (The Second Floor). There were also two Yiddish theaters: *Eldorado* and *New Azazel.* In addition, there was a Yiddish drama studio under the auspices of the Zionist *DROR Hechalutz* movement, but founded and directed by Yitzhak Katzenelson. In the Lodz ghetto a group of adolescents created a Yiddish theater called the *Avant-Guard,* and the Vilna ghetto Yiddish theater was known as *Der Kleyner Shtot Zal* (The Small City Theater). Later, when these places no longer existed, poetry was circulated among many persons and read both in slave factories that were established in the larger ghettos and at "literary evenings."[25] In concentration camps oral poetry, as mentioned above, was composed on barrack bunk beds during coveted moments of rest.

Theory and Canon

Although I have mentioned several major poets, not all of them figure in this work. Mine is not an attempt to survey the work produced by all well-known poets in the Holocaust. Nor are my choices prompted by a superimposed order, an effort to balance the number of Yiddish and Polish poets. Instead, my purpose is to provide an in-depth analysis of representative poems that because of their artistic maturity and their special historical significance seem best to reflect the Jewish response to the mass destruction. Since there was a spontaneous explosion of folk poets and street singers, who were moved by a compulsion to bear witness, and since their endeavors, however unsophisticated or lachrymose, reflect a simple truth, some very brief examples of their work are provided.

The methodology I have employed is a textual explication, for a close reading seems to allow the poems to reveal their own historical compass, to speak their own truth, to communicate their nature, meaning, and significance in their own terms. This technique of criticism seems best suited to a poetry that, because it evolved from and is peculiar to its own unusual epoch, reveals profound shifts of sensibility. And yet this writing is tangentially linked to other literatures. Although shaped by the "daily dread of experience" (if a pun be permitted), some of this poetry has its roots in various biblical motifs, as noted above, including the Lamentations tradition. Other poetry derives from romanticism and pantheism. There is also writing that is grounded in modernist traditions and that anticipates such postmodernist trends as minimalism, providing a pivotal nexus within the literary continuum.

Like all the literature in and of the Holocaust, this poetry does not signal a new poetic genre. Nor has it occasioned new kinds of idioms that would reflect the radical evil of this event. For as Czesław Miłosz writes in his discussion of Michał Borwicz's evaluation of the literature in the concentration camps, these poems "belong stylistically to the prewar period, but at the same time they try to express 'the new' which cannot be grasped by any of the available notions and means of expression."[26]

It is for this reason that the literature both in and of the Holocaust has greatly complicated theoretic approaches to it, causing various scholars to embark on quests of new critical methodologies with which to interpret, analyze, and evaluate it. The problem is obvious: the imagination of those who were not there has no point of reference; and even those who were there have not been able to provide new modes of expression to bridge the gap.

Nonetheless, poetry in the Holocaust can and, in my judgment, should be subjected to the most rigorous literary scrutiny. New critical methodologies are not imperative to its interpretation, analysis, and evaluation. Indeed, the inherent existential, historical, contextual, and aesthetic resonances of this corpus of literature can be redeemed from neglect and obscurity only by reading and studying it. The writers in the Holocaust who left this legacy for posterity apparently were not worried about canons or theories of interpretation; their concern was that we read, as Szlengel put it, "what he read to the dead."[27] The poetry's eloquence is intrinsic. Much of it is characterized by a high degree of poetic craft and artistic organization. Often devoid of extrinsic metaphors, it is, nonetheless, marked by various rhetorical figures, including anaphoras, asyndetons, zeugmas, and the like. Above all, it lays bare insiders' perspectives on the events in the very process of their unfolding. Thus this body of writing provides precise correlatives for states of consciousness in relation to the unfolding cataclysm; it shows how the condemned people felt and what they thought, how they responded to life and death, and what they did with their hope and despair, how they fought back and what they did when traditional vehicles of resistance were disintegrating one after another.

To facilitate a discussion of this body of creative writing, the thematic division of the book is tripartite. This schema proved compelling, because the themes derive from their textual compass. Part 1 is an exploration of testimonial or documentary poetry. Part 2 examines poetry concerned with the morale of the people, with forms of moral resistance, and the crisis of faith. Part 3 is an exegesis of political and resistance poetry. I have also included a fourth part, an autobiographical epilogue, that is obliquely related to this entire project, but most notably to part 2.

It should be noted that most of the poetry in the Holocaust reveals an underlying principle: the primacy of testimony. Like historians, the poets, therefore, addressing various issues, wanted chiefly to bear witness. But unlike historians, they have transformed monstrous reality into art. Admittedly, this art does not conform to the assumption that the purpose of art is to assuage the anguish of reality or that it must transcend the abyss through a moral vision, one that seeks redemption by striving for perfection and excellence. But this art is art by virtue of its ability to express the unspeakable in ways that surpass most other contextualizing methods. It is thus that this poetry often provided a measure of catharsis for some of those who were in the ghettos and camps at the time, keeping at bay the despair that threatened to overwhelm them.

If poetry in the Holocaust managed to document and thereby to reveal—as only poetry can—patterns of human response to terror, despair, and death, then it fought against them, even if it did not conquer them, and it provided for its immediate readers as well as for posterity a form of temporary solace. For the readers in the Holocaust this meant spiritual succor and catharsis; and for post-Holocaust readers it might also translate into spiritual succor, a sense of awe that it was written at all: that human beings can have the moral fortitude to write poetry, this most sublime of literary expressions, in the darkest of nights.

◻

PART ONE

Poetry as Documentation

Wołanie w Nocy

Wiersze lipiec-wrzesień 1942
Wiersze te, napisane między jednym
A drugim wtrząsem, w dniach konania
Największej w Europie Gminy Żydowkiej
Między końcem lipca a wrześniem 1942,
Poświęcam ludziom, o których mogłem się
Oprzeć w godzinach zawiei i kompletnego chaosu.
Tym nielicznym, którzy umieli w wirze zdażen,
W tańcu przypadku śmierci i protekcyjek
Pamiętać, że nie tylko rodzina . . . nie tylko
Kolegacje. . . . Nie tylko pieniądze. . . .
Ale nalerzy ratować tych nielicznych ostatnich
Mohikanów, których całym kapitałem i jedyną
Bronią jest słowo.
Do tych, to których dotarło moje. . . .

. . . WOŁANIE W NOCY . . .

◻ ◻ ◻

Call in the Night

Poems, July-September 1942
I dedicate these poems—written between one
And another cataclysm, when
The largest Jewish community in Europe was dying
Between the end of July and September 1942—

To those people on whom I could
Lean during this tempest and total chaos.
To those few in number who
Were able to remember
In the whirlwind of events,
In the death dance of accident and favoritism,
That not only members of the family, not only
Friends, not only money,
But also the handful Last of the Mohicans
Must be rescued,
Those whose entire capital and sole
Weapon is the word.
To those reached by my

CALL IN THE NIGHT

Władysław Szlengel,
Warsaw ghetto

Chapter One

In the Beginning

Poetry often derives its eloquence from the longing of the imagination to bring order to chaos, to bridle the apocalyptic and demonic worlds, and to render the incomprehensible intelligible. In the chaos of the Holocaust, this lyrical yearning sought fulfillment in the whole spectrum of poetic genres, one of which was documentary poetry.

Since in this habitation of death, history was conspiring with the poets in unusual ways, poetics of testimony assumed unusual meanings. Frequently, its purpose was to focus attention upon the various aspects of the crisis, so that activities toward its containment might be generated. Thus documentary poetry often attempted to identify or name the facts in order to comprehend the exploding chaos and to galvanize those mechanisms that might help to cope with or resist it. When despair and terror overwhelmed the poet or reader, some of the poetry became a form of exorcism. Thus naming or describing hunger and grief, for example, was an attempt to control their domination.

Above all, testimonial poetry was a day-to-day chronicle of the unfolding cataclysm. Rooted in Jewish literary tradition, some of the poetry—even that which was written in Polish—takes its analogue, form, and lexicon from such antecedents as elegaic liturgy, the iconography of pogroms, and the general Jewish literature of destruction. Nonetheless, many of the documentary as well as other poems show unmistakable modernistic influences. Not all the poetry, however, is marked by the same literary quality. An abundance of literary amateurs, compelled to bear witness, resolved to record events for posterity. Consequently, there was a spontaneous explosion of folk poetry—a kind of simple *Urdich-*

tung and balladry, the chief of which was the *kina* or *kloglid* (dirge)—that documented while it lamented.

The testimonial imperative of both the literary poems and the simple folk songs reflects, more often than not, the collective destiny of the Jews. Although by no means all, much of this poetry eschews the narrow concerns of private struggles and subordinates them to the problems facing the community. Where personal hardships or individual grief are the center of the poems, they often belong to the author's early writings.

Władysław Szlengel: Initial Forms of Distancing

Early attempts to grasp the significance of the unfolding events are exemplified in Władysław Szlengel's "Telefon" (Telephone). Not much is known about Szlengel or the other poets writing in the Holocaust, although some of their poetry was saved. Most of their biographical data is, therefore, conjectural; for, like other persons who knew them, the poets vanished.

In fact, of Szlengel we know more than about most of the other poets. Born in 1914 in Warsaw, he began to write poems, songs, and skits for the stage at an early age. His youthful writings appeared in school papers, while his mature work was published in various literary journals. Shortly before the war, Szlengel worked as literary consultant to and was director of a theater in Bialystok. He returned to Warsaw in 1940, before the ghetto was sealed off, both because he was consumed by longing for the capital and by anxiety about the fate of his wife who remained there. Irena Maciejewska, the anthologist of Szlengel's ghetto poetry, writes that Szlengel took part in the September 1939 defense of his country. This fact is corroborated by Emanuel Ringelblum, the historian and Warsaw ghetto archivist.[1]

In collaboration with other writers in the ghetto, Szlengel founded and ultimately became the central figure of both an underground literary journal, *Żywy Dziennik* (Living Daily), and a cabaret, *Sztuka* (Art). Szlengel died during the Warsaw ghetto uprising, having produced a large body of poetry, songs, and other writings, of which only a handful was saved. But this handful is very compelling, for it includes poetry written during the unfolding events in the ghetto and, therefore, constitutes a spectrum of the stages of a poet's consciousness in its relation to these events. Like many ghetto poets, he regarded poetry as the most appropriate idiom with which to immortalize the memory of the living, the dying, and the dead. Apparently, the power of his poetry was of such intensity that it resonated in various parts of the ghetto and in all its stages. Articulating despair, hope, and opposition, his poems and songs secretly circulated among many people and were recited by the poet himself not only in *Sztuka* and in literary circles in the earlier period of the ghetto but also in slave labor factories that were established later, after July 1942, the commencement of the final liquidation of the ghetto.

Szlengel's early ghetto poetry is marked by parodic, jocular, and often nostalgic tones, all of which achieved for himself and his readers a measure of distance from an intolerable reality. The inverse relationship between the escalating atrocities and Szlengel's parodic and comic temper produced an irony of singular corrosiveness. This discrepancy has its roots in the Jewish folk tradition that evolved a talent to "laugh off the trauma of history,"[2] as David Roskies writes, by comic juxtapositions perfected by Sholem Aleichem.

Although Szlengel probably had more than a passing familiarity with the Yiddish folk idiom, he is first and foremost grounded in the Polish literary tradition. His early ghetto poetry shares with the *Skamander* movement, popular in the first decade of the interwar period, a predilection for colloquial idioms, a lighthearted poetic voice, as well as satiric and ironic modes. His use of macabre buffoonery and the morosely grotesque, both of which dominate his later ghetto period, shows an affinity with the poets of the 1930s known as the "catastrophists." These writers divined from historical events not only the crisis of the individual and Western civilization but that of the entire world. In Szlengel's world their catastrophic vision was a prophecy fulfilled. Yet when Szlengel wrote his early poem "Telephone," he probably envisioned, like the rest of the incredulous world, neither the savagery nor the extent of the tragedy that was to come.

A long poem (twenty-four stanzas of four lines each with an uneven rhyme scheme), "Telefon," like all Szlengel's ghetto poetry, is marked by "unpoetic" language. From the very beginning of his incarceration in the Warsaw ghetto and his determination to record events, Szlengel apparently had the prescience to realize that he was writing his "documentary poems" (*wiersze-dokumenty*), as he called them, for and about the dying and the dead. For them, Szlengel probably thought, high rhetoric was absurd. Since the world in which they lived could hardly be compared to any other one, metaphors and analogies were highly inappropriate.

Catapulted into the enclosed ghetto, Szlengel projects a vision of it, even in its early days (Szlengel did not date his poems, but we can surmise the dates from the poems' contexts), as a planet cast out of the universe. Suddenly separated from the world he once knew, his lyric imagination strains to recapture the lost world. But it is crushed by an awareness that for a Jew all lines of communication have been broken. Long-standing friendships with gentiles have been dissolved, as the Jew is forced to take "a different road" in 1939. Nonetheless, the poet reaches for the telephone to realize once again that the human nexus he had established with the Poles has been irrevocably severed.

Telefon

Z sercem rozbitem i chorem,
z myślami o tamtej stronie
siedziałem sobie wieczorem
przy telefonie—

I myślę sobie: zadzwonię
do kogoś po tamtej stronie,
gdy dyżur mam przy telefonie
wieczorem—

Nagle myślę: na Boga—
nie mam właściwie do kogo,
w roku trzydziestym dziewiątym
poszedłem inną drogą—

Rozeszły się nasze drogi,
przyjaźni ugrzęzły w toni
i teraz, no proszę—nie mam
nawet do kogo zadzwonić.[3]

◻ ◻ ◻

Telephone

With heart rent and sick,
and thoughts on the other side

I sat one evening
by the telephone—

And so I thought: let me call
someone on the other side,
when I'm on telephone duty
in the evening—

Suddenly I realized: by God—
there is actually no one to call,
in nineteen thirty nine
I turned a different corner—

Our ways have parted,
friendships have sunk in a swamp
and now it's plain to see—there is
no one I can reach.

Szlengel's bitter intoning of his growing sense of despair and isolation are reminiscent, but ironically so, of the writings of the Polish poet Jan Lechoń, whose sense of despair caused him to write the following famous lines:

Nie ma nieba ni ziemi, otchłani ni piekła,
Jest tylko Beatrycze. I właśnie jej nie ma.

❑ ❑ ❑

There is neither heaven nor earth, no abyss nor hell,
There is only Beatrice. But she does not exist.

Since Lechoń's fame and influence were well established in Poland, Szlengel was probably thoroughly familiar with Lechoń's famous epiphany. This would render his influence on Szlengel singularly ironic. For while Lechoń's metaphysical loneliness reflects an interwar form of anguish, Szlengel's mirrors the deadly isolation of the Jew in the Holocaust. While Lechoń's anguish arises from the implacable cosmic void—a form of Sartrean "nothingness"—Szlengel's pain springs from the palpable fullness of an expanding hell. Szlengel obviously exploited the ironic juxtaposition of his and Lechoń's sense of isolation, showing the glaring absurdity of prewar influences on wartime poetry and on wartime reality. This mode—the ironic and parodic—came of age in the

Holocaust and was, therefore, in the tradition of both Yiddish and Polish ghetto writing.

In "Telephone" the only dialogue Szlengel is able to establish with the prewar world is the telephone dial-a-time whose naming of the passing minutes is a bittersweet evocation of memories from before the war. The long cataloguing of simple human pleasures is rendered in a rhythmic crescendo of dazzling, montagelike images. These include the poet's returning from a Gary Cooper film; buying a newspaper while noting the dawnlike neon reflections on the evening pavement; watching the strolling couples headed toward "Café Club"; inhaling the piquant aroma of sausages wafting from "Café Quick"; observing the after-dinner crowds; and listening to the cacaphony produced by speeding taxis and streetcars, counterpointed by the amplified voice of a popular crooner, Mieczysław Fogg. These memories, idealized by longing, increase the distance between the lost world and the infernal present.

Doomed to converse wholly with himself, the poet seeks to defend his integrity against self-pity by a progressive amplification of his comic voice. Hence the cadences of the closing strophes resonate with a blend of self-mockery and bitter irony, as he bids the dial-a-time, the only lady who did not reject his overtures, farewell:

> *Jak dobrze się z tobą rozmawia*
> *bez sporu, bez rożnych zdań,*
> *jesteś najmilsza zegarynko—*
> *ze wszystkich znajomych pań—*

> *Już lżej teraz sercu będzię,*
> *gdy wiem, że kiedy zadzwonię,*
> *ktoś mnie spokojnie wysłucha,*
> *choć po tamtej stronie.*

> *Że ktoś to wszystko pamięta,*
> *że wspólnie łączył nas los,*
> *i mowić się ze mną nie boi,*
> *i tak spokojny ma głos.*

> *Noc jesienna pluszcze*
> *i wiatr nad murkami gna,*

gwarzymy sobie, marzymy
zegarynka i ja. . . .

Bądź zdrowa moja daleka,
są serca, gdzie nic się nie zmienia,
za pięć dwunasta—powiadasz
masz rację . . . więc do widzenia.[4]

❑ ❑ ❑

How pleasant it is to chat with you
without arguments, without any opinion,
you are the most agreeable, dial-a-time—
of all my lady friends.

My heart is less heavy,
for I know that should I call,
someone will calmly listen,
even on the other side.

That someone remembers it all,
that we were joined by the same fate,
and is not afraid to chat with me,
and has so calm a voice.

The autumn night is pouring in
and the wind blows above the wall,
we prattle and daydream
the dial-a-time and I. . . .

Be well my distant one,
there are hearts that always remain constant,
five to twelve—you declare—
right you are . . . well, so long for now.

Such daydreams and reminiscences as Szlengel's, while obvi-
ously painful, were also healing. They nourished the starving
spirit with a kind of idealized remembrance of the past. This prac-
tice was widespread during the entire Holocaust period—in the
ghettos and, perhaps even more, in concentration camps. Some of
the inmates in both engaged, whenever possible, in various rever-
ies, composing poems and songs, and re-creating in them the lost

world as a realm of perfection. In doing this, they were immortalizing and sanctifying the past and, at the same time, creating oral epithets for fugitive tombstones. Moreover, these imaginative reconstructions had, as it were, the magic power associated with shamanistic rites. The incantations of the sacred images and the paeans in praise of the murdered family, friends, and shtetl had the authority to exorcise, even if for an hour, whether in the ghettos or concentration camps, the specter of starvation or the terror of the chimney. Listeners knew that the confabulating imagination was creating idealized verbal universes. Yet this did not break the spell of conjuration. Casting out stalking death and evil, even if for a moment, these romanticized verbal worlds returned to the exhausted people the past, sustaining the present moment by purging it of its cruelty.

Writing about human perceptions, Ernest Cassirer notes that adaptation to our world is contingent on our ability to create a symbolic superstructure that intervenes between the environment and ourselves. As a result of this, "no longer can man confront reality immediately; he cannot see it, as it were, face to face. Physical reality seems to recede in proportion as man's symbolic activity advances."[5] Interestingly, such symbolic activity is a function not only of poets and ordinary people in extreme situations, but of those in normal and obviously primitive worlds as well. Apparently, both writers and their readers often seek in verbal superstructures compensations for an intolerable reality.

For the poets in the Holocaust, the paradox is that the painful memory of the past often generated a symbolic past-future axis. Moving backward in time and breaking through the wall of pain, the creative imagination was able to use the memory of a lost Eden as a possibility and perhaps even a promise of a regained one. Such symbolic processes helped not only to adapt to but also to transcend the wretchedness of the present moment. To remember the idealized past was to strain toward the future, toward the life-sustaining belief in the return of the prewar world. Hence, the evocative power of such simple, bittersweet poems as Szlengel's "Telephone" often had a cathartic and redemptive effect on the poet and reader alike.

Discussing Hiroshima and Holocaust survivors, Robert Lifton observes that the loving ruminations on painful details of their "death immersions" is an attempt on the part of survivors to break out of their psychic numbing. "For these memories are unique in that they enable one to transcend both the psychic numbing of the actual death encounter and the 'ordinary numbing' of the moment."[6]

Abraham Sutzkever:
To Live Both for Oneself and for the Dead

A related idea is expressed in Abraham Sutzkever's "Di Er-shte Nakht in Ghetto" (The First Night in the Ghetto), a poem that takes its title from a slim anthology of poetry written in Vilna between 1941 and 1943, shortly after this city's ghetto was established (September 1941). "The First Night in the Ghetto," like most of Sutzkever's wartime poetry, both partakes of and stands in sharp relief against his prewar work. The latter shows not only refined and often delicate stylistic devices of versification but also brilliant linguistic manipulations and rhyming schemes of singular inventiveness. Coupled with these is the poet's penchant for pantheism, especially notable in his early work, and a predilection for things romantic: introspection, a preoccupation with the relationship between the external and his inner worlds, sensual lyricism, and a devotion to nature in all its multifarious splendors. In the highly politicized Vilna of the 1930s, Sutzkever was an avowed stranger. His poems, devoid of ideology, were rejected by the popular, leftist literary group "Young Vilna."

While his wartime poems were to undergo dramatic permutations, they retained their antebellum artistic integrity, allegiances, and proclivities. Much of his writing in the ghetto and the Narotch Forest, where he joined the resistance and survived the war, plays numerous variations on the theme of resistance, both armed and moral; on Jewish tradition as a vehicle of that resistance; and on nature as a source of succor and transcendence. Many of these poems reveal mythic, prophetic, oracular, and nature images that are structured toward a promise of redemption.

Other poems, notably those comprising the collection *The First Night in the Ghetto*, are informed by confessions of singular existential anguish and personal and communal chastisement for the "sin" of traditional pacifism that marked diaspora Judaism. In this he reflects Chaim Nachman Bialik, who in his famous Hebrew poem "The City of Slaughter," written in 1903 in response to the bloody Kishinev pogrom, pours execrations not only on the murderers but also on the victims for not having armed themselves, for having forfeited their right to self-respect and human dignity, because they saved their lives without fighting back.

Sutzkever's admonition also takes its analogue from Moyshe Leib Halpern's "A Night." The imprecations that mark this poem are similar to those expressed in "The City of Slaughter" and are directed not only against the murderers, against God, and against faith in religious and social redemption, but also against the victims for allowing themselves to be victims during the pogroms after World War I.

The phenomenon of self-blame, a form of "disaster complex," as Yitzhak Yanasowicz calls it, is peculiar to modern, assimilated Jews, who blame themselves for not being able to extricate themselves from their fate as Jews and, hence, scapegoats of history. In his discussion of *The First Night in the Ghetto*, Yanasowicz further notes that religious Jews are not subject to this self-implicating logic and do not feel guilty when they are able to save their lives. On the other hand, modern, wordly Jews are afraid both of the slaughter itself and of perishing in it like sheep.[7]

Consigned by history and choice to the class of modern Jews, as Yanasowicz suggests, Sutzkever lays bare in *The First Night in the Ghetto* his sense of shame and guilt for having saved his life while others, some of them members of his own family—his mother and child—were killed. These poems, therefore, reveal his resentment against the terrible reality into which he was thrust as much as they express vituperations against his faintheartedness and egotism, his perception that he bought his life at the price of others—a phenomenon rather typical of survivors of all disasters, small and large. "The Circus," for example, articulates the poet's deepening despair, his perception that his existence is bereft of sense, just as is the value of his heretofore cherished beliefs. Not surprisingly, both this and his confrontation with the mass death that accompanied the establishment of the Vilna ghetto, the inner turmoil associated with facing his own death and human dread of it—all these were pivotal in Sutzkever's development as poet and human being.

Apparently the turbulent emotions that mark *The First Night in the Ghetto* were the root cause of Sutzkever's reluctance to publish the book. One must assume that in the end the poet came to terms with this dilemma, for he resolved to publish the anthology in 1979, but not before he revised most of the poems in it. Indeed, Sutzkever is alleged to have edited not only these but also most of his ghetto poems before submitting them for publication. Although, as Roskies notes, the poet was moved by reasons of aestheticism, his chief motives were ideological "when he consigned to oblivion the anger, guilt, and despair expressed in such poems as 'The Circus' and the 'Three Roses' [both contained in the anthology]. The survivor-poet wished to allow only his lyrical and dramatic voices to speak for the ghetto experience."[8]

Roskies further states that Sutzkever's self-censorship, much like that of other survivor-poets, was largely motivated by a reluctance to offend the memory of the dead. This concern was especially rife immediately after the war when the few thousand survivors were faced with a new peril: the Soviet secret police as well as the anti-Semitic Poles, Lithuanians, and a motley crew of former Nazi collaborators—"all of whom had good reasons to suppress the crimes perpetrated against the Jews."[9]

"The First Night in the Ghetto" is one of the best poems of this period, documenting as it does Sutzkever's initial response to the German commencement of the terror that swept Jewish Vilna. Like Szlengel's "Telephone," the opening stanzas of "The First Night in the Ghetto" are an evocation of the bewilderment of a poet, the integrity of whose youth has been violated. Yet Sutzkever's poem is mediated by an inner vision and cultural retina that are radically different from those of Szlengel. While Sutzkever was anchored in Jewish culture and the Yiddish language, the more assimilated Szlengel was rooted in both Polish and Yiddish cultures. When immured in the Warsaw ghetto, Szlengel experienced a bereavement at the separation that was alien to Sutzkever. Although Sutzkever keenly felt the loss of the world outside the ghetto, notably nature with the primeval forests and the splendid pastoral landscapes of Poland, he did not bewail the loss of the non-Jewish social world of prewar Vilna, for his link with it was tenuous. His anguish seems to derive from the terrifying realization that the destruction of his people began with the establishment of the Vilna ghetto. Sutzkever's sense of doom stands in some relief against Szlengel's perception of the events, for the enclosing of the Vilna ghetto ushered in with full force the technology of the Final Solution, measures that were to be applied to the Warsaw ghetto in the summer of 1943, a year later.

Di Ershte Nakht in Ghetto

'Di ershte nakht in ghetto iz di ershte nakht in keyver,
Dernokh geveynt men zikh shoyn tsu'—dos treyst azoy mayn

shokhn
Di grine gliverdike gufim, oysgeshpreyt oyf dr'erd.

Tsi kenen oykh fazunken vern shifn in yaboshe?
Ikh fil: se zinken shifn unter mir un bloyz di zeglen,
Tseflikte un tsetrotene, zey valgern zikh oybn:
Di grine gliverdike gufim oysgeshpreyt oyf dr'erd.

S'iz bizn haltz—
Es hengt iber mayn kop a lange rine
Mit zumer-fedem tsugeshpunen tsu a khurve. Keyner
Bavoynt nit ire kamern. Bloyz brumendike tsigl
Aroysgerisene mit shtiker fleysh fun ire vent.

Araynshpiln in rine flegt an ander tsayt a regn,
A linder, veykher bentshndiker. Mames flegn untn
Anidershteln emers far der ziser volknmilkh
Tsu tsvogn tekhter, glantsn zoln mazldik di tsep.
Atsind—nito di mames, nit di tekhter, nit kayn regn,
Bloyz tsigl in di khurve. Bloyz di brumendike tsigl,
Aroysgerisene mit shtiker fleysh fun ire vent.

S'iz nakht. Es rint a shvartser sam. Ikh bin a holoveshke,
Farratn funem letstn funk un tomik oysgeloshn.
A shvester iz mir bloyz di hurva. Un der faykhter vint,
On-otem tsugefaln tsu mayn moyl mit mildn khesed,
Bagleyt mayn gayst, vos teylt zikh oys fun shmatikn gebeyn,
Vi s'teylt zikh dos flaterl fun vorem. Un di rine
Hengt alts iber mayn kop an oysgehoybene in kholel
Un s'rint durkh ir der shvartser sam a tropn nokh a tropn.

Un plutsem—yeder tropn vert an oyg. Ikh bin in gantsn
Adurkhgeoygt mit likht. A nets fun likht baym shepn likht.
Un iber mir di rine tsu der khurve tsugeshpunen,
A teleskop. Ikh shvim arayn in zayn geshlif un blikn
Fareynikn zikh likhtike. Ot zenen zey, vi nekhtn,
Di heymishe, di lebendike shtern fun mayn shtot.
Un tsvishn zey—oykh yener nokhhavdoliker shtern
Vos mamelipn hobn im aroyfgevuntshn: gut-vokh.

Un s'vert mir gut. Nito ver s'zol fartunklen im, tseshtern,
Un lebn muz ikh, vayl es lebt mayn mames guter shtern.[10]

❑ ❑ ❑

The First Night in the Ghetto

"The first night in the ghetto is the first night in the grave,
Later one gets used to it"—thus comforts my neighbor
The green, stiff corpses strewn on the ground.

Can ships actually sink on land?
I know: ships do sink under me, and only the sails,
Ripped and trampled, are scattered above:
The green stiff corpses strewn on the ground.

I have it up to my throat—
A long gutter hangs above my head
Woven into the ruins with gossamer. No one
Dwells in its rooms. Only roaring bricks,
Torn from their walls with chunks of flesh.

Playful was the rain in the gutter in other times,
Supple, soft, blessed. Mothers used to put out
Pails to catch the sweet cloudmilk
And shampoo their daughters' hair to bring luck's luster to the
     braids.
Now—there are no mothers, no daughters, no rain,
Only bricks in the ruins. Only roaring bricks,
Torn from their walls with chunks of flesh.

It's night. Black poison oozes. I am a piece of ember,
Betrayed by the last spark precipitously extinguished.
The ruins alone are my sister. And the moist wind,
Without breath falls upon my mouth with gentle grace,
Escorting my spirit which detaches itself from my tattered
     skeleton
Like a butterfly emerging from a caterpillar. And the gutter
Still hangs over my head raised above the void,
And from it black poison oozes drop after drop.

And suddenly—each drop becomes an eye. My entire being is
     wholly
Permeated with eye-light. I scoop up the light.
And above me the gutter woven into the ruins.
A telescope. I swim into its smoothness and the eye-glances

Unite brightly. Here they are, just like yesterday,
The familiar, the living stars of my town.
And among them—the after-Sabbath star
That motherlips used to bless: a happy new week.

And I am resuscitated. There is no one to cast darkness over it,
to destroy it,
And live I must, for my mother's good star is alive.

While in "Telephone" the promise of redemption is merely implied, in "The First Night in the Ghetto" this promise is formulated as an unequivocal assertion. It comes at the end of the poem as the poet gazes at yesterday's luminous sky and at yesterday's stars, notably at the "after-Sabbath star that motherlips used to bless: a happy new week."

This affirmation of life, variously orchestrated in Sutzkever's wartime poetry, is not only an act of personal survival, but one of cultural continuity as well, an imperative that derives from the poet's fear that only a dying "ember" might be left of the Jewish community in Europe. In Sutzkever's poetic world, the primacy of individual survival is metaphysically and ideologically linked to Jewish continuity—a responsibility that is communally redemptive. Thus the dying "ember," Sutzkever intimates, will be ignited again; and his dead mother's star, among "the familiar, the living stars of my town," is a symbol of Jewish continuity that, he believes, is unextinguishable.

There is yet another purpose in rekindling the dying "ember"—namely, to bear witness, an imperative as commanding in the early stages of the occupation as in its later ones, when the poet feared that the very memory of European Jewry might be obliterated. The perception of an "ember" as historical witness is neither new nor peculiar to Sutzkever alone. In other times of disaster, other Jews, fearing the destruction of their community also perceived themselves as an "ember" morally bound to bear witness. One such prototype of a dying "ember" as historical chronicler is a medieval fragment that, as Sidra DeKoven Ezrahi writes:

> has survived from Hebrew Lamentation literature of the fourteenth century, written by a man who returned to his hometown after a trip only to discover that a pogrom had wiped out every inhabitant and destroyed all the holy books, except one Bible. This one remaining man, who refers to himself as

the "last ember," wrote a brief account of the destruction of his town on the pages of the one remaining Bible.[11]

The impact of the poet's perception of the hell into which he and his neighbors have been hurled is immediate, even if conveyed by a neighbor. The neighbor persona is a device that allows the poet to distance himself from and ultimately to take cognizance of the brutality with which the Nazis established the Vilna ghetto. The reign of terror was such that it caused the trapped Jews to experience a form of mental catalepsy, which oscillated between a clear perception of the truth and an inability to assimilate it. Sutzkever reflects this phenomenon both in his assertion that "the first night in the ghetto is the first night in the grave" and in the bitter consolation that "later one gets used to it." The tension between the dawning of an extreme knowledge—namely, the possible destruction of the Jews in Europe—and the denial of this realization—expressed in the assertion that one can live in a grave—is singularly ironic. For this tension recalls the traditional optimism and pacifism of diaspora Judaism that had learned to adjust to calamity in order to survive. But since prewar disasters stand in sharp relief against the present assault, the two are implicitly and ironically juxtaposed. The irony also derives from Sutzkever's condemnation of this very pacifism, which is articulated in other poems of this and even later periods and is discussed in another chapter.

Moreover, there is a form of dramatic irony[12] in Sutzkever's apprehension of the end of the world in which "green, / stiff corpses strewn on the ground" are assured that life can continue. This peculiar kind of irony derives from the fact that terrible as the situation was in 1941, it pales by comparison with the conditions in the following years. The same irony is evident in the early entries of Chaim Kaplan's Warsaw ghetto diary. As early as September 12, 1939, Kaplan writes, "it is beyond my pen to describe the destruction and the ruin that the enemy planes have wrought on our lovely capital. . . . Dante's description of the *Inferno* is mild compared to the inferno raging in the streets of Warsaw."[13] Because of the growing daily horrors, each successive entry reveals yesterday's naivety, while the diary as a whole lays bare the shock Kaplan sustained in his confrontation with the *anus mundi*. The early writings of Kaplan, just like the early poetry of Sutzkever, reveal a truth most succinctly expressed by Edgar in *King Lear*:

And worse it may be yet: the worst is not,
So long as we can say, "this is the worst."

Both Kaplan's and Sutzkever's later writings, however, recall
Dante's agitation during his symbolic pilgrimage in hell: his fear
of encroaching madness, his failing spirit and revulsion, his moral
indignation and concern that he will not be able to record what
he saw.

In Sutzkever's earthly hell, unlike Dante's metaphoric con-
struct, nothing is symbolic, nothing allegorical, moral, or anagogi-
cal. Indeed so real is irreality that Sutzkever seeks moorings in
such conceits as "ships sinking on land." This oxymoron height-
ens the irony of the assertion in the catechismal structure of the
second strophe—namely, that it is possible for Jews, even when
transformed into "green, stiff corpses," to survive in a disintegrat-
ing world.

The irony and the paradox of such assertions arise not only
from the traditional optimism of Judaism, but also from those psy-
chic phenomena associated by Robert Lifton with "extreme death
immersion" or "death imprint." Speaking of Holocaust and Hi-
roshima survivors, Dr. Lifton suggests that their sense of vulnera-
bility can be seen in two ways. One group manifests a heightened
sense of vulnerability, resulting from

> the jarring awareness of the fact of death, as well as of its
> extent and violence . . . Yet as we have also observed, the sur-
> vivors can retain an opposite image of having met death and
> conquered it, a sense of *reinforced invulnerability*. He may
> feel himself to be one of those rare beings who has crossed
> over to the other side and come back—one who has lived out
> the universal psychic theme of death and rebirth.[14]

Since Sutzkever is keenly aware that, like nature, Jewish history is
replete with ritual reenactments of death and rebirth, he may be
drawing sustenance from this cyclical promise, even in the present
terror.

It is this promise that makes its presence manifest in the po-
et's rebellious words: "I have it up to my throat." And it is this
declaration that initiates the process of restorative mourning, for it
allows the cognitive faculties to comprehend and evaluate the full
weight of the tragedy, without which the process of individual or
collective rebirth cannot be initiated. The grotesque nature of

death, often including daily enactments of mass murder, militated against the healing rituals of traditional mourning. This problem was exacerbated by a host of bizarre situations. All too often there were not enough individual graves to bury the dead or else there were no dead for burial, for the victims either vanished with the smoke or disappeared into some other void.

Sutzkever, however, alone among the other "green, stiff corpses," under a gutter of a building in ruins, strains the limits of his will and rises to lament the building's empty rooms. Only the inanimate "roaring bricks, / Torn out of their walls with chunks of flesh," join him in his solitary mourning. This surrealistic image augments both the poet's anguish and the silence of the world outside his own. Furthermore, this image conveys the savagery with which the buildings in the ghetto were emptied of their inhabitants. Singling out but one of the buildings, Sutzkever renders the barbarism of the *Aktion* all the more palpable. The confined space and energies inherent in the ensuing images and associations break forth in an elegaic outpouring:

Playful was the rain in the gutter in other times,
Supple, soft, blessed. Mothers used to put out
Pails to catch the sweet cloudmilk
And shampoo their daughters' hair to bring luck's luster to the
  braids.
Now—there are no mothers, no daughters, no rain,
Only bricks in the ruins. Only roaring bricks,
Torn from their walls with chunks of flesh.

The world for which the poet grieves and the vehicle of his mourning reflect each other in a complementary relationship of solitary anguish and an isolated world.

Significantly, the lamentation for the vanished world, the poem itself, is the poet's temporary verbal shelter. Much like Szlengel's, Sutzkever's memory is a defense against psychic and spiritual disintegration. Thus the world suddenly destroyed is returned, albeit in ruins—ruins, however, that are sacrosanct and canonized into a transcendental spirit: "the ruins alone are my sister." This feminine image resembles the Shekhina,[15] the feminine emanation of the divine, who was alleged to have shared in Israel's exile and suffering (Megillah 29a). She is the generative source of creative energy whose divine presence prompts the redemptive "moist wind without breath" to fall upon the poet's mouth "with

gentle grace / escorting my spirit that detaches itself from my tat-
tered skeleton / Like a butterfly."

The image of the "moist wind without breath" is a metaphor
(and such metaphors abound in Jewish lore) of the souls of marty-
red Jews, the recent inhabitants of the now ruined buildings. They
are the midrashic reminder that the events of Jewish ancestors are
a sign to their descendants. They are, therefore, the phantom pres-
ence that transmigrates through the ruins to the poet's conscious-
ness. Transfigured into wind and later into eyes and stars, this
mystical transmigration of souls lifts the poet's spirit from the
communal grave of the ghetto, linking it with the living spirit of
Israel. The metamorphosis of the souls into stars is conveyed in
the evocative images:

> Here they are, just like yesterday
> The familiar, the living stars of my town.
> And among them—that after-Sabbath star,
> The one motherlips used to bless: a happy new week.

The transcendental presence of both the Shekhina and the
martyred Jews is absorbed by Sutzkever not only in a mystical act,
but one of conscious will as well. This union of spirit and will—a
union that reflects Judaic theodicy, reenacted in the Holocaust—
initiates the poet's rebirth process. In his organic universe, the
murderers remain unnamed. Death is personified as "black poi-
son" oozing from "the gutter," an intimation of a womb. These
symbols are transfigured into the all-illuminating eyes and a tele-
scope: into life and its womb:

> And suddenly each drop [of black poison] becomes an eye. My
>   entire being is wholly
> Permeated with eye light. A network of light as I scoop up the
>   light.
> And above me the gutter woven into the ruins.
> A telescope. I swim into its smoothness and the eye glances
> Unite brightly.

In these transformations, the eyes become the living stars of the
poet's town.

Sutzkever's rebirth is not only metaphysical but physical as
well. The dying "ember" is reignited by both the promptings of the
numinous souls of murdered Jews and his personal, telescopically

focused will. "And live I must, for my mother's star is alive." So the dead and the reborn are united in their consecration of life and, therefore, Jewish continuity. For in the Holocaust, the stubborn struggle to stay alive was often as much for those who were already killed as for oneself.

Even when documenting facts, Sutzkever's poems derive their power from their spirituality rather than graphic detail. Like many other poets of the period, Sutzkever eschews the mean and horrific. He seems unwilling to defile his aesthetic structures and, above all, the ethical world of the Jews with the sordid realism of the Holocaust. Moreover, Sutzkever was determined to uphold the highest criteria of art despite or perhaps because of the wretchedness of the ghetto. As Ruth Wisse writes:

> Even before the war he had determined that the failure of humanity could not alter the basic criterion of art. In the living hell that followed, the uncorruptible standards of the good poem became, for Sutzkever, the touchstone of a former, higher sanity and a psychological means of self-protection against ignominy and despair. Even beyond this, he seems to have developed a belief in the mystical power of art to save, literally *save* the good singer from death.[16]

In a world gone up in smoke, the poet refused to surrender the thing one would expect he needed least. For in the end, art, for Sutzkever the regenerative power, helped him to sustain his belief in the supreme value of surviving, of living.

Chapter Two

The Great Chain of Being

Although an avowed Jew, Władysław Szlengel was not as deeply rooted in Jewish culture and its literature as was Abraham Sutzkever. Moreover, while Sutzkever sought an idiom within aesthetic structures, and while he fine tuned his own lyric voice, finding in art a source of redemption and a vehicle of immortalizing evanescent Jewish life, Szlengel intuitively, rather than programmatically, seemed to avoid the aesthetic, recoiling from traditional poetics, which he apparently regarded as inappropriate for ghetto reality. Since this reality was a function not of familiar norms and values but rather of unimagined daily catastrophes, familiar terminology often sounded absurd and meaningless. The ghetto lexicon was, therefore, in a process of continuous change, providing nuances of meaning that the register of common language could no longer transmit. And it is in these linguistic transmutations that Szlengel found the most precise correlatives for ghetto surreality. Hence, Szlengel's poetic idiom is simple but ironic, conversational, and prosaic, imploding ghetto slang and deliberate Yiddishisms to destroy the perfect diction of prewar Polish poetry. Unsymbolic and concrete, unimaginative and *sachlich*, his images mean what they are. Yet no less than Sutzkever, Szlengel intended his poetry to immortalize fugitive life. This he did by casting that life into poetic form.

The Last Ember and the Document Poem

Both Szlengel's nostalgia, a tone that marks such early ghetto poems as "Telephone," and his preoccupation with the pain of cultural truncation were to undergo rapid and radical changes. His later poems, notably those written from 1942 to 1943, reveal concerns that dominate the poetry of those poets who like Sutzkever are rooted in Jewish tradition. Szlengel's transformation was probably a result of the inverse relationship between the growing atrocities and his intensified sense of Jewish identity—a phenomenon not unusual among assimilated Jews in both the Holocaust and other oppressions.

Catapulted from his non-Jewish heritage into the ghetto, Szlengel, like the others, realized the bankruptcy of assimilation. His later ghetto poetry shows the dissolution of the lines between personal and communal grief. In this Szlengel reflects Jewish liturgy of destruction that tends to avoid individual grief and tragedy. Moreover, this tradition mourns not the individual victim or martyr but rather invokes the memory of communal suffering. Indeed, Judaic theodicy includes no saints' days, and whether it is individual martyrs, exalted leaders, or the mass destruction of thousands of Jews, they are all incorporated into Yom Kippur commemoration services.[1]

Like Sutzkever's, Szlengel's later poetry is in the tradition of the duty of the "last ember" to leave a chapter of martyrology for posterity. As Irena Maciejewska states, his poems—like the notes of Adam Czerniakow, chairman of the Warsaw Judenrat, and the diary of the famous physician, educator, and writer Janusz Korczak or the entries of the noted historian Emanuel Ringelblum—became the self-conscious chronicles of the condemned. Szlengel is now the poet of "documentary poems" (*wierszy dokumentów*), the recorder of "terrifying events" (*straszliwych zdarzeń*). "*Te określenia raz po raz pojawiają się u samego Szlengla i w nich zawarta jest najpełniejsza autodefinacja rodzaju jego twórczości.*"[2] (These descriptions repeatedly appear in the writings of Szlengel himself and embody the most comprehensive self-definition of the character of his work.)

In an essay, a form of prose-poem, Szlengel writes:

Wszystkimi nerwami czuję się duszony coraz mniej dawkowanym powietrzem w łodzi, która nie odwołalnie idzie na dno. Rożnica jest minimalna: jestem w łodzi nie niesiony gestem bohaterstwa, ale wtrącony bez woli, winy czy wyższej racji.

Ale jestem w tej łodzi i czuję się jeśli nie kapitanem, to w każdym razie kronikarzem tonących. Nie chcę zostawić

tylko cyfr dla statystyki, chcę przyszłą historję wzbogacić
(złe słowo) w przyczynki, dokumenty i ilustracje.

Na ścienie mojej łodzi piszę wiersze dokumenty, towarzysz-
om mego grobowca czytałem elaboraty poety, poety anno
domini 1943, szukającego natchnienia w ponurej kronice
swoich dni.[3]

□ □ □

With all my senses I feel myself being suffocated by the di-
minishing air in a boat that is irrevocably going down. The
distinction is minimal: I'm in this boat not carried by heroic
gestures but rather thrown in without volition, guilt, or
higher law.

Still, I am in this boat; and if I don't perceive myself as its
captain, I am nonetheless the chronicler of the drowning. I
don't want to leave mere statistical ciphers. I want to enrich
(wrong word) future history with a legacy, documents, and il-
lustrations.

I write document-poems on the wall of my boat. To the com-
panions of my tomb, I read elaborations of a poet, a poet *anno
domini* 1943, who sought inspiration in the dismal chronicle
of his day.

One such "document poem" written on the wall of a sinking
boat is "Rzeczy" (Things). Despite Szlegel's rejection of prewar lit-
erary standards, this tripartite, 126-line poem shows influences of
the Polish Jewish poet laureate, Julian Tuwim (1894–1956).
"Things" resonates with echoes of Tuwim's *Bal w operze* (*The
Ball at the Opera*), a powerful poem of 1936 full of forebodings of
the Holocaust. Like *The Ball at the Opera*, "Things" vibrates with
dazzling rhythms, the metallic ring of colloquialisms, as well as
the ironic and grotesque. While *The Ball at the Opera* is an encap-
sulated history of the interwar period in Poland, "Things" is a
contraction of the history of the Warsaw ghetto. Written late (the
end of 1942 or beginning of 1943), this poem is an evocation of a
Dantesque hell into which the condemned are irrevocably driven.
Invoking the grotesque, Szlengel's projection of this descent is not
of individuals but rather of their possessions. In doing this, he re-

flects the Nazi perception of Jews as having somehow been divested of their humanity:

Rzeczy

Z Hożej i Wspólnej, i Marszałkowskiej
Jechały wozy . . . wozy żydowskie . . .
    meble, stoły, i stołki,
    walizeczki, tobołki,
    kufry, skrzynki, i bety,
    garnitury, portrety,
    pościel, garnki, dywany,
    i drapiery ze ściany.
    Wiśniak, słoje, słoiki,
    szklanki, plater, czajniki,
    książki, cacka, i wszystko
    jedzie z Hożej na Śliską.
    W palcie wódki butelka
    i kawałek serdelka.
    Na wozach, rikszach, i furach
    jedzie zgraja ponura. . . .
A ze Śliskiej na Niską
znów jechało to wszystko.
    Meble, stoły, i stołki,
    walizeczki, tobołki.
    pościel, garnki—psze panów,
    ale już bez dywanów.
    Po platerach ni znaku
    i już nie ma wiśniaków,
    garniturów ni betów,
    i słoików, potretów.
    Już zostały na Śliskiej
    drobnosteczki te wszystkie,
    w palcie wódki butelka
    i kawałek serdelka.
    Na wozach, rikszach, i furach
    jedzie zgraja ponura.
Opuścili znów Niską
i do bloków szło wszystko.
    Nie ma mebli i stołków,
    garnków oraz tobołków.
    Zaginęły czajniki,

książki, bety słoiki.
Poszły gdzieś do cholery
garnitury, platery.
Razem w rikszę to wal to . . .
Jest walizka i palto,
jest herbaty butelka,
jest ogryzek karmelka.
Na piechotę, bez fury
jedzie orszak ponury . . .
Potem z bloków na Ostrowską
jedzie drogą żydowską
 bez tobołów, tobołków,
 i bez mebli czy stołków,
 bez dywanów, czajników,
 bez platerów, słoików,
 w ręce z jedną walizką
 ciepły szalik to wszystko,
 jeszcze wody butelka
 i chlebaczek na szelkach,
 depcząc rzeczy—stadami
 nocą szli ulicami.
A z Ostrowkiej do bloku
szli w dzień chmurny o zmroku—
 walizeczka i chlebak,
 teraz więcej nie trzeba—
 równo . . . równo piątkami
 marszem szli ulicami.

Noce chłodne dni krutsze,
jutro . . . może pojutrze . . .
na gwizd, krzyk albo rozkaz
znowu droga żydowska . . .
 Ręce wolne i tylko
 woda—z mocną pastylką . . . [4]

☐ ☐ ☐

Things

From Hoża and Wspólna and Marszałkowska Streets
cartloads . . . Jewish cartloads on the move . . .
 furniture, tables, and stools,
 small valises and bundles,
 trunks, boxes, and featherbeds,

suits, portraits,
bedding, pots, rugs,
and draperies.
Cherry wine, big jars, little jars,
glasses, silverware, teapots,
books, toys, knicknacks
moved from Hoża Street to Street Śliska.
In the pocket a bottle of vodka
and a chunk of sausage.
In carts, rickshaws, and wagons
the gloomy motley rides . . .
Then from Śliska to Niska
again everything moved.
Furniture, tables, and stools,
small valises and bundles.
Bedding, pots—yessirree—
but already without rugs.
No sign of silverware,
no more cherry wine,
no suits, no featherbeds,
no little jars, no portraits.
All these trifles
left on Śliska,
in the coat-pocket a bottle of vodka
and a chunk of sausage.
In carts, rickshaws, and wagons
the gloomy motley rides . . .
Again they left Niska
all heading toward the blocks.
No more furniture, no stools,
no pots, no bundles.
Lost are the teapots,
books, featherbeds, little jars.
To the devil went
the suits and knicknacks.
Dumped together in a rickshaw . . .
a valise and a coat,
a bottle of tea,
a bite of caramel.
On foot without wagons
the gloomy mob rides . . .
Then from the blocks to Ostrowska
moving along a Jewish road

without big or small bundles,
without furniture or stools,
without rugs and teapots,
without silverware and little jars,
a valise in the hand,
a warm scarf . . . that's it,
still a bottle of water,
a chunk of bread tied to suspenders,
things trampled underfoot—herdlike
they walked the street at night.
And from Ostrowska to the blocks
they walked on a cloudy day at dusk—
a small valise and a chunk of bread,
no other needs they had—
straight, straight in rows of five
they marched through the streets.

Cool nights, shorter days,
tomorrow . . . maybe the day after . . .
to a whistle, shout or order
again a Jewish road . . .
the hand free but for
water—and a strong pill . . .

In his projection of the uninterrupted tableau of the daily movement of human possessions, Szlengel shows the relentless contraction of the Warsaw ghetto. Initially the "Things" moved from the elegant streets of Warsaw (Hoża, Wspólna, and Marszał-kowska). Many possessions, as well as their owners, pouring into the narrowing funnel of the ghetto in an endless caravan of wagons drawn or pushed by humans, were unable to find housing; for virtually each apartment had already been shared by several families. The homeless were either frantically seeking shelter or meandering dazed in a state of bewildered exhaustion. Roaming the fetid, crowded, and noisy streets, some persons and "things" managed to establish residence against the walls of buildings. But they had to compete with corpses strewing the streets. The swollen corpses, some with ballooning bellies and legs—a result of exposure or starvation and typhus—were the remains of individuals who had been earlier driven into the ghetto, dragging their worldly possessions in their "Jewish wagons."

Those "things" and their owners who could find shelter realized, soon enough, that it was very temporary. For they were forced to move in a rapidly descending succession of streets to

Roman Kramsztyk, "Street Family in the Warsaw Ghetto." (Charcoal)

Śliska and from there to Niska, the lower circles of the ghetto. As "things" were squeezed into the bottoming cone, they became fewer and smaller. Yet their value was high, for their loss symbolized the loss of life's anchors and ultimately life itself. In resuming the descent from Niska to the "blocks"—factories in which only those who secured permits to work and hence to live worked as slaves—all that is left of the human possessions "is a suitcase and a coat, / . . . a bottle of tea, / . . . a bite of caramel." Reflecting the meaning of the content in the poem's structure, both the long list of "things" that are no longer there and each successive strophe become shorter.

Setting again upon the "Jewish road," the handful of "things" and the decimated ranks of the "gloomy mob" move from the "blocks" to Ostrowska Street. In his poetic compression of the beginning and the end of the Warsaw ghetto, Szlengel provides cryptic signs intelligible only to those who are familiar with the cosmological system of the ghetto. Ostrowska Street constituted the bottom of the "cauldron," an area of seven blocks into which the Jews were forced on September 6, 1942. The Germans dubbed that area, and the *Aktion, Einkesselung* (encircling). The apt Yiddish and Polish translations of it were, respectively, *kesl* and *kocioł* (cauldron). The psychological appropriateness of this translation derives from the fact that the *Einkesselung* was a veritable witch's cauldron, a Walpurgis Night during which all the evil forces were unloosed on the seven square blocks. Having been allowed to bring food and drink for two days, that is "a bottle of water" and a chunk of bread tied to suspenders, the Jews were told that the *Aktion* was for registration purposes. Although few believed this ruse, most Jews complied with the order for fear of being shot. The *Aktion* lasted a whole week.

Szlengel deliberately avoids any description of the encirclement. Nor, for that matter, does he provide a graphic mise-en-scene of the events that preceded the *Einkesselung*. He probably regarded silence more appropriate for the unspeakable. To mention "blocks" or "Niska" or "Ostrowska" was enough. After all, as his essay-poem "This I Read to the Dead" indicates, he wrote for the dead who were thoroughly familiar with his allusions. Apparently he had little hope that anyone else in the world of the living would read his work. Yet current readers need to understand his images and punch-line phrases. Hurled at dawn into the "cauldron," amid flying feathers unloosed from bayoneted pillows, the bewildered Jews waded through puddles of blood, stepping over corpses. According to German statistics, 2,648 people were shot in the seven days of destruction.[5] In this seething "cauldron" the Jews were made to form orderly columns, "straight, straight in rows of five," out of which ten thousand people were selected daily and deported to gas chambers in Treblinka. At the conclusion of the *Aktion*, those who survived the selection—parents whose children or adolescents whose forty-year-old parents were the selected—and who managed to recover from their cataleptic state and had the energy to summon the will to live were marched from Ostrowska Street back to the "blocks."

If Szlengel ever entertained the hope of Jewish survival, at this crossroad he seems to have considered that notion absurd. The experience of the "cauldron," from which he returned to the "blocks," apparently confirmed the rumors that the Jews were not being resettled in the East for agricultural work, as they were led to believe, but rather transported to gas chambers in Treblinka and other mass murder factories. Isolated from the outside world and receiving scanty and false information regarding the destination of the Jews deported heretofore, Szlengel, like the rest of the Warsaw ghetto denizens, was probably incredulous when rumors of gas chambers and other forms of mass murder began to seep into the ghetto. By July 1942 the Jews had little doubt that thousands were killed, but the fact of gas chambers or total destruction was largely disbelieved, just as it was disbelieved in the rest of the world when the first reports of death camps were smuggled out of Poland.

The few witnesses who managed to stagger back from the death centers were thought to be demented, their minds unhinged by the horrors of the ghetto itself and by the anguish connected with the deportations of their families. When the July 1942 deportations began, it was reported that the SS gave their word of honor to the Judenrat that not one of the deported Jews had been killed. Moreover, to assuage the alarm in the ghetto, the Judenrat was directed to issue a proclamation assuring the panic-stricken Jews that the resettlement in the Eastern territories was not a lie, as they suspected. At the same time, letters to relatives from Jews purported to be in Białystok, Brześć, Pińsk, and even as far east as Mińsk and Smoleńks, began to arrive daily, further confounding the population. These messages, actually written under duress at Treblinka, urged starving relatives in the ghetto to volunteer for resettlement.

In the absence of a viable defense system and in the face of absolute starvation as well as the inherent inability to face one's own imminent death, the credulity of the Jews was a form of adaptation to an intolerable situation. But the "cauldron" apparently caused Szlengel to have little doubt of the imminent destruction of the Jews. He realized that "tomorrow . . . maybe the day after . . . / to a whistle, shout, or order / again a Jewish road." And at this, the last time, "the hands [will be] free but for / water—and a strong pill." That pill was poison.

Self-Implicating Logic

The first part of "Things" is marked by a play of tone, images, and words that suggests a self-implicating attitude—one that is dominated, on a subrational level, by the myth of the victim's guilt. This attitude is evoked in the thematic variations of the grotesque image "gloomy motley," "gloomy mob," "herdlike they walked," and "straight, straight in rows of five they marched." The ironic specificity of the Jewishness of the "Jewish wagons," "Jewish road," and "again a Jewish road," amplify Szlengel's perception of Jewish culpability. Szlengel seems to see this guilt rooted in the status of the Jews as the world's *pharmaki*, the scapegoats of history, a perception that informs many of Szlengel's poems.

Such manifestations of displaced guilt are not peculiar to Szlengel alone. Victims of other crimes are frequently subject to feelings of guilt and shame that rightfully belong to, but are rejected by, perpetrators and bystanders alike. The motives of the victim, criminal, and passive bystander are obviously complex. Yet some of Szlengel's motives can be gleaned from both the unique predicament of the Jews and the role Szlengel chose for himself as a ghetto poet.

Szlengel obviously knew that because the shtetl Jews had little recourse to law and justice even before the war, they were often forced to resist total destruction by appeasement. But at this moment in Jewish history and his personal despair, Szlengel began to regard the policy of appeasement as bankrupt. He was, therefore, determined to reveal this to his fellow Jews, for he felt morally bound to show them what he believed—namely, that the road of acquiescence and accommodation has led to "a whistle, shout, or order." Even in this late hour, or perhaps because of it, he wanted to extricate his people from their historical acquiescence in the face of atrocity. To this end, he held up a mirror, his poem, to them.

Another reason for Szlengel's self-implicating logic is the human longing for reason and causality. Chaim Kaplan, too, notes in his diary that "the worst part of this kind of death is that you don't know the reason for it. . . . The lack of reason for the murders especially troubles the inhabitants of the ghetto. . . . People do not want to die without a cause."[6]

The abrogation of causality robs victims of their own sense of power and their ability to direct their own destinies. Sometimes in their helplessness, they prefer to believe that had they but willed it, they might have exerted some influence over their own fate. Such displaced guilt allows victims to see a measure of reason in a world they cannot fathom. Apparently, any comfort found in the recognition of one's own powerlessness was difficult for Szlengel to accept lest it provoke self-pity. This Szlengel would not countenance. Indeed the bristling irony that pervades Szlengel's ghetto poems is probably a bridle with which he restrains this inclination. The tension between these polar impulses is reflected in the first part of the poem.

The six stanzas are marked by a flow of nearly impeccable couplets and trochaic meter. The nervous inner rhythms stand in sharp contrast to the Apollonian form. The dazzling beat of the metrical units is augmented by asyndetic lines. The concrete, massive nouns fall almost unconnected, as if in a heavy torrent, getting ahead of the poet himself; and are only held together in the first strophe by three verbs (move, moved, and rides). In the following five strophes the verbs increase in direct proportion to the increased frequency with which "things" are made to move from street to street and in inverse proportion to the decreasing number of possessions. The contrasting syndeton in the first couplet of the opening strophe amplifies the emotional cataloguing of elegant Warsaw streets from which the piled up "things" were forced to move.

Both the irony and the grotesque in these stanzas derive from the poet's bitter awareness that the perpetual Jewish wagons, traveling an endless Jewish road of persecution, have come to an end. The ironic sensibility of the poet, who seems to have a clear vision of what he adumbrates, conjures up images of the "Wandering Jew" and a long diaspora road: a road that commenced with the expulsion from the Holy Land, passed through the first ghetto in medieval Venice, through inquisitions and pogroms to the last ghetto in twentieth-century Warsaw—the end of the road.

If the first part of the poem is informed by muffled cadences of the tragic, in the second part these tones are silenced. Szlengel ultimately avoids the tragic, precisely because the tragic was of such magnitude that it allowed for no verbal approximation. Any poetic imitation of the tragic would perforce become a metaphor devoid of reality. For Szlengel the ironic, absurd, and grotesque are devices more useful in transforming ghetto reality into the logos of speech.

In a Swiftian tour de force (a world in which suits of clothes perform all the offices of human life[7]), Jewish "things" are animated with Jewish life and thus perform all the offices of that life, revenge included. The Jews are gone; but their "things" accrue (*narasta*) to the forsaken houses, waiting for the coming of the "Aryans," presumably the Poles. The latter will reclaim the abandoned apartments, put an order to the mass of scattered "things," and begin a carefree life. However, lest one get carried away, this vision of bliss is replaced by an image of an unfinished bottle of water and a strong pill left in some freight car:

> *Tylko w jakimś wagonie*
> *pozostanie to tylko:*
> *nie dopita butelka*
> *z jakąś mocną pastylką....* [8]

❑ ❑ ❑

> But in some freight car
> only this will remain:
> A bottle half-full
> and some strong pill....

The bottle and the poison presumably belonged to someone who either suffocated in a cattle car on its way to Treblinka, before he or she had time to end his or her life, or who foolishly hoped to the last moment that somehow he or she might be spared. In either case what is left for posterity is a legacy of trains carrying people to death centers and a "bottle half-full / and some strong pill."

Moreover, lest the "Aryans" expect to gorge themselves on Jewish possessions, believing that the reductivity and subsequent extermination of Jewish human beings will go unavenged, their "things" will shatter this illusion:

> *A w noc grozy, co przyjdzie*
> *po dniach kul oraz mieczy,*
> *wyjdą z kufrów i domów*
> *wszystkie żydowskie rzeczy.*
> *I wybiegną oknami,*
> *będą szły ulicami,*
> *aż się zejdą na szosach*
> *nad czarnymi szynami.*
> *Wszystkie stoły i stołki,*
> *walizeczki, tobołki*
> *garnitury, słoiki,*
> *i platery, czajniki,*
> *i odejdą i zginą,*
> *nikt nie zgadnie, co znaczy,*
> *że tak rzeczy odeszły,*
> *i nikt ich nie zobaczy.*[9]

☐ ☐ ☐

And in the night of awe that is to come
after days of bullets and swords,
all the Jewish things
will leave the trunks and houses.
And they'll run out the windows,
walk down the streets,
till they'll meet on the highways
along the black rail-tracks.
All the tables and stools,
and valises, and bundles,
suits, little jars,
and silverware, and teapots,
and they'll leave and perish,
and no one will guess the meaning
of disappearing things,
and no one will see them again.

Projecting a world of grotesque metaphysical justice, the poet creates a circuit of energy between himself and his ghetto reader. In this fusion both come face-to-face with the ultimate absurd: the deadly isolation of the Jews on whose behalf neither God nor humanity lifted a finger. Only inanimate "things," mystically empowered with the spirit of the murdered Jews (resembling in a parodic sense the ruins in Sutzkever's "The First Night in the Ghetto"), will exact vengeance. Such grotesque revenge reflects and befits the cosmic chaos.

Both the breathless inventory of "things" and the dazzling rhythms, augmented by three enjambents (11. 1, 3, 7), reflect the agitation and amplify the grotesque in the first part of the poem. Yet Szlengel returns for a moment to the world of recognizable phenomena. This is expressed in the assertion that the metaphysical revenge will come "after days of bullets and swords," an event he envisioned, inspired, and lived to see in the Warsaw ghetto uprising.[10]

The ironic, absurd, and grotesque crowd and pressure the concluding four line stanza:

> *Lecz na stole sędziowskim*
> *(jeśli veritas Victi . . .)*
> *pozostanie pastylka*
> *jako corpus delicti.*[11]

❏ ❏ ❏

> But on the judgment table
> (if *veritas victi . . .*)
> the pill will remain
> as *corpus delicti.*

Contained in this conclusion is a vision of justice and truth, each of which is contingent on the other. Szlengel probably laughed at both of these possibilities with bitter irony. Having been transformed into smoke, but for a ridiculous pill of poison, nothing will remain of the Jews, not even a *corpus delicti.*

Sutzkever:
The World Turned Upside-Down

Another poem that reflects the supremacy of Jewish possessions is Abraham Sutzkever's "A Vogn Shikh" (A Cartload of

Shoes), written in the Vilna ghetto on January 1, 1943. While
"Things" is a historical compression of the Warsaw ghetto, "A
Cartload of Shoes" focuses on one event in the Vilna ghetto—
namely, a trainload of murdered Jews' shoes sent to needy Ger-
mans in Berlin:

A Vogn Shikh

Di reder yogn, yogn,
Vos brengen zey mit zikh?
Zey brengen mir a vogn
Mit tsaplendike shikh.

Der vogn vi a khupe
in ovntikn glants;
Di shikh—a fule kupe
Vi mentshn in a tants.

A khasena, a yontef?
Tsi hot mir ver farblendt?
Di shikh azoyne nonte
Oyf s'nay ikh hob derkent.

Es klapn di optsasn:
Vuhin, vuhin, vuhin?
Fun alte Vilna gasn
Me traybt undz kayn Berlin.

Ikh darf nit fregn vemes,
Nor s'tut in harts a ris:
Oh, zogt mir shikh, dem emes,
Vu zenen zey di fis?

Di fis fun yene tufl
Mit knepelekh vi toy,—
Un do—vi iz dos gufl
Un dort vu iz di froy?

In kindershikh in alle
Vos ze ikh nit kayn kind?
Vos tut nit on di kale
Di shikhelekh atsind?

Durkh kindershikh un shkrabes
Kh'derken mayn mames shikh!
Zi flegt zey bloyz oyf Shabes
Aroyftsiyen oyf zikh.

Un s'klapn di obtsasn:
Vuhin, vuhin, vuhin?
Fun alte Vilna gassn
me traybt undz kayn Berlin.[12]

❑ ❑ ❑

A Cartload of Shoes

The wheels are turning, turning,
What are they bringing there?
They are bringing *me* a cartload
Of quivering footwear.

A cartload like a wedding
In the evening glow;
The shoes—in heaps, dancing
Like people at a ball.

Is it a holiday, a wedding dance?
Or have I been misled?
I know these shoes at a glance
And look at them with dread.

The heels are tapping:
Where to, where to, what in?
From the old Vilna streets
They ship us to Berlin.

I need not ask whose,
But my heart is rent:
Oh, tell me shoes the truth,
Where were the feet sent?

The feet of those boots
With buttons like dew,—
The child of those slippers,
The woman of that shoe?

And children's shoes everywhere,
Why don't I see a child?
Why are the bridal shoes there
Not worn by the bride?

Among the children's worn out boots
My mother's shoes so fair!
Sabbath was the only day
She donned this footwear.

And the heels are tapping:
Where to, where to, what in?
From the old Vilna streets
They chase us to Berlin.

Perhaps most central to both "Things" and "A Cartload of Shoes" is the metaphoric comprehension of the "Great Chain of Being" ladder, the lowest rung of which is occupied by inanimate matter. In the Holocaust this vision of the cosmic order was turned on its head. For people were either reduced to the lowest order of animal—exterminable vermin—or transformed into inanimate matter—soap or lampshades. Conversely, inanimate things—shoes, for example—received the highest value.

The major difference between the two poems is their tone. Szlengel's poem quivers with bitter irony and fury, both propelled by his anguish. Sutzkever's voice, on the other hand, is muffled by the very weight of his grief. All intellectual or aesthetic considerations capitulate to his pain. Although the poems are further marked by different architectonic patterns, they draw surprisingly close in diction, revealing similar recurrent images and rhythms.

In his evocation of the Warsaw ghetto, Szlengel adheres to his documentary grammar, one that uses unadorned ghetto colloquialisms and derives its images from the surreality of the ghetto landscape. Deviating from his usual elegant associations of images, allusions to scriptures, and graceful vocabulary, in "A Cartload of Shoes," Sutzkever, like Szlengel, speaks in artless language, drawing his imagery from "the daily bread of his experience." Perhaps stunned by the eerie sight of shoes of murdered Jews being transported in huge piles to Germany, Sutzkever seeks an appropriate tongue in the simpler folk analogues and antecedents.

The folk character of these precursors animated the spirit of anonymous poets who wrote in Yiddish, the vernacular of the Jewish masses in Slavonic countries in the late eighteenth and early nineteenth centuries. Heretofore, Hebrew was the literary idiom. Sutzkever's early pantheistic experimentations and later brilliant linguistic manipulations as well as sensual lyricism did not prevent him from locating an axis between the folk beginnings of modern Yiddish poetry, earlier medieval liturgical lamentations, and the tragedy he writes about in "A Cartload of Shoes." In this, Sutzkever reflects the ethos of his people who, in recalling historical antecedents, project a vision of hope for the future and find consolation in their ability to survive disasters.

Another feature of "A Cartload of Shoes" is its proximity to the ballad, a genre popular in the Holocaust and used by both Yiddish and Polish poets. This poem shares with the ballad an unembellished vocabulary and directness of narrative line. Metaphoric language is replaced by incremental repetitions of significant words (turning, wagon, shoes, feet) and a repeated questioning pattern in seven out of the nine stanzas. The poem's effect derives from the fusion of lyrical, epic, and dramatic qualities. It starts in medias res and moves episodically in abrupt leaps, focusing on a single event—namely, the shipment of shoes to Berlin. There are no allusions to what preceded this; nor do extensive descriptions burden the story line. Thus the narrative is carried forward with mounting tension to its dramatic *pointe.* This sudden twist occurs not at the conclusion of the poem, as it does in many ballads, but rather at its center, as the poet realizes the cargo's contents. Furthermore, the poem is marked by an eeriness that evokes both uneasiness and suspense. These elements are sustained over the lines, including the balladic refrain. The meter is distinguished by its artlessness. The stanza form is a quatrain, mostly of alternating three- and two-stress lines with an *a b a b* rhyme scheme.

The surrealistic, grotesque, and eerie modes arise as much from the spectral reality that Sutzkever witnesses as from his poetic sensibility. The phantasmagoric cartload of shoes, "quivering" with their owners' death—as the image suggests—is sealed in time and space as in a nightmare. The sense of the nightmarish is augmented by the suspense and eeriness of "a cartload of shoes" likened to "a wedding / In the evening glow." And as in a nightmare, the ghostly train, heaped high with the grotesquely tapping shoes, as if it were a "holiday, a wedding dance," moves with inexorable precision and deadly speed toward the terror-stricken witness as the line, "they bring *me* a cartload / of quivering shoes," suggests. The personal pronoun is an intimation of the grief and horror experienced by those who managed (so they thought) to trick fate or take flight from the present destiny of the Jews. More-over, there is a sense of incredulity, expressed in the rhetorical questions, that the murder of the brides, the children, and the mothers actually happened. And there is the guilt that one saw it all reenacted daily and yet could summon one's will to live, or that one deserves the life not vouchsafed to others. Finally, there is the terror that the train is in the end bound to carry one's own tapping shoes to Berlin.

"A Cartload of Shoes" is, in the final analysis, a communal jeremiad in which the poet laments not only his murdered mother, but also the children, the brides, and the countless numbers of Jews killed daily. As an eyewitness, then, Sutzkever is the interpre-tive mediator whose poem produces a fusion of agony and testi-mony. This lament, like many of its kind, is therefore a synthesis of personal responses to the tragedy and careful documentation of objective fact.

Józef Bau:
A Way of Existence

The torment and bereavement of the trapped Jews were ex-pressed in a whole spectrum of poetic tendencies, including mod-ernistic ones. The collapse of the last vestiges of morality and the concomitant bankruptcy of language (discussed above), caused some poets to seek a vocabulary within the wave of modernistic influences, just as they did within the framework of other literary archetypes. For the convincing verisimilitude with which the po-ets were able to transcribe the human condition into art and which derived from the availability of familiar images was hardly applicable to a knowledge that had no antecedents and no ana-logues. Above all, the language they found arose from the spectral reality of the world in which they were dying.

One such poem is Józef Bau's "Szpital Obozowy" (Camp Hos-pital), written in the Gross-Rosen concentration camp in 1944:

Szpital Obozowy

Leżą na półkach pryczach,
wychudli, błyszczący emalią potu
umierający "muzulmanie"

Ciężkim, monotonnym krokiem
madejowych godzin,
wzdłuż i wszerz baraku-namiotu,
przechadza się
w pokrwawionym fartuchu felczera . . .
"Kapo-wyczekiwanie"
—i ostatnie minuty oblicza
—i miejsca rachuje, które za chwilę
zwolnione zostaną:
. . . tych tak . . . tych tak . . . tych jeszcze nie,
. . . tych tak . . . tych jutro rano. . . .

Widzi: gorączka porzera
niedojedzone przez wszy szkielety
śmierci na sprzedaż wystawione
i przez okno patrzy;—na pobliskim
kominie, przysmarzone dusze
tańczą z czarnym dymem upiorne minuety.
. . . więc przekreśla numery, obok kładzie dopiski:
"zmarli na własne życzenie."[13]

❑ ❑ ❑

Camp Hospital

On shelf bunks lie
emaciated, glistening with sweat's enamel,
dying "Mussulmen."

With heavy monotonous step
of creaking hours,
treads
the length and breadth of the barrack-tent
in the blood-stained apron of a medic . . .
a "Kapo-watch"
—and counts the last minutes
—and figures who soon will
be released:
. . . these yes . . . these yes . . . those not yet
. . . these yes . . . those tomorrow morning. . . .

Sees: fever consumes
the not yet lice-devoured skeletons

displayed for death to buy,
and stares out the window;—in the nearby
chimney, lightly roasted souls
dance a spectral minuet with the black smoke.
. . . then crosses out the numbers, jots down some footnote:
"died voluntarily."

"Camp Hospital" exhibits unusual patterns that repudiate standard grammatical structures, punctuations, and strophic architectonics. The three stanzas of uneven length and unrhymed verses are marked by dissonant rhythms and fragmented diction, which trail off into silence.

In language recalling stenographic notation, the first stanza establishes both the interior of the hospital, "the shelf-bunks," and its patients, the "Mussulmen." Bau's language, however, is so constricted that it explains nothing to those who are not familiar with the world to which he alludes and the language spoken there. The rigidity of his vocabulary is a form of silence, one that signals his capitulation to the incommunicability of his experience. Yet the poem, even the condensed first strophe, conveys a whole way of existence.

The image of the "shelf-bunks" derives from the endless rows of bunk beds, three stories high, that conjure up an image of a morgue. At best the loosely fitted boards of the bunks were equipped with a lice-ridden, often blood-stiffened blanket and an equally filthy sack usually empty of its intended straw. To avoid the lice, the boards were frequently naked. The appellation "Mussulman" was bestowed on those prisoners who were so emaciated and tortured or psychically so exhausted that they could no longer endure the agony of living. They were the living dead. Only their "sweat's enamel" distinguished them from the actually dead.

This "barrack-tent" resembled no hospital known to human experience. The stench alone of the languishing and putrefying "Mussulmen," most of them like lepers, covered with festering sores—wounds produced as much by the ubiquitous lice, the epidemics of scabies, mange, and typhus as by malnutrition or beatings and various forms of torture—defies description. So does the itch of the scabies, a form that settled between the fingers, causing the skin to crack, and pus and blood continually to ooze. The scratching was often so uncontrollable and violent that it scraped off scabs on large portions of the body. The mange too was of a special kind. It settled in the hair, the preferred nesting of the lice.

It was imperative to shave the head and those areas of the body that tend to grow most hair to get rid of the pestilence; but these vermin nested in the sores as well.

The "hospital" echoed with a muffled din: the whimpering and wailing of those who could summon enough will and energy to utter these elemental sounds. The prisoners afflicted with typhus or galloping consumption and wracked by raging fever often fell off their bunks. Landing on top of each other, they sometimes brought about an end to their wretchedness. Both these and other corpses usually lay unburied or uncremated for days. The general putrefaction of the dead and the dying was further increased by the barrels into which the sick relieved themselves. These open barrels were generally kept inside the "hospital." Again one is tempted to invoke the lower ditches of Dante's *Inferno* to convey a measure of the palpable hell of a concentration camp hospital:

> When we
> were above the last cloister of Melabolge so that
> its lay-brothers could be seen by us, strange
> lamentations assailed me that had their shafts
> barbed with pity, at which I covered my ears with
> my hands. As the pain would be if the diseases of
> the hospital of Val di Chiana between July and
> September, and of the Maremma and Sardinia,
> were altogether in one ditch, such was it there,
> and such stench issued from it as is wont to come
> from festered limbs. . . .
> Step by step we went without speech, watching and
> listening to the sick, who had not strength to
> raise themselves. I saw two sitting propped against
> each other as pan is propped on pan to warm,
> spotted from head to foot with scabs; and I never
> saw curry-comb plied by a stable-boy whose master
> waits for him or by one kept unwillingly awake as
> each plied on himself continually the bite of his
> nails for the great fury of the itch that has no other
> relief, and the nails were scraping off the scabs as
> the knife does the scales of the bream or other fish
> that has them larger.[14]

The Germans stayed clear of such hospitals as described by Bau. The "Kapo-watch" alone reigned supreme in this place. It is, therefore, from his evocative point of view, as he stares out the window, that we see the system of *l'univers concentrationnaire,* as David Rousset dubbed it. And it is through the Kapo's consciousness, as he "treads the length and breadth of the barrack-tent / in the blood-stained apron of a medic," that we perceive the hospital. The term "medic" is as deceptive and ironic a reductio ad absurdum as is the term "hospital." Both words arouse a sense of cognitive insecurity; for having lost their familiar meaning, both words are invested with sinister connotations. The "medic" is a Kapo, a prisoner designated by the Nazis to perform some of the most odious and cruel camp offices. For this, the Kapo received a bit more food and some other privileges, among them, a dubious promise of life. The Kapo is personified as a solitary, lowly demon, himself relegated to duty in the lowest ditches of the camp's hell. He keeps a careful record of the passage of the souls. Thus he "counts the last minutes / and figures who soon will be released," crossing out numbers and scribbling something in his book of death. For in this mad chaos, a kingdom of strange paradoxes, *Ordnung muss sein,* and the fervent efficiency is such that a careful record must be kept of the "Mussulmen" who "died voluntarily."

The disjunctive sentences of the poem, their elliptical phrasing and suspension of normal grammar and standard punctuations, recall the distraught stammering of one who recognizes the futility of transcribing unspeakable horror into language. Here the lyric voice is constricted. It trusts itself to communicate neither the truths that evade its human understanding nor the grief and anguish that, if permitted to surface, would surely unhinge the mind. The poetic consciousness is so stunned that its ability to communicate its states, as poetry inherently does, is occluded. Only the recording voice is heard, as it stiffly recounts what the eyewitness sees.

Nonetheless, both grief and anguish are conveyed by such pictorial correlatives as "the not yet lice-devoured skeletons / displayed for death to buy" or "in the nearby chimney, lightly roasted souls / dance a spectral minuet with the black smoke." Although both images are marked by the grotesque, they derive their palpability from the intrinsic surreality of the concentration camp. Here death, for example, conspires with the unloosed demonic forces. Contrary to its traditional eagerness, it is reluctant to claim the souls of the resigned "Mussulmen." Death is therefore personified as a capricious or sadistic customer who must be cajoled to purchase the displayed wares. The image of "lightly roasted souls"

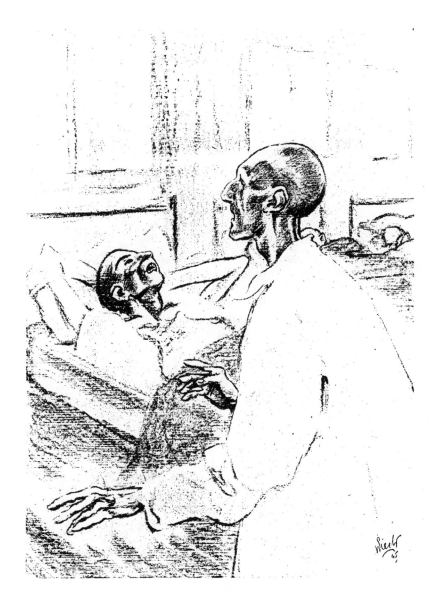

Henri Pieck, "Buchenwald." (Sketch)

suggests that some of the people who were removed from the gas chambers were still alive when hurled into the crematorium.

The evocation of ontological unhinging and the intimation that the unspeakable suffering seems to find its most resonant voice in silence or in language devoid of metaphor and comparison are conveyed in other poems by Bau—Głód (Hunger), for example:

Głód

Mąka skrzepnięta w bochen betonu,
—skondenzowana zapłata za dzień męki,
oto chleb.

Osiem żołądków wypełzających przez oczy,
dzieli go na osiem równych części.
z dokładnością do jednej kruszyny;
—oto bóstwo,
do którego modli się myśl,
poprzez potrójny mur drutów kolczastych.

. . . a dalej, dalej poza splotem
drutów i męki, podobno istnieje świat.
Lecz my zaszachowani
karabinami maszynowymi
wież strażniczych—nie wiemy o tym,
nam wytatuowano na skroni: "Szach mat!"[15]

❑ ❑ ❑

Hunger

Flour coagulated into a loaf of cement
—condensed wages for a day's torment
—that's bread.

Eight stomachs creeping through the eyes
divide it into eight even parts,
the exactness of each crumb;
—that's the godhead
to which thought prays
behind the triple barbed-wire wall.

. . . and farther, farther, beyond the braid
of wires and torment, apparently a world exists.

Henri Pieck, "Buchenwald." (Sketch)

But we checkmated
by watch tower
machine guns—know it not,
our temples are branded "checkmate."

Written in 1943 in Płaszów, a camp near Cracow, this com-
pelling articulation of hunger is almost completely devoid of ex-
trinsic imagery. The sole superimposed metaphor is the word
"cement" to which the daily bread of the prisoners of Płaszów is
likened. That the coveted bread is transubstantiated into the very
godhead by one of the most excrutiating of tortures, starvation, is
not an extravagant conceit. It is rather a faithful recording of fact.
For in this world, a slice of cementlike bread was often perceived
as the sole redemption to which body and soul bowed in reverence
and supplication. Indeed, starvation here is so intense that there is
a veritable dissolution of selfhood. The austere language has lost
one of its essential words, "man," and consciousness is an embod-
ied sensation of hunger, a stomach "creeping through the eyes." In
this godless realm, victims are condemned to death not only by
starvation, but also by machine guns trained in numerous watch-
towers that dot the triple barbed-wire walls. This image, too, de-
rives from the language of concentrationary realism, just as does
the suspicion that the condemned in Płaszów are inhabiting a land
disconnected from the rest of the world: " . . . and farther, beyond
the braid / of wires and torment, apparently a world exists."

Sutzkever:
The Entombing of the Manuscripts

Fervid attempts to record the unfolding events in testimonial
poetry were coupled with equally fervid attempts to save the
manuscripts from destruction. In most cases this was achieved by
depositing them in hermetically sealed containers and burying
them in the ground. Sutzkever, who like many other writers hoped
that the manuscripts would one day be unearthed, actively worked
to save the most valuable books and manuscripts. This he did as
an employee of the YIVO Institute for Jewish Research in the
Vilna ghetto, where his official job was to prepare material to be
sent to Germany. His "Kerndlekh Veyts" (Grains of Wheat), nota-

bly the poem's conclusion, expresses the hope that the hidden treasures will, some day, be recovered.

In the imaginative world of the poet, the manuscripts he hides in the earth become grains of wheat sown for an uncertain future. When overcome with despair, he recalls an Egyptian tale about a king who ordered his servants to fill a gold urn with grains of wheat. This urn was deposited in a pyramid built for the king. Nine thousand years later, when the seeds were unearthed, they blossomed into golden wheat. In pensive tones the poet muses:

> *Efsher oykh veln di verter*
> *Dervartn zikh ven oyf dem likht—*
> *Veln in sho in basherter*
> *Tsebliyen zikh oykh umgerikht?*
>
> *Un vi der uralter kern*
> *Vos hot zikh farvandlt in zang,—*
> *Vern di verter oykh nern,*
> *Vern di verter gehern*
> *Dem folk, in zayn eybikn gang.*[16]

❑ ❑ ❑

> Perhaps in destiny's hour
> Even these words may
> Suddenly grow into flower
> In the light of day.
>
> And like the prehistoric seed,
> transformed into sheaves of wheat—
> These words will nourish,
> These words will belong
> To my people, the eternal throng.

Fortunately, Sutzkever's poetry, written both in the Vilna ghetto and in the forests where he joined the partisans, saw "the light of the day." Unhappily, this cannot be said for most of the literature written in the Holocaust. Although some of it miraculously survived, most of it was destroyed, just as were its authors, both well known and anonymous.

❑

PART TWO

Morale, Moral Resistance, and the Crisis of Faith

Un atsind Blimele, kind-leb,
Tsoym dayn kinderishe freyd—
S'kvekzilberdike taykhl in dir—
Un tsum umbakantn veg lomir zayn greyt.

❑ ❑ ❑

And now Blimele, sweet child,
Contain your childish joy—
The rivulate of quicksilver within you—
And let us be ready for the unknown road.

Simkhe-Bunem Shayevitsh,

Lekh-lekho,
Lodz ghetto, February 1942

Chapter Three

Breaking through the Wall of Silence

Because both self-conscious and folk poetry had among Polish as well as other East European Jews a long and rich tradition—much of it in response to waves of destruction that periodically ravaged Jewish communities—it may not be surprising that the first to react to the German occupation were the Yiddish and Polish Jewish poets.[1] From the beginning, their poetry was a vehicle of moral and cultural sustenance as well as an expression of spiritual defiance that kept the souls of the condemned from dying. It was, furthermore, a quest for reaffirmation of traditional values in a disintegrating world.

That tradition was rebelliously alive is reflected in the very act of writing or composing poetry in the mind and committing it to memory when writing materials were not available. As an affirmation of life, all attempts to write had a measure of success in transcending the wretchedness of the present moment. Since it articulated for many their thoughts and feelings, this poetry was often a means of catharsis as well as an expression of revulsion and opposition against the oppressor. Hence, the greater the threat to the physical and cultural existence of the immured Jews, the more determined was their literary activity. Indeed, after waves of mass deportations to death centers, those who temporarily held onto life in the ghettos, in various hiding places, fighting with the partisans, posing as Christians on the "Aryan side," and even in some of the concentration camps, feverishly turned to writing. As the poet Michał Borwicz writes:

*Po każdej "akcji wysiedleńczej," kiedy uliczki ghetta wypeł-
niał krzyk krwawej ciszy, kiedy mieszkania wiały pustką po
tysiąchych ofiar, a meble i rzeczy po nich "konfiskował" nie-
miecki skarb, na progach, chodnikach i podłogach wałęsały
się strzępy i odpadki rabowanego mienia. Wśród nich bardzo
często można było dojrzeć zapisane kartki. Wyprute przez
niemieckich rzezimieszków z szuflad i skrytek oraz przez
nich—jako pozbawione materjalnej wartości— podeptane z
pogardliwą nieuwagą.[2]*

◻ ◻ ◻

After each deportation—when the narrow ghetto streets
echoed with a cry of bleeding silence, when the dwellings
blew with the emptiness of thousands of martyrs, and the
furniture and belongings were "confiscated" by the German
treasury—the thresholds, floors, and sidewalks were strewn
with tatters and scraps of plundered property. In the midst
of it, it was often easy to see handwritten slips of paper.
Ripped out of drawers and hiding places, these notes, devoid
of material value, were disdainfully trampled by the German
looters.

Like their predecessors, the poets in the Holocaust apparently
knew that the objective chronicler of events needs the comple-
ment of a truth that transcends historical fact: the truth of the
poets. For it is their poetry that reveals—perhaps more eloquently
than any other literary genre—the most precise correlatives for
states of consciousness: the human response to life and death,
hope and despair. A cogent formulation of this idea appears in
Chaim Kaplan's *The Warsaw Diary of Chaim Kaplan:*

> Who will immortalize our troubles? The national splendor
> inherent in religious poetry is not expressed in newspaper re-
> ports.... A catastrophe that becomes part of poetry...
> spreads among the people and is transmitted to future gener-
> ations. A poet who clothes adversity in poetic form immor-
> talizes it in an everlasting monument. And this monument
> provides historic material from which future generations are
> nourished.... Poet of the people where art thou?[3]

Such mandates and exhortations as Kaplan's were hardly
necessary, for most poets—self-conscious and established ones,

amateurs and simple folk-song writers—regarded it as morally imperative to immortalize the unfolding cataclysm and at the same time to provide a scaffolding with which to support the morale of the people.

Julian Przyboś:
The Solitary and Salutary Voice

This sense of grave responsibility on the part of the poets became itself a poetic topos. Abraham Sutzkever's poetry, for example, abounds in such themes. Occasionally, gentile Polish poets, horrified eyewitnesses, articulate in their poetry indignation and revulsion and, hence, by extension, moral support for the isolated and entrapped Jews. One such poet, who was to become a Nobel laureate, is Czesław Miłosz. His "Campo Di Fiori" and "A Poor Christian Looks at the Ghetto" are discussed in part 4 of this study. Another poet is Julian Przyboś. Born in 1901, in a small village, he began to publish poetry in the avant-guard review *Switch*, and was later to join a group known as the "A.R." ("revolutionary artists"). Przyboś was a socialist for whom, as Czesław Miłosz writes in *The History of Polish Literature*, "artistic creativity signified a man's elan toward universal happiness through the realization of all human potentialities."[4] But Przyboś also knew that "an artist's first duty toward mankind is to create good art and not to renounce high standards in the name of any supra-artistic goal."[5]

These lofty artistic resolutions apparently seemed absurd to Przyboś in the apocalypse ushered in by Germany. The following untitled and undated poem reflects Przyboś's transformed artistic standards. Furthermore, it reveals his anguish as both a poet and human being, while it places the Holocaust in its unique relationship to the Jews:

> *Jestem pracownikiem słowa, które kształtuję,*
> *którym władam—a gdy sięgam teraz po słowo, zamyka*
> *mnie szczelnie niepokonane milczenie.*
>   *Jestem poetą—ale nie znajduję na całym obszarze*
> *doświadczonych przez siebie uczuć—nawet przeczucia*
> *tej grozy, od której, gdyby ją dopuścić do serca—*
> *stanęłoby serce.*

Jestem Polakiem, który—jak wielu, jak prawie
wszyscy patrioci polscy—przerzył moralnie śmierć
w więzieniu gestapo, ale nie mogę, nie czuję w sobie
uprawnienia i siły do objęcia myslą męczeństwa
narodu żydowskiego.

We wczesnej mojej młodości byłem żołnierzem,
patrzyłem na wojenną śmierć przyjaciół—lecz nie
mam w sobie tyle hartu, by móc obiektywnie, twardo
uświadomić sobie los Żydów zamkniętych w ghetto i
więzionych do komór gazowych.

Będąc z dala od Warszawy w bohaterskie dni
powstania i zagłady stolicy—przecież pojąłem,
przekrwawiłem w sobie i myslę że czcią, bólem i
przekleństwem o tej największej tragedii w polskich
dziejach.

Ale opuszcza mnie wszystka ludzka zdolność
reakcji, nie potrafię, jestem bezradny i przerażony,
ilekroć wspomnę o rzeczy najokropniejszej od
istnienia naszej planety.

I nie liczba ofiar, nie to że tyle milionów
Żydów zginęło niewinnie—zgineły przecież miliony
Polaków czy Rosjan—
  i nie sam fakt fizycznego uniceństwa,
  —śmierć niezawiniona; męczeńska śmierć była
  nieraz w dziejach ludzkości udziałem tysięcy—
  ale wyważenie ostatniej zasady człowieczeństwa,
zburzenie do fundamentów już nie tylko etyki,
rozumu, prawa—
  ale zamach na ostateczną resztę człowieczeństwa,
na to że człowiek, nie mając swojej śmierci,
śmiercią męczeńską coś znaczył, w imię czegoś
umierał.

Hitlerowcy śmierci mordowanych Żydów chcieli
odjąc nawet znaczenie, nawet miano śmierci.

Kiedy ogarniemy pomyśleniem, kiedy wytrzymamy tę
grozę moralną?

Pióro moje drży i muszę milczeć. Dziś pisząc te
słowa w drugą rocznicę wysiedlenia Żydów z Krakowa,
wiem jedno:

Dopuki nie udźwignę choć jednym słowem w
poezji—ciężaru tej najstraszliwszej sprawy—
nie będę się czuł poetą zupełnie wolnym, tym, który

przeżył, a nie umarł
w owym czasie pogardy, męczeństwa i walki.[6]

❏ ❏ ❏

I am a craftsman of words. I forge them, I
master them. And now when I reach for a word, I
feel myself enclosed in impenetrable silence.

I am a poet. Yet I am unable to discover in the
entire spectrum of my experienced emotions even an
inkling of the terror which, if permitted to reach
the heart, would surely cause the heart to stop.

I am a Pole who—like many, like almost all
Polish patriots—morally experienced death in a
Gestapo prison. Yet I cannot, I feel neither
justified nor strong enough to comprehend the
martyrdom of the Jewish people.

In my early youth I was a soldier and witnessed
the death of many comrades in arms. Yet I haven't
been tempered enough to apprehend objectively the
fate of the Jews incarcerated in the ghetto and
shipped to gas chambers.

Although I was not present in Warsaw during the
capital's heroic days of resistance and destruction,
I nonetheless experienced—I think with reverence as
well as with agony and execrations—this most
terrible tragedy in the annals of Poland.

Yet I am bereft of any human ability to react: I
cannot. I am rendered helpless and frightened
whenever I think about this most terrifying event
since the creation of our planet.

And it's not the number of victims, not that so
many innocent Jews perished—after all, millions of
Poles and Russians perished too—
and not only the physical destruction,
the undeserved death; in human history violent
death has often been the destiny of thousands—
but the obliteration of the basic human
principles, the destruction of the very foundation
not only of ethics, reason, justice—
but the assault on the last semblance of that
which is human, on the fact that a human being had

some worth when he died the death of a martyr, when
he died in the name of something.
The Nazis were determined to rob the murdered
Jews of the very meaning, the very name, of death.
When will we comprehend, how will we endure this
total moral disintegration?
My pen trembles, and I must be silent. Today,
writing these words on the second anniversary of the
deportation of the Jews from Cracow, I know one
thing:
As long as I will not lift with at least one
word in poetry the weight of this most terrible
thing, I will not be a totally free poet—one who
survived, who did not die in this age of
degradation, martyrdom, and struggle.

Both the word images and the structure of this poem project
Przyboś's dilemma. Before the war, words were the element with
which Przyboś shaped his perceptions of and responses to reality.
As "a craftsman of words," he sought to transmute their compo-
nents in such a way that they would distill the truth and illumi-
nate reality. Because he distrusted everyday language, he exerted
great effort to breathe or hammer into words meanings that liber-
ated them from the triteness imposed upon them. This he did, in
the words of Czesław Miłosz, "by striking one word against the
other . . . ," in order "to kindle the spark of a new apprehension of
reality."[7]

It is ironic that the "new apprehension of reality" Przyboś
sought was ushered in not by the metaphysics of language, his pur-
gation of words, but rather by the Holocaust. In the face of its un-
imaginable reality, both the poet's language and imagination
capitulate. Although at the time when he writes his poem he has
already internalized the various aspects of the cataclysm, he can-
not fathom its unique significance in relationship to the Jews.
Words, the tools of his craft, whether wrenched from their trite
dependence on everyday language or whose timelessness he seeks
"enclose [him] in impenetrable silence." His poetic imagination,
informed as it is by a whole spectrum of "experienced emotions"
(including his vicarious death in a Gestapo prison, his anguish at
seeing both the death of his "comrades-in-arms," and the tragic if
heroic Warsaw uprising) shrinks before the "terror" facing the
Jews. Indeed, the very consideration or contemplation of

that "terror," which "if permitted to reach the heart would surely cause the heart to stop," obliterates whatever impotent power language might still possess.

Przyboś's awareness of the moral implication of the present evil—its unique significance with respect to the Jews and his own impotence as a human being and poet—seems to paralyze his natural human ability to respond to the tragedy. Because he is not sharing their destiny, he is painfully conscious of the chasm that separates him from the Jews. Humbled by the most "terrifying event since the creation of our planet," he feels bereft of the ability to react. It is thus that he defends his human essence as well as his lyric imagination from the threat of total disintegration. He cannot and will not fathom a depravity so heinous that it robs the murdered of "the very meaning, the very name, of death." Przyboś probably alludes to death in extermination centers, a system that engendered the warped illusion in the minds of the murderers that their victims were not entirely human. It is this perverse perception that, among other things, probably helped to expedite the final solution.

The bounded space of Przyboś's poem, its metaphorless images and unpoetic structure, seem to congeal into rigid letters, dead words, as his "pen trembles" and he must surrender to "silence." Yet his associations and analogies, his understanding of the unparalleled fate of the Jews, break forth creatively, conveying nuances of feeling and moral backbone that are more than facile communication. And so Przyboś's sense of moral revulsion, indignation, and anguish, on behalf of both the Jews and the destroyed fundamental human principles, transcends the silence that seeks to enclose him. The final constellation of words—his solemn vow to unveil even with "one word in poetry the truth about this most terrible event"—reflects his prophetic spirit. But these words are also a ritual of expiation that he must enact again and again for having "survived . . . this age of degradation, martyrdom, and struggle."

Abraham Sutzkever:
Guardian of the Songs Left Behind

The image of a solitary Christian poet breaking through the wall of silence on behalf of the entrapped and forgotten Jews is unusual. Nonetheless, or perhaps because of it, it is salutary, an anima figure in a world bereft of soul. The poetry of the immured Jews, on the other hand, is replete with such images; the very act of writing is as much a reflection of it as it is its canon. Abraham Sutzkever's work, in fact, resonates with themes of spiritual resistance and moral fortitude. In this he pitted his responsibility to uphold the morale of the Jews and, as discussed in the preceding chapter, the life of his own mind against death. These abiding concerns are expressed, among other poems, in "Gezang fun Yiddishn Dikhter in 1943" (Chant of a Jewish Poet in 1943):

Gezang fun Yiddishn Dikhter in 1943

Tsi bin ikh der letster poet in Erope?
Tsi zing ikh far meysim, tsi zing ikh far kroen?
Ikh trink zikh in fayer, in zumpn, in rope
Gefangen fun gele gelatete shoen.

Kh'tsebays mayne shoen mit khayishe tseyner
Geshtarkt fun mayn mames a trer. Durkhn tropn—
Derze ikh s'milionike harts, fun di beyner,
Vos yogn tsu mir fun der erd in galopn.

Ikh bin dos milionike harts! Bin der hiter
Fun zeyere ibergeloste nigunim.
Un Got, vos der mentsh hot farbrent zayne giter,
Bahalt zikh in mir, vi di zun in a brunem.

Zay ofn mayn harts! Un farnem vi se shprotsn
Geheylikte shoen in tsukunfts makhshove
Fargikher, farayl zeyer makhtikn rotsn
Un zay in dayn tsar zeyer onzoger, novi.

Un zing fun di zumpn, un zing fun der nider,
Biz vanen es lebt nokh a trer fun der mamen!
Derhern dayn kol zoln beynerne brider,
Di brandike ghetto un s'folk hinter yamen. . . . [8]

❏❏❏

Chant of a Jewish Poet in 1943

Am I the last poet in Europe?
Am I singing for corpses, am I singing for crows?

I am drowning in fire, in swamps, in pus,
Captive of yellow-patch hours.

I gnaw my hours with teeth of a beast,
Strengthened by my mother's tear. Through the teardrops
I behold the millionth heart of the skeletons,
Rushing in a gallop from the earth toward me.

I am that millionth heart! The guardian
Of the songs they left behind,
And God, whose estates man had burned down.
Is hidden within me like the sun in a well.

Be open, my heart! And know that the hollowed hours
Sprout forth in the thoughts of posterity.
Hasten, hold not back their mighty will
And in your grief become their herald, their prophet.

And sing from swamps, and sing from netherworlds,
As long as a mother's tear is still alive!
So that your voice will be heard by the skeletonlike
brothers, the burning ghetto and the people beyond the seas.

Unlike the deliberately unpoetic lexicon, dissonant rhythms, and disjunctive structure of Przyboś's poem, Sutzkever's "Chant of a Jewish Poet in 1943" is in the tradition of standard devices of versification. The meter of the five stanzas is distinguished by its artlessness, and the stanza form is a quatrain, mostly of five stress lines and an *a b a b* rhyme scheme.

The opening stanza establishes a different aspect of a dilemma facing the poet in the Holocaust from that posited by Przyboś. At the core of Sutzkever's dilemma is an agonizing question, "Am I the last poet in Europe? / Am I singing for corpses, am I singing for crows?" This riddle is directed not only at himself and all the murdered Jewish poets, but also at the other, implicitly evoked, creative energies that might reanimate the conscience of the silent world.

The forthcoming reply to the query, formulated in the catechismal structure of the first stanza, springs from the occasion, calling forth crowded images of death and violence. The synesthesia "I am drowning in fire" and the other images of suffering, "[I am drowning] in swamps, in pus / Captive of yellow-patch hours," project a hermetically sealed world (a vision pervasive in both Sutzkever's and other Holocaust writers' work) in which neither the silent aspect of humankind nor God will be provoked. The images of violence and suffering leap at us like metaphysical conceits. Yet Sutzkever's language, while imagistic, is not metaphorical. Despite the figurative synesthesia, the images are signals of a palpable, if new, reality. In the Holocaust, the reign of terror—the burning of the ghettos and people, the putrefying skeletons of the dead and the dying, and all the other tortures—was so boundless and oceanic that the evocation of drowning in them reflects an aspect of reality.

The set of images in the next stanza shows a paradoxical relationship between the poet's rage and frustration as he "gnaw[s] the yellow-patch hours" of ghetto existence "with teeth of a beast," and the tender image of his mother's sustenance-giving tears. Since Sutzkever has a deep affinity with mysticism, the mother image recalls Rachel or the Shekhina, archetypal anima mothers, both of whom appear in various feminine guises in Sutzkever's poetry. The Shekhina, for example, appears in "Di Ershte Nakht in di Ghetto" (The First Night in the Ghetto), discussed in the preceding chapter. In both poems, as in the old myth, the Shekhina is the feminine emanation of God in all creation, individuation, and separation from God. She is the transcendental companion and source of succor to the children of Israel in their exile and dispersion. Giving new life to the archetypal myth, Sutzkever has the generative source of the anima mother transmigrate through Sutzkever's mother's teardrops. And it is because of their mystic intervention that Sutzkever's ego and poetic imagination transform his impotent rage and frustration into the psychic process of death and rebirth, a theme that abounds in Sutzkever's poetry, including "The First Night in the Ghetto."

One among a host of skeletons, he perceives himself as the anointed "millionth heart of the skeletons / That in a gallop rush from the earth toward me." His absorption of his mother's sacrosanct tears helps him to project a mystical link between God and himself, as poet. Because of it, the helpless poet who "gnaws the . . . hours with teeth of a beast," is reborn as a prophet of his people in whom God is "hidden . . . like the sun in a well." But this God-poet axis has secularist underpinnings that resemble Jung's concept of the striving of the ego to establish a relationship with God—one that has the power to transform humankind into man-God. Or as Sartre sees it, the fundamental human project is to become one's own God.

This form of self-divinization causes the oracular albeit anxious voice of the poet to fill the silent cosmos. Henceforth, he will be "the guardian," if not of his people's lives as God might have been, then at least of the songs they left behind—that is, of the memory of a whole way of life, tradition, and culture, the "estates man had burned down." Significantly, Sutzkever prostrates himself not before God but rather before himself and entreats his own heart to "be open.... And [to] know that the hollowed hours / Sprout forth in the thoughts of posterity." For it is, in the end, posterity's prophet that he must be, because he knows in the agony of 1943 that this is all he can do for his dying people. So, in the words of Przyboś, Sutzkever tries "to lift with at least one word in poetry the weight of this most terrible thing."

Moreover, his attempt to link "the skeletonlike brothers / the burning ghetto, and the people beyond the sea" reflects his moral resolve to uphold the spirit of the dying by linking them with the living spirit of Israel, a pervasive theme in his poetry. This form of consecration of life (*Kiddush ha-Hayym*) not only defines Sutzkever as a poet-prophet in the Holocaust; it also heightens our awareness of the abiding optimism that informs most of the ghetto and concentration camp poetry. His self-exhortation to sing "so that your voice will be heard . . . by the people beyond the seas" might be an expression of hope that some form of intervention on the part of the world beyond the condemned ground of the Holocaust might yet come forth.

Sutzkever's belief in the possibility of salvation arises not as much from his trust in the mediating will of God as from the tradition of hope and faith in continuity that marks the ethos and the history of the Jews. This trust in Jewish continuity often prevailed in the darkest hours, even when God's silence seemed to be most inscrutable. Sutzkever was aware that the symbols, signs, and rituals—the whole spectrum of semiotic structures connected with Jewish theodicy—miraculously participated in and realized the sacred in the apparent absence of God's intervention. These symbols, signs, and rituals, as articulated in "Chant of a Jewish Poet in 1943" and a host of the poet's other works, manage to transform themselves into a vision of divine grace—when in reality Sutzkever uses revelatory language and speaks to the minds and religious sensibilities of his people and himself in order to bolster their morale.

As noted in chapter 1 of this study, Sutzkever's wartime poetry, of which "Chant of a Jewish Poet in 1943" is but one example, stands in sharp relief against his prewar work. The latter, devoid as it was of ideology, was greeted with little approval by the popular and highly politicized literary group "Yung Vilna." They rejected Sutzkever's predilection for refined stylistic devices of versification, his lyricism, introspection, and preoccupation with the relationship between the external world and his inner landscape. During the war, Sutzkever's poetic voice took on new resonance, producing endless variations on the theme of resistance—both armed and spiritual—and Judaic tradition as a vehicle of that resistance. Much of this poetry is marked by a mythic and prophetic vision that proffers some hope of redemption. In "Chant of a Jewish Poet in 1943," this hope resonates in his self-exhortation to "sing from the swamps, to sing from the netherworlds / As long as a mother's tear is still alive."

The very exhortation to "sing" became itself a moral mandate in much of this world of radical evil, for singing and writing were citadels that often protected, even if only temporarily, against moral and physical disintegration. As a vehicle of spiritual resistance such activity is in the tradition of Jewish eschatology and ethos, appearing in diverse writings and commentaries. In *The Tales of Hasidim*, for example, Martin Buber cites the following story:

> Once when Jews were passing through a period of great stress, the rabbi of Apt, who was then the eldest of his generation, issued a command for a universal fast in order to call down God's mercy. But Rabbi Israel summoned his musicians, whom he carefully selected from a number of different towns, and night after night he had them play their most beautiful melodies on the balcony of his house. Whenever the sound of the clarinet and the delicate tinkle of the little bells floated down from above, the Hasidim began to gather in the garden, until there was a whole crowd of them. The music would soon triumph over their dejection and they would dance, stamping their feet and clapping their hands. People who were indignant at these doings reported to the rabbi of Apt that the day of fasting he had ordered had been turned into a day of rejoicing. He answered: "It is not up to me to call him to account who kept the memory of the command of the Scriptures green in his heart. And when you go to war in your land against the adversary that oppresseth you, then ye shall sound an alarm with the trumpets; and ye shall be remembered before the Lord your God."[9]

Some of the intelligentsia of virtually every ghetto were determined to keep "the memory of the command of the scriptures green in . . . [the] heart[s] of the people." But one of countless examples of such triumph is provided by Michał Borwicz. He recounts a story about a concert in the Vilna ghetto he heard from S. Kaczerginski, poet and anthologist of *Lider fun Ghettos un Lagern* (Songs in the Ghettos and Concentration Camps). The spirit of this event draws particularly close to the one cited by Buber.

The concert, spearheaded by Sutzkever, took place on January 18, 1942, one month after a singularly bloody *Aktion*. Many in the ghetto responded with bitterness to the concert, adding to the posted announcements: "No Concerts on a Cemetery!" Nonetheless, on the day of the event, the Vilna ghetto theater was filled beyond capacity, and the audience quickly realized that the program had little to do with an ordinary "concert." From the stage came some of the most evocative poems of such venerated Jewish bards as Chaim Nachman Bialik (1873–1934). These poems as well as selections from the works of such luminaries as Peretz (1851–1915, poet and novelist) resembled liturgical laments for martyred Jews. But a seeming non sequitur followed—namely, recitations of some of the most humorous passages from the folktales of Sholem Aleichem (1859–1916), the beloved author of the Jewish masses. The consternation that swept the theater was total. The audience could not bear Sholem Aleichem's humor after the solemn and funereal mood evoked by Bialik's poems. Nevertheless, the audience quickly fell under the spell of the inimitable Yiddish storyteller. His protagonists' tales of woe were perceived as allusions—however remote in time, space, and intensity—to the sorrow and terror that reigned in the Vilna ghetto.[10] So the Jews of the Vilna ghetto kept the "memory of the command of the Scriptures green in their hearts," and in sounding "an alarm with the trumpets" of both solemn and humorous literature, they managed to "triumph over their dejection."

Władysław Szlengel:
The Abrogation of the Covenant and the Day of Judgment

Although the Jews of the Vilna and other ghettos often triumphed over their dejection by "sounding an alarm" of both solemn and humorous literature as well as other forms of cultural sustenance, the radical evil of the Germans and the silent aspect of God and humanity produced a religious crisis (intimated in Sutzkever's secularization of the command of the scriptures), though rarely absolute apostasy. In the work of many poets, God is inscrutable, unaccountable, and indifferent, while terror, chimneys, and death appear to be consecrated by divine will and are manifest in the exploding chaos. In other poetry, the religious despair is transformed into outright blasphemy.

The poets express the suspicion that the omnipotent, just, and wise God of their fathers has turned His back on the chosen people either because of their sinfulness or because God has been reduced to craven pusillanimity in the shadow of the swastika. God is, therefore, no longer able to protect them. In the first case, God's wisdom and justice are challenged, for a punishment that calls for living children to be thrown into flames exceeds any conceivable form of sin. In the second case, God is charged with bad faith, for God misled the people into believing in divine omnipotence and promise of redemption. Thus in some poems, Szlengel's "Już czas" (It's High Time), for example, the universe is stood on its head, and it is God who, on Judgment Day, is judged by God's children.

One of the few poems dated by Szlengel, "It's High Time" was written in December 1942, probably upon the poet's learning about the gas chambers in Treblinka:

Już czas

Już czas! Czas!
Długo nas dniem obrachunku straszył!
Mamy już dosyć modlitw i pokut.
Dzisiaj Ty staniesz przed sądem naszym
I będziesz czekał pokornie wyroku.
Rzucim Ci w serce potężnym kamieniem
Bluźniercze, straszne, krwawe oskarżenie.
—Ostrzem potoru, brzeszczotem szabel
Wedrze się w niebo jak wierza Babel.
I Ty, tam w górze, wielki skazaniec,
Tam w międzygwiezdnej straszliwej ciszy,
Ty każde słowo nasze usłyszysz,
Jak Cię oskarża naród wybraniec,
—Nie ma zapłaty, nie ma zapłaty!
To, żeś nas kiedyś, dawnymi laty,

Wywiódł z Egiptu do naszej ziemi.
To nic nie zmieni! To nic nie zmieni!
Teraz Ci tego juz nie przebaczym,
Że Tyś nas wydał w rece siepaczy—
Za to, że w czasie tysięcoleci
Byliśmy Tobie jak wierne dzieci.
Z Twoim imieniem każdy z nas konał
W cyrkach cezarów, w cyrku Nerona.
Na krzyżach Rzymian, stosach Hiszpanii
Bici i lżeni poniewierani.
I Tyś nas wydał w ręce Kozakom,
Co rwali w strzępy święty Twój zakon.
Z męki getta, widma szubienic
My, upodleni, my—umęczeni—
Za smierć w Treblince, zgięci pod batem,
Damy zapłatę!! Damy Zapłatę!!
—Teraz nie ujrzesz już swego końca!
Gdy Cię sprowadzim na miejsce kaźni,
100-dolarowym krążkiem słońca
Ty nie przekupisz wartownika łaźni.
I kiedy kat Cię popędzi i zmusi,
Zagna i wypchnie w komorę parową,
Zamknie za Tobą hermatyczne wieka,
Gorąca para zacznie dusić, dusić,
I będziesz krzyczał, będziesz chciał uciekać—
Kiedy się skończą już konania męki,
Zawloką, wrzucą, tam potwórnym dołem
Wyrwą, Ci gwiazdy—złote zęby z szczęki—
A potem spalą.
———— I będziesz popiołem.[11]

❑ ❑ ❑

It's High Time

It's high time! High time!
Endlessly threatened with a day of reckoning!
Enough prayers and penance.
Today You will face our judgment
And humbly await our verdict.
We'll strike Your heart with a mighty rock
Of blasphemous, terrifying, bloody charges.
With the sharpness of hatchets, with the clash of swords

The skies will be sundered like the tower of Babel.
And You, up there, Almighty convict,
There in the awesome silence of the galaxies,
You will hear every single word of ours,
When sentenced by us, Your chosen people.
There is no absolution, no absolution!!!
That sometime in the distant past,
You delivered us from Egypt and brought us to our land,
Will change nothing! nothing!
We won't forgive You now
That You have delivered us
Into the hands of the killers—
Because during the millennia
We had been Your loyal children.
With Your name on our lips each one of us expired
In the circuses of caesars, in the circus of Nero.
On the crosses of the Romans, pyres of Spain—
Whipped, cursed, and scorned.
And You delivered us into the hands of the Cossacks,
Who tore Your Law into shreds.
For tortures in the ghetto, specter of the gallows,
We, the degraded, we, the exhausted,
For death in Treblinka, bent under the whip,
We'll pay You back!! We'll pay You back!!
You won't escape Your end now!
When we'll bring You to the place of execution,
You won't bribe the guard of the showers,
With the sunlike glitter of a hundred-dollar coin.
And when the executioner will chase and force You,
Drive and push You onto the steam room floor,
And seal behind You the hermetic door,
Hot vapors will choke You, You'll see,
And You will scream and weep and want to flee—
And when Your death agony will come to an end,
You'll be dragged, and in a monstrous pit land,
Then they'll tear out Your stars—the gold teeth from Your
     flesh—
Then they will burn You.
     And You'll be ash.

Szlengel's bitter invective is rooted in traditional liturgy, no-
tably in the right to judge God for trespasses. The logic of such an

inversion has its antecedents in Hasidic, kabbalistic, and rabbinic literature. The right to judge God is implicit in the relationship between God and Israel—a relationship established by God's insistence that Israel accept the covenant (Deuteronomy 5:3). Thus, as Byron Sherwin writes:

> In Jewish law, God can be tried for his crimes because he is party to an agreement. . . . In this respect he is a "person" in Jewish law. The trials of God narrated by Hasidic literature [and] Holocaust literature . . . are not only aggadically [theologically] defensible, but halakahically [legally] viable. As man is required to bear witness before God, he may also bear witness against God.[12]

Thus protests, even when expressing anger and disappointment, are rooted in faith. It is precisely because of the accusations that they are expressions of reverence and love for God and trust in the covenant. They are, further, signals of belief that disasters are followed by salvation and are, therefore, inherently transient.

Horrified by the systematic murder of the Jews, Szlengel walks the thin line between this faith and apostasy, holding on to God only by dint of his rage against God and the antiworld, which seems to be God's creation. Although Szlengel mirrors the tradition initiated by Abraham—one that expects God to do justice by the chosen people ("Shall not the judge of the earth do justice?" (Gn. 18:25)—in the current crisis Szlengel finds it fit to stand that whole tradition on its head. He is, therefore, not merely indicting God for not having honored the terms of the covenant, nor merely hurling execrations at God ("we'll strike Your heart with a mighty rock of blasphemous, terrifying bloody charges"), but actually punishing God with the very fate of the chosen people. But even in his relegation of God to the status and hence fate of the Jew, Szlengel does not reject divine existence. He rather inverts the belief that God's divinity is a function of omnipotence, benevolence, and justice—however tempered they may be by wrath.

The inversion of the traditional conception of God seems forced upon the poet by God's actions, which resemble the ingratitude and cruelty peculiar to humankind. For in their exile from the land into which God had delivered them, the Jews had served their host countries in secular proportion to the way they served God. Yet with God's acquiescence, complicity, or active participation, as Szlengel charges, they invariably rejected the Jews, often expelling or murdering them "In the circuses of caesars, in the circus of Nero. / On the crosses of the Romans, pyres of Spain / Whipped, cursed, and scorned. / . . . delivered . . . [by God] into the hands of the Cossacks, / Who tore Your Law into shreds." And if this were not enough, Szlengel charges, God had "delivered us into the hands of the killers— / Because during the millennia we had been Your loyal children."

Implicit in this bitter accusation is a form of divine perversity—a perversity that is manifest in God's punishing the Jews not because they were refractory but rather because they were "loyal children." Szlengel was, no doubt, familiar with the terms of the covenant. He knew that it contained a promise of both redemption and retribution, each of which was commensurate with the Jews' adherence to or violation of the covenant. But as Szlengel sees it, only God's curse, not God's blessing, had been fulfilled. God's professions of love for the chosen people as articulated in the prayer book, "with everlasting love hast thou loved the house of Israel," are a blatant contradiction to the tortures inflicted upon the Jews during the centuries of exile. These tortures have now culminated in God's complicity in the total destruction of the Jews, a perception that dominated the thinking of Szlengel, as well as that of many others, when "It's High Time" was written.

The final blow to the covenantal relation between God and Israel, Szlengel implies, is the total destruction of the Jews. This violates the promise that regardless of transgressions, God's retribution would not include the absolute obliteration of the Jews; a remnant would always survive. To the despairing Szlengel, who witnessed the deportation of most of the Warsaw ghetto Jews—including his family and friends—to the ovens of Treblinka, this promise seemed apocryphal.

Moreover, according to classical midrashic tradition, two conditions are necessary for redemption: either total righteousness or total wickedness of humankind. Clearly, to the religious sensibilities of Szlengel as well as that of other writers in the Holocaust, both conditions were realized. As they saw it, the Jews sacrificed on the altars of the world with God's name on their lips were wholly innocent—an innocence that stems from the inherent saintliness of Jews who die, as Maimonides is alleged to have said, for no other reason than their Jewishness. The Nazis, on the other hand, were wholly guilty. Yet neither condition could call forth the intervention of God.

In *Dos Lid funem Oysgekhargetn Yiddish Folk* (1944) (The Song of the Murdered Jewish People) Yitzhak Katzenelson expresses a similar idea of intrinsic Jewish innocence—one that is ultimately godlier than God—in the following imprecations:

> Don't you know us, recognize us? Have we changed so?
> Are we so different? We are the same Jews we were,
> Even better. . . .
> All the martyred Jews taken to their death, the millions
>   murdered here—
> They are better. They suffered more and were purified here
>   in exile.
> How can a great Jew of long ago be compared with a small,
>   simple, common Jew
> In present-day Poland, Lithuania, Volhynia? In every one
>   of them
> A Jeremiah wails, a tormented Job cries, a disillusioned king
>   intones Ecclesiastes. . . .
> An entire crucified, grief-laden people
> Is about to enter the [heavens]. O any one of my murdered
>   children is fit to be their God![13]

Szlengel rages at God because he perceives God as perverse, impotent, and malevolent. God does not walk with the righteous and penitent Jews, but rather with the diabolical Germans, as Nazis took pleasure in reminding the Jews. That "sometime in the distant past," Szlengel vituperates, God "delivered us from Egypt and brought us to our land. / Will change nothing! Will change nothing!" There is no absolution even for God—or perhaps because God is God—for such an abrogation of the basic covenantal terms. "The day of reckoning," with which God had "endlessly threatened" the Jews, was ushered in with unmediated and unexpected vengeance. Indeed, the day of reckoning itself was unexpected. For as Szlengel insists, it is not the Jews, sacrificed in ritualistic autos-da-fé as well as spontaneous pogroms with God's name on their lips, who have been refractory.

Perhaps the most elaborate images in this poem are God's culpability: God's perversity, malevolence, and impotence. Szlengel conveys with the immediacy of an eyewitness the sustained attempt to assimilate into poetic and human consciousness as well as into Jewish history a catastrophe that stands outside these realms. The success of this attempt is contingent on the belief in divine complicity and malevolence. In *The Jewish Return to History: Reflections in the Age of Auschwitz and a New Jerusalem,* Emil Fackenheim writes that the classical pre-Holocaust midrash was aware of the discrepancy between God's omnipotence and omnibenevolence, and a world that takes its worldliness precisely from its opposition to these divine attributes. For the human world contains human attributes: evil and freedom. In the framework of classical Jewish life, however fraught it had always been with endless calamities, this tension was accepted as one of the paradoxes of life. But for Szlengel the catastrophe that has swallowed up most of Europe's Jews stands outside any recognizable or assimilatable tragedy.

Szlengel sees—just as Katzenelson does and as Jacob Glatstein, writing after the Holocaust in "My Brother Refugee" notes— that the Jews had been godlier than God. Certainly, they had been more loyal to God and the covenant than God had been to them. For whereas for "millennia we had been Your loyal children," as Szlengel bitterly writes, expiring "with Your name on our lips," God had "delivered us into the hands of the killers," into the terror of the ghetto and death in Treblinka. The dawning of this knowledge is enough to make Szlengel hurl into "the awesome silence of the galaxies" a verdict of death. "It's high time" that the "Almighty sentenced one" be judged, "and humbly await our verdict," for both the terrible death and the degradation of God's loyal children. "It's high time," too, that God "hear every single word of ours," which will "sunder the skies like the tower of Babel." God's threats of "a day of reckoning" will now come to an end, even as the chosen people, and even God, will come to an end. For as Szlengel implies and Glatstein explicitly states in another poem, "Without Jews there is no Jewish God. / If we leave this world / The light will go out in your tent."

In the imaginative world of Szlengel, the "degraded" and "exhausted" Jews will avenge themselves against their refractory God. But their retribution will go beyond the mere bearing of witness against their revered adversary. Nor will the Jews invoke the tradition of mere accusations against or quarrels and pleas with God, all of which provided solace and sustained faith in the past. "Enough prayers and penance." Paradoxically, while Szlengel rejects the tradition of pleas and contentions—that is, dialogue with God—the language of his poem reflects it. For in it, Szlengel establishes a dialogue with God, even if its denouement deviates sharply from tradition. Paradoxical also is the very deviation, because, reflecting midrashic tradition, Szlengel shows implicitly

B. Linke, "El Mole Rachamim."

the irrevocable link that ties the fate of God to that of God's people.

On some level, Szlengel's poem is a modern—perhaps uniquely Holocaust, parodic, and grotesque—derivative of the traditional midrash. Like its classic antecedents, it attempts to comprehend and interpret an apocalyptic event whose consequences justify the questioning and rejecting of divine purpose. Reflecting the midrashic canon, the poem is rooted in historical fact, and central to it is communal experience that includes elements of realism and the miraculous. But the miracle is not God's. Consistent with Szlengel's inversion of the cosmic order, the miracle is that of Szlengel, the modern and somewhat absurd representative-prophet of his people.

Demonstrating the inscrutable malevolence of God and the irredeemable catastrophe of the Jews, Szlengel sentences God to a Jewish death in Treblinka. Thus God will not only share the destiny of the Jewish people, but will also be paid in kind for bad faith, as Szlengel iterates in the acrimonious anaphora, "We'll pay You back!! We'll pay You back!!" And so the Jews will deliver their transgressing God "to the place of execution," just as God had delivered them before. Since aggadically and halakahically, God can be regarded as having been implicated as a "person" in history, and since the results of divine actions are monstrous, God "won't escape . . . [the] end now!"

The logical conclusion of both divine reductivity and divine necessity to share in the fate of the Jews is evoked in the image of God failing to "bribe the guard of the showers, / With the sunlike glitter of a hundred-dollar coin." The pressure of emotion contained in this and the ensuing images bears witness to both the panic and hope with which the victims, who can no longer speak for themselves, died in the "steam room" of Treblinka. Intuiting, rather than *knowing*—at the early stages of Treblinka's history—the demise that awaited them, the victims tried to bribe the guards with whatever treasures they saved for extreme situations. The guards, of course, never failed to accept the bribes, sending the somewhat reassured Jews into "showers," as they were led to believe. Szlengel's carefully chosen words—his deliberate avoidance of the words "gas" and "gas chambers" with and in which, respectively, the "almighty, sentenced one" will die—adumbrate the naivety of the victims and the lies of the murderers. Nonetheless, the euphemistic appositives, "the steam room floor," the sealed "hermetic door," and the "hot vapors [that] will choke you, you'll see, / And you will scream and weep and want to flee," convey the protracted death agony of the victims. At the same time they are an intimation of the grief of the living, the poet who writes about it and who can never really cease thinking about the torment of his people. The rage that marks these lines springs as much from this anguish as from the anger directed at God for allowing such atrocities.

The sensibility of the poet, who seems to have a clear vision of what he describes, results in an amplification of the explicit images of God's death and implicit ones of that of the Jews. The description of death is divided into several sections, each of which allows for renewed beginnings of its agony. The effect of the images derives from their copious reinforcement and skillful control of actions and feelings, all of which strike us with continually augmented power. The amassing of the different stages of death in Treblinka, including terror at the sudden realization on the part of the duped victims that the "vapors" choking them are not steam or water from the showers, culminates in the poet's lingering on the image of the emasculated God who, like the helpless people, "scream[s] and weep[s] and tr[ies] to flee." Amplifying further the impotence of the convicted Jewish God dying a Jewish death in Treblinka, the poem ends in a torrent of fury, augmented by dazzling rhythms. The images of the dead God who will "be dragged and in a monstrous pit land," whose "stars—the gold teeth" ... will be torn out, and who like God's children will "burn ... and ... be ash" crowd and pressure the conclusion of the poem, reminding us again of the passionate anger that characterizes a body of poetry of which "It's High Time" is an example.

Although the role of God in this supreme catastrophe delivered a heavy blow to Szlengel's morale, it did not destroy it. Like most of the ghetto Jews, he was determined to carry on despite the destruction of religious moorings and hence familiar norms of value. Rebelling against a cosmic order that is challenged by the reality of the ghetto and Treblinka, the poet, like the other Jews, seemed determined to live or to die not in the name of God, but despite God. Perhaps at this crossroad, some of the Jews felt that to worship God was to betray the murdered. For as the poet, Yitzhak Katzenelson put it, it is "all the better that there is no God. . . . To be sure, it's bad without Him, very bad. / But if He existed it would be even worse!"[14]

Chapter Four

The Cultural Ferment and the Moral Mandate

If neither Szlengel, Katzenelson, Sutzkever, nor any other poet could invent new values to enable them to restore order either to their own or their reader's lives, at least by continuing to write, they often succeeded in keeping at bay the despair that probably would have helped to expedite their destruction. Thus like Orpheus, the poets gained passage for themselves (and their readers) through their songs. Zivia Lubetkin, one of the leaders of the resistance movement in the Warsaw ghetto, writes that the creativity of the poets was "evidence that despite everything, the Nazis couldn't break our spirit; there were still creative forces among us. Even the most realistic who prophesied catastrophe thought: 'perhaps we will not be overcome.' "[1]

Such established poets as Szlengel, Katzenelson, or Sutzkever gave frequent readings of their works at various private and public gatherings. The public readings were sponsored by clandestine cultural organizations that proliferated in the larger ghettos. In the Warsaw ghetto, for example, YIKOR (Yiddishe Kultur Organizatsye; Yiddish Cultural Organization) and the Zionist-Socialist DROR (Freedom) undertook a wide spectrum of literary and theatrical productions, concerts, ballets, and lectures. Perhaps the most striking productions involved children. Often under the tutelage of experienced actors and choreographers, children dazzled the audience with their creativity. The proceeds derived from these performances were almost always earmarked for soup kitchens.

"Postwar Unearthing of Secret Archives under the Ruins of the Warsaw Ghetto and Attempts to Restore Them."

Another popular activity, often actively encouraged by cultural organizations, was reading in Polish and Yiddish both among children and adults. YIKOR especially promoted the use of the Yiddish language and its literature. Reading in both languages as well as in other tongues, Lucy Dawidowicz writes:

> was not only narcotic and escape, but also a discipline of the mind, an attempt to retain the habits of civilized existence. Reading about wars and catastrophes involving other people and nations universalized the Jewish experience and transcended the misery within the ghetto walls.[2]

For that reason, well-organized underground libraries proliferated in the ghetto, and the practice of personal book exchanges was also widespread.

Oneg Shabbat (Joys of the Sabbath), a secret Jewish archive founded by the historian Emanuel Ringelblum, as well as YIKOR, established secret, central Jewish archives. About twenty boxes of documents concerning the martyrology of Polish Jews, as Borwicz writes in *Pieśń ujdzie cało*, were collected by archivists and buried under the ruins of the ghetto.[3] In the Vilna ghetto, YIVO (Yiddish Visenshaftliche Organizatsye; Institute for Jewish Research) was engaged in similar activities. Some of the hidden treasure of both organizations was recovered after the war. There was, furthermore, a vital Yiddish and Polish underground press as well as hectographic printing of various literary works, published by such organizations as DROR.

Poetry of Humble Fact

Not only were libraries and literary cafés an integral part of the ghetto scene, but so also were street singers. These famished, half-naked minstrels improvised songs that dealt with the cataclysmic events and the Jewish response to them. The street singers were ingenious word coiners, and their songs were testimony to the endless linguistic changes brought about by the growing brutality. As mentioned in the preceding chapter, neologisms were a commonplace, and both familiar language and idiomatic expressions were either rendered meaningless or else assumed derisive connotations. Not only was common terminology corrupted by the German used by the Nazis, but also by ghetto and concentration camp slang of both Yiddish and Polish provenance.

Rubinsztajn, the notorious Warsaw ghetto clown and master punster, was particularly adept at coining new words and making droll puns. One of the pithy apothegms in the Yiddish dialect of Warsaw I heard Rubinsztajn chant as he begged in the streets of the ghetto was: *"Alle glaakh—urem n'raakh. Geb nish avek d'bonne!"* (rich and poor—all's equal. Don't give up your ration card). This was a particularly appropriate maxim, for in the eyes of the Nazis all Jews were equally guilty and hence equally punished. The trick, as Rubinsztajn counseled, was to hang on to one's ration card, here meant as a metaphor for life. Thus like the poets and such spiritual leaders as rabbis, the wise ghetto fool exhorted passersby to live.

The following is another example of his terse wit:

> *A groshn iz gunish,*
> *A tsvayer iz gunish,*
> *A dryer iz gunish,*
> *A fihrer zol paygern!*

(A penny ain't nothin', / two ain't nothin', / three ain't nothin', / four [which in the Warsaw dialect sounded like Führer], drop dead!)

Although fearful of Rubinsztajn's open audacity, onlookers silently cheered the clown on.

Typically, the street songs and sometimes even the more literary poems were sung to popular melodies. The clash between the highly charged ghetto poems and the sentimental tunes was startling. The irony was especially bitter when carefully wrought poetic diction or even artless songs of despair or hope or moral teachings stood in sharp contrast to a vulgar love tune. The dissonance made more emphatic the chasm between the landscape of endless terror and a world where sentimental songs had been and still were being crooned in nightclubs.[4] The following unpublished excerpt of a song, written by an anonymous woman and very popular in the Warsaw ghetto where I learned it, is an example of this genre:

> *Świat w grózy się wali,*
> *pożogą płonie.*
> *Już nic nie ocali,*
> *Już wszystko tonie.*

❑ ❑ ❑

The world collapses in ruins,
Immolated in the conflagration.
Nothing will save it,
All drowns in the devastation.

The young songwriter witnesses the literal incineration of her uni-
verse, but she cannot fathom it. Nor can she understand the cos-
mic silence that envelops her burning world:

O *ludzie gdzie są sumienia,*
Gdzie wasze serca i duszy treść?
Kiedy się skończą cierpienia,
Kto to może dłużej tak znieść?

❑ ❑ ❑

O people where is your conscience,
Where are your hearts and divine essence?
When will this suffering come to an end,
Who can longer under it bend?

This simple lament, devoid as it is of any aesthetic compul-
sion, other than rhyme, iterates in successive strophes both the in-
tolerable agony and the impossible task of recording the suffering.
But this emaciated, sore-covered, shuffling, and rag-clad ingénue
writes and sings. However tentative, these acts are by their very
nature expressions of hope and affirmation, even if her stomach
and her consciousness are deliberately and desperately focused on
earning bread. In this she mirrors the teachings of religious tradi-
tion, which, as Lucy Dawidowicz writes, were incorporated in the
folk wisdom: "A Jew lives with hope." "While there is life, there is
hope." "Even when the slaughtering knife is at your throat, don't
lose hope." "As long as you draw breath, don't lose hope" or
"don't think of the grave."[5] One might add: "When does a Jew
sing? When he is good and hungry" or "Why is the Jew still
around? Because he is good and stubborn." Dawidowicz further
notes that these teachings, "permeating every ghetto in Eastern
Europe, supplied the antidote to depression and despair. Every-
where the phrase 'hold on' and 'hold out' epitomized the value of
life and survival."[6]

This sanctification of life was in itself a moral mandate. As an example of spiritual defiance, it was cogently articulated in the clandestine culture of the ghettos. In the Vilna ghetto not only did this secret culture flourish, but in 1942 prizes were awarded for the best sculpture, poetry, and drama. Such organizations as CENTOS in Warsaw established clandestine schools, including higher education. Both the soup kitchens and the children's homes, proliferating in the ghettos, were often a front for these schools. There were, in addition, numerous "private schools" (*komplety*), consisting of small groups of children and teachers who met for instruction in the homes of the students and teachers on alternating days. The number of children and teachers alike invariably dwindled, for they were either deported or died from malnutrition and exposure. Certainly, in the Warsaw ghetto by the middle of 1942, most of the *komplety* disappeared, although there were still some obstinate cases of instruction even in the bunkers as late as April 1943. But these involved only one or two children and a stray teacher who happened to find shelter in one of these catacombs.[7]

Built in the secrecy of night, mostly in the cellars of ghetto tenements by "prudent" individuals who, as Szlengel writes, believed in outlasting the war (*wierzyli w przetrwanie*),[8] these hideouts began to crop up in the Warsaw ghetto by the end of 1942. Each shelter—some of them quite ingenious and elaborate—was initially intended for two or three families. However, at the time of the uprising, most were open both to the ghetto combatants and to those shelterless persons who got wind of them. Among the latter were solitary individuals whose families had already disappeared. Some of them were less resented because they were able to render a useful service, such as teaching, for example.

W*ł*adys*ł*aw Szlengel:
Bunkers: Architecture of Despair

Writing about this period in "This I Read to the Dead," Szlengel conveys the hope and naiveté as well as despair and frenzy of the builders of these places. In this narrative poem, Szlengel projects a vision of the obliteration of twenty centuries of Western civilization and a return to the cave age. This he does as he reviews and classifies the poetry he wrote for those who had vanished:

Zwozi się cement, cegły, noce rozbrzmiewają
stukiem młotów i oskardów. Pompuje się wodę, robi
się studnie podziemne. Schrony. Mania, pęd,
nerwice serca getta warszawskiego.
  Swiatło, kable podziemne, przebyjanie wylotów,
znów cegły, sznury, piach . . . Dużo piachu . . . Piach . . .
  Nary, prycze. Aprowizacja na miesiące.
Prezekreśla się elektryczność, wodociągi, wszystko.
Dwadzieścia wieków przekreślonych przez pejcz esesmana.
Epoka jaskiniowa. Kaganki. Studnie wiejskie.
Długa noc. Ludzie wracają pod ziemię.
  Przed zwierzętami.
  A za oknem coraz wyższe słońce.
  Wyjątkowo ciepły luty.
  Przeglądam i segreguję wiersze pisane dla tych,
których nie ma. Te wiersze czytałem ciepłym, żywym
ludziom, pełen wiary w przetrwanie, w koniec, w jutro,
w ZĘMSTWĘ, *w radość i budowanie.*
  Czytajcie.
  To nasza historia.
  To czytałem umarłym . . . [9]

❏ ❏ ❏

Carting of cement, bricks, nights reverberate
with the din of hammers and axes. Pumping of water,
constructing of underground wells. Bunkers, mania,
running, the heart of the Warsaw Ghetto palpitates
violently.
  Light, underground cables, escape routes, again
bricks, ropes, sand . . . Lots of sand . . . Sand . . .
  Board-beds, bunk-beds. Provisions for months.
  Crossing of electrical wires, faucets, everything.
Twenty centuries crossed out by the whip of an
SS-man. Cave Age. Muzzles. Village wells. Long
night. People are returning to the caves.
  Before the animals.
  And beyond the window, the sun is ever higher.

An exceptionally mild February.
I am reviewing and classifying poems I wrote
for those who are no longer here. I read these
poems to warm, living people, full of hope in
outlasting, in an end, in tomorrow,
IN REVENGE, in joy and creativity.
Read.
This is our history . . .
This I read to the dead . . .

More than Szlengel's other wartime writing, this passage
(like the rest of "This I Read to the Dead"), is poetry of humble
fact, poetry of remembered reality. "Reality as it is remembered,"
Czesław Miłosz writes, "is the most humble art of mimesis."
Reality "is paramount and dictates the means of expression."[10]
Perhaps it occurred to Szlengel, even before it struck, among
others, Czesław Miłosz, Elie Wiesel, Tadeusz Różewicz, Tadeusz
Borowski, T. W. Adorno, and George Steiner, that the idea of liter-
ature about the Holocaust is impossible and indecent. Perhaps,
too, Szlengel realized that the ability of art to transform anguish
and moral chaos into carefully wrought poetic diction would, in
the end, pervert their truth.

Szlengel's style, his "poetry of fact," as Irena Maciejewska ob-
serves, "derives from an awareness that the business of a writer is
to record what was and how it was, a bequest of the 'conventional'
fulfillment of an apocalypse that unfolds without the blast of
trumpets" (" 'Poezja faktu' wyrosła ze świadomości, że sprawa
pisarza jest zapisać to, co było i jak było, jest przekazanie 'zwy-
czajności' spełniającej się apokalipsy, która dokonuje się bez grz-
motu trąb"[11]). Maciejewska further writes that if read today,
Szlengel's work seems an obvious antecedent of the changes in
postwar Polish poetry.[12] Thus Szlengel's simple "reportage-poems"
(donosy poetyckie), as the poet labeled them, born on the far side
of evil, are a precursor of the minimalism of Tadeusz Różewicz
and Tadeusz Borowski as well as of the antipoetry of Miron Bia
łoszewski—although both the poets and the writer of the tales of
Auschwitz probably evolved their poetics independent of Szlen-
gel's legacy. Rożewicz, for example, writes in 1966:

Czułem ze coś skończyło się na zawsze dla mnie i dla ludz-
kości. . . . W tym czasie, a więc w roku 1945, w kilka
miesięcy od zakończenia drugiej wojny światowej i okupacji

hitlerowkiej, takie określenia, jak "przeżycie estetyczne,"
"przeżycie artystyczne," wydawały mi się śmieszne i pode-
jrzane. Potem w sierpniu zrzucono pierwszą bombę
atomową. Do dnia dzisiejszego tzw. przeżycie estetyczne
ciągle wydaje mi się śmieszne, choć już nie godne pogardy.
To przekonanie o śmierć dawnego "przeżycia estetycznego"
leży ciągle u podstaw mojej praktyki pisarskiej.[13]

☐ ☐ ☐

I felt that both for me and humanity something came to a
permanent end. . . . At this time, in 1945, a few months after
the end of World War II and the German occupation, such
definitions as "aesthetic experience," "artistic experience,"
seemed to me laughable and suspicious. Later, in August, the
atom bomb was dropped. To this day, this so-called aesthetic
experience still seems to me laughable, though unworthy
even of scorn. This conviction of the death of the former
"aesthetic experience" continues to underlie the principles
and practice of my writing.

Such writers as Różewicz apparently arrived at their convic-
tion by means of reflection—a cogitation that allows for a tem-
poral and spatial distance between "the man who suffers and
the mind that creates." This distinction is regarded as necessary
to perfect aesthetic forms, even if Różewicz scorned aesthetics.
Szlengel, on the other hand, not having had the benefit of this dis-
tance, arrived at his epiphany more intuitively, pressed by the ne-
cessity of a final knowledge.

Because "This I Read to the Dead" was written for the dead,
there is a constriction of the poet's inherently lyrical voice. Indeed,
much as in Julian Przyboś's untitled poem, discussed above, there
is an obliteration of the very shape and structure associated with
poetry. Szlengel's intuition, tempered as it is by the ghetto experi-
ence, seeks in verbal and structural asceticism a means of commu-
nicating his grief and wrath. But his terse lexicon and episodic
structure generate connotations that go beyond these states of feel-
ing. The quoted passage vibrates with the energy of despair. There
is nothing melancholy about his grief. In this he reflects the mo-
rale of the ghetto, for few people surrendered to total depression.
Although the suffering that followed each *Aktion*, which like an
elemental force swept the ghettos, left indelible memories on that

portion of the population who escaped it, incidents of suicide were very rare, and the determination to carry on rarely waned.

Some in the ghettos interpreted this behavior as a form of emotional atrophy or mental occlusion.[14] But the determination to "pick up the pieces" was in no small measure a form of spiritual resistance, a tradition encoded in the Jewish collective unconscious and engendered both by Judaic theodicy and the regularity of catastrophes visited upon the Jews. For Judaism teaches and, indeed, orders Jews not to yield to despair. There was, for example, a Hasidic rabbi in the Warsaw ghetto, whose famous exhortations not to give up were emblazoned above the entrance of his small *shul* (*shtibl*) in these words: "In God's name, Jews, do not despair." Thus, Jewish history, as already noted, is an endless rehearsal of the essential exhortations to celebrate life and to proclaim hope despite the recurrent waves of destruction.

Both the feverish building of bunkers and Szlengel's literary mimesis reflect aspects of the rabbi's injunction, for they are articles of hope. But Szlengel, a master ironist and parodist, probably more doubtful than the rabbi about the possibility of deliverance, seems to imply that the frenetic activity resembles the ordeal of Sisyphus. The sense of futility is intimated in the reiterated image of bricks, "carting of cement, bricks.... / again bricks.... " The accretion of this image suggests not only the feverish smuggling of bricks in the secrecy of night, but also the attempts to improve the safety of the bunkers. To that end the ghetto architects and engineers, some of them homegrown, were urged to add yet another "brick," to devise yet a more ingenious entrance.

Although ultimately proved futile, the inventiveness of the architects was reassuring, for some of the bunkers, notably those built in the cellars, had not only emergency exits ("escape routes"), but also emergency chambers excavated under the initial level of the bunker. The lower level was accessible through crawl-in tunnels, the entrance to which, in some cases, was as ingenious as the camouflage to the upper level, in some cases a swiveling toilet bowl. The more elaborate shelters were furnished with "underground wells," as Szlengel breathlessly lists, "underground cables ..., board-beds, bunk beds. Provisions for months. / ... electrical wires, faucets, everything." One might also add that some of them included burial places.

Yet despite the faith of the desperate people in these hide-outs, Szlengel, like many other Jews, knew they were castles of sand. The "sand ... lots of sand ... Sand ... ," like the reiterated image of "bricks," is not only a recording of the amounts of sand required for the construction of the bunkers, but also an allusion to the futility of the very attempt. The sense of futility is heightened by the ellipses, an ironic preterition that signals not the idea that "sand . . . , lots of sand . . . " is required as dependable building material, but rather the truncation of that idea. Thus, the meaning is reflected in the form.

The reciprocal relationship between content and structure is what makes this passage cohere. For the verbal and emotional frenzy that marks it, hampering and at the same time rendering the poet's expressions more rapid, threatens the total destruction of the already disjunctive poetic form. The fierce diction of the one-word sentences, their nervous, staccato rhythms, the elliptical phrasing and asyndetic construction, and not least the irony—all of these cause the words to fall unconnected as if out of the poet's control. In fact, the disconnected string of nouns and appositives— "bunkers, mania, running . . . " "light, underground cables, escape routes, again bricks, rope, sand . . . ," and the like—are merely held together by a few abstract and impersonal verbals, *Zwozi się, pompuje się, robi się, przekreśla się,* which, incidentally, do not have a grammatical equivalent in English but are translated as gerunds: "carting of cement," "pumping of water," "constructing of wells," "Crossing of electrical wires." Laying bare the poet's agitation and grief, all the rhetorical forms, a language of despair, are an echo of the poem's sense.

Szlengel's anguish and rage are not only a function of his personal loss—the disappearance of his family, friends, the Jews—but also of the obliteration of twenty centuries of Western civilization. His is an elegy written "for those who are no longer here . . . [the] warm, living people, full of hope in outlasting, in an end, in tomorrow, *in revenge,* in joy and creativity." But, like Julian Przyboś's poem, "This I Read to the Dead" is also a dirge for the destroyed human principles, the "twenty centuries crossed out by the whip of an SS-man," the "Cave Age," to which "people are returning." / "Before the animals," and the "long night," ushered in by Germany.

The ironic image of the sun rising outside the "long night" that has swallowed up the Jews ("And beyond the window, the sun is increasingly higher. / An exceptionally mild February,") is obviously a conventional topos, conveying the incongruity between human suffering and nature's neutral beauty. For Szlengel, however, it is also a verbal bridge that helps his aroused psyche to move from the world of the dead to that of the living. For him, this image connotes less nature's neutrality than the indifference of those beyond the landscape of death. The conclusion of "This I Read to the Dead" is clearly addressed to those who inhabit this side of the Styx. "Read. / This is our history... / This I read to the dead...." Contained therein is an implied message whose meaning is articulated in more precise terms in a postscript to "This I Read to the Dead." It reads thus: *"To były wiersze, które nie dotarły sumień.... / A żywi... / No, cóż... / ... żywi niech nie tracą nadzei.... "*[15] (These were poems that did not reach the conscience... / And the living... / Well, the living... / the living must not lose heart.)

Abraham Sutzkever: Citadels against Despair

Like Szlengel's, and like most of the poetry in the Holocaust, Sutzkever's poems, including the most lyrical, are rooted in fact, born of the actual, as Ruth Wiesse writes in "The Ghetto Poems of Abraham Sutzkever," the situation and vocabulary riveting the art to its "concrete origin in fact."[16] The factual nature of Sutzkever's poetry rendered it more public and hence more accessible to the sensibilities of readers in the ghetto. This phenomenon, a "poem of community," as Northrop Frye calls it in his discussion of the "Theory of Genres," made it seem to rise from the collective as well as personal experience of readers, uniting them in a form of "participation mystique." Such a participation mystique, Frye writes, marks not only sacred and oracular literature, but the panegyric, elegy or threnody as well.[17] Because much of Sutzkever's poetry is marked by oracular and prophetic resonances, they tended to absorb readers in communal participation, summoning them to spiritual or armed resistance. Even the pure threnodies had an intended didactic bias or were perceived, according to ghetto testimony, to be morally instructive. Such a threnody is "Di Lererin Mire" (The Teacher Mire):

Di Lererin Mire

Mit lates oyf layber, tseshnitn in pasn,
Me traybt undz in ghetto, es geyen di gasn.

Di hayzer bagleytn oyf eybik gezegnt
Un shteynerdik vert yeder gzeyre bagegnt.

In tfilin vi kroynen marshirn di zkeynim,
A kelbele geyt mit a dorfsyid in eynem.
A froy shlept a goyses farklemt in di negl,
A tsvayter—a bintele holts oyf a vegl.

Un tsvishn zey ale—di lererin Mire.
A kind oyf ir orem—a gildene lire.
A kind oyf ir orem, baym hentl—a tsveytn,
Arum di talmidim, bagleytn, bagleytn.

Un kumt men tsu Yiddisher gas, iz a toyer,
Nokh varem dos holts vi a kerper a royer.
Un glaykh vi a shloyz far getribene shtromen,
Er tut zikh an efn, farshlingt in di tomen.

Me yogt iber hurves on broyt on fayer,
Dos broyt iz a bukh un dos likht iz a blayer.
Farzamlt di kinder in hurver dire,
Es lernt zey vayter di lererin Mire.

Zi leyent zey Sholem Aleichems a mayse,
Es finklen di kinder un lakhn bes-mayse.
Zi flekht zey mit bloyene stenges di tseplekh
Un tseylt ir farmegn: hundert draysik di keplekh.

Tsu glaykh mit der zun iz di larerin Mire
Shoyn vakh un zi vart oyf di kinderlekh ire.
Zey kumen. Zi tseylt. O, nit tseyln zey beser!—
Durkh nakht hot do tsvantsik farshnitn a meser.

Ir hoyt vert a shoyb in farnakhtike flekn,
Nor s'tor zey nit Mire di kinder antplekn.
Farbayst zi a lip un mit gvure banayter
Dertseylt zi fun Lekertn, muntert zey vayter.

Durkh nakht hot a grokayt batsoygn di heyfn,
Un gro vert di lererins hor oyf di shleyfn:
Zi zukht inem keller ir mamen der blinder—
Tsuzamen mit ir feln zibetsn kinder.

Ven zun hot di blutn getriknt, hot Mire
Bahangen mit grins di faryosemte dire:
—Gekumen der lerer Gershtein, me vet zingen
Der khor zol ariber di toyern klingen.

Shoyn klingt es: "nit vayt iz der friling." Nor untn
Di hek un bagnetn tsetreyslen di gruntn.
Me shlept far di hor fun di kellers un lekher.
"Nit vayt iz der friling" farklingt ober hekher.

Shoyn zekhtsik farblibn on shvester, on mames
Di lererin Mire iz alle tsuzamen.
S'iz noent a yontef, iz, taybelekh, kinder,
A forshtelung darf men bavayzn geshwinder!

Tsum yontef—nito mer vi fertsik—nor itlekh—
Mit vaysikn hemdl, mit likhtike tritlekh.
Di bine iz frish mit a zun, mit a gortn,
Me ken azh in taykhl zikh oysbodn dortn.

Baym Leyenen Peretses Drite Matone
Hot untergezegt dos geboy di sakone.
Zey hobn gekhapt! Un fartog iz geblibn
Fun hundert mit draysik, bloyz Mire un zibn.

Azoy, biz di hak hot tseshpoltn dem zinen,
Iz Mire a blum un di kinderlekh—binen.
Shoyn gro iz di blum farvelkt ihre glider
Nor morgn in toy vet zi oyfblien vider.[18]

❑ ❑ ❑

The Teacher Mire

With patches on our flesh, cut into stripes,
We are driven into the ghetto, streets run ahead.
Buildings escort us forever left behind
And each draconic law is met like a stone.

In phylacteries like crowns old men march,
A little calf and a country-Jew walk side-by-side.
A woman drags someone dying clasped between her nails,
Another one pulls a wagon filled with wood.

And among them all is the Teacher Mire.
A child in her arms like a golden lyre.
A child in her arms, a second one hand-in-hand,
And around them the pupils, an escorting band.

And when they reach Yiddish Street,
They come upon a gate of wood as warm as raw flesh.
And just like a sluice before rushing streams,
It breaks open, sucking all into its darkness.

Driven through ruins without fire without bread,
Bread is a book and light a pencil's lead.
The children are gathered in a tenement ruin,
And the Teacher Mire resumes her teaching.

She reads to them a Sholem-Aleichem story,
The children all sparkle and laugh at the tale,
She plaits into braids blue ribbons
And counts her treasure: a hundred thirty little heads.

Like the very sun is the Teacher Mire.
Already awake she awaits her small fry.
They are coming. She counts. O, much better not to count!
During the night twenty were cut down by a knife.

Her skin turns to glass in the stain of dusk,
But Mire must not reveal it to the children.
She bites her lip and with fortitude renewed,
She tells them about Lekert, and cheers them up anew.

During the night grayness enveloped the courtyards,
And gray has turned the teacher's hair around the temples:
She looks for her blind mother hidden in the cellar—
Along with her seventeen children have vanished.

When the sun had dried the blood, Mire
Hung the orphaned ruin with outdoor green.
In came Teacher Gerstein and announced a song.
The chorus above the gates must resound.

It's ringing: "Not Far is Spring." But below
The axes and bayonets shatter the walls,

And people are pulled from cellars and holes.
But "Not Far is Spring" resounds ever louder.

Only sixty are left without sisters or mothers,
The Teacher Mire is all of them together.
Children, soon there'll be a holiday, little sparrows,
We must quickly, quickly prepare a show!

The holiday comes—there are no more than forty. But each one—
In the whitest of shirts, with luminous childish steps.
The stage is aglow with a sun, and a garden,
One can actually bathe in the stream.

During the reading of Perets's "The Third Gift,"
The building was sawed down by the fiend.
They caught them! And at dawn, of
the hundred and thirty, only Mire and seven were still alive.

And so, as the axe had cleaved the mind,
Mire turned flower and the little kids—bees.
And grayed has the flower, wilted her core
But tomorrow in the dew she will blossom once more.

Unlike Szlengel who rarely dates his poems, yet invariably
locates them in concrete fact that is deliberately projected as time-
less and undifferentiated hell, Sutzkever locates his poem in a spe-
cific time frame and thus also welds it to its concrete origin in
fact. "The Teacher Mire," dated May 10, 1943, shortly before the
total elimination of the Vilna ghetto in September of that year, is a
factual account of the beginning and near end of that place. In this
it resembles Szlengel's poem "Things," discussed in the preceding
chapter. Like "Things"—a contraction of the history of the War-
saw ghetto—"The Teacher Mire" is a compressed history of the
Vilna ghetto. But whereas the central image of Szlengel's poem is
the descent of human possessions into the narrowing funnel of the
ghetto, the focus of Sutzkever's poem is people, notably, a woman
whose boundless love and courage not only kept her pupils alive as
long as possible, but also inspired moral fortitude in most others
who knew her. Moreover, while "Things" resonates with fury,
irony, and the grotesque, all stoked by the poet's anguish, the voice
of "The Teacher Mire" is marked by muted grief, bounded by the
Apollonian patterns of the poem. Although the structure of each

work is vastly different, they are both narrative poems. What further distinguishes the two poems is the balladic *feeling* of "The Teacher Mire."

Although clearly not a pure ballad, this poem shares certain conventions with the literary ballad. Like the latter, it is a song poem that tells a story and that, in the sophisticated handling of established balladic techniques, rhetorical devices, and themes of a reflective nature, towers over its earlier prototypes. Yet it retains the eerie and the sinister. But these, significantly, derive not from deliberate poetic inventions, but, as already discussed, from the surreality of the events. "The Teacher Mire" is further marked by directness of narrative and exposition, allowing for an unhindered development of the story line, all of which are associated with the ballad. In these features it resembles that class of Sutzkever's poems to which "A Cartload of Shoes" belongs, although the latter is a more self-conscious ballad (see chapter 1). The meter of both poems is distinguished by its simplicity. The stanza form of "The Teacher Mire" is a quatrain, mostly of four stress lines with an impeccable *a b a b* rhyme scheme.

The expository opening scenes of the poem unveil the turbulent events that drive Mire and her charges into oblivion. Since these events are by their very nature the poet's demonic epiphany, he uses surreal images to convey them. The surreal is, at rock bottom, a mechanism of translation or preservation of essentially unutterable truths.

In the first stanza, images of dehumanization, pauperization, and perplexity establish the violence with which the Jews were herded into the ghetto on September 6, 1941. Driven from their homes and robbed of their possessions, they were further humiliated by two yellow patches with an inscribed letter "J" in the center of each. The ambiguous image, "with patches on our flesh, cut into stripes," alludes either to the yellow patch decree or to the poverty to which the Jews had already been reduced. The syntactical strategy of this line produces a form of metonymy and is, therefore, an intimation of both. Moreover, the image of "patches on the flesh, cut into stripes," rather than on clothes, conjures up a picture of stigmata burned or cut into the flesh, or else of suddenly appearing protrusions. "The large piece of yellow material on . . . [the] shoulders seemed to be burning me. . . . I felt a hump, as though I had two frogs on me,"[19] reads "The 8th of July, 1941" diary entry of the fourteen-year-old Yitskhak Rudashevski. But Sutzkever's verbal strategy evokes with equal power that kind of unique wretchedness that is associated with people in patches and rags on a death march. This sense is further augmented by an intimation of stoning, "and each draconic decree is met like a stone." These emblems of violence and damnation are amplified by the surreal tableau of "streets [that] run ahead" or "buildings [that] escort us forever left behind." Each of these images suggests the shock sustained by the human mind—a state of frozen suspension produced by that violence. Thus the condemned appear to be riveted in place, while the streets and buildings seem to do the running and the escorting; it is much like the impression one gets in a madly speeding vehicle.

Like a roving camera or the retina of a painter, Sutzkever's poetic eye fastens here on one, there on another subject in this eerie procession. Singled out in this motley humanity are pious old men, who, both defying the peril and invoking divine tempering mercy, wear "phylacteries like crowns." These cameos of majesty and faith are etched with veneration and anguish. And so is the portrayal of a simple country Jew and a little calf, presumably the man's only possession, who walk side-by-side. Following this, is a more sinister scene of a dying person, pulled along by a woman whose despair is registered in the image of clutching nails. The use of the Hebrew term *goyses* for the dying person lends further weight to the woman's grief. This is juxtaposed by an image of another woman dragging a bundle of wood in a wagon, an incongruity with which the poet probably alludes to the breakdown of some of the basic human values among the Jews themselves.

The last image is, however, redeemed by the pictorial power of the Teacher Mire, executed in the manner of an allegorical emblem. Carrying "a child in her arms—a golden lyre," clutching another one's hand, and encircled by a retinue of orphans, the image of this woman parallels that of the old men in "phylacteries like crowns." She is like an anima figure whose very presence seems numinous, transcending the wretchedness of the doomed people. But like the rest of the nightmarish procession, "a rushing stream"—with the implied thousands of men, women, and children, some shuffling along apathetically, many shoving and pushing, but virtually all dazed, clutching each other for comfort, while harnessed to large bundles, many of which are abandoned by falling persons who are driven on by the Lithuanians—Mire and her pupils are swallowed by the ghetto gate. The confusion and helplessness of the unsuspecting, unprepared, and unarmed procession is embodied in the image of a "rushing stream" that breaks the "sluice" and drowns each and every one. The impression of brutality with which the bewildered are hurled into oblivion is further heightened by the evocative image of the gate, the "wood" of which "is still warm like raw flesh."

With a subtle shift of technique, notably in tone and collocation of imagery, the fifth strophe shows the established ghetto, through the ruins of which Mire and her small charges are endlessly driven. Since hardly any residence in the ghetto was permanent, the teacher and the orphans were forced to settle in one or another tenement ruin, in each room of which it was not unusual to find fifteen people, as young Rudashevski testifies.[20] Although the ruins are factual, they are also used to signify the destruction that was wrought by the systematic deportations to such death pits as Ponary. But during the interludes, the darkness of the ruins and the children's world were illuminated by the love of Teacher Mire, and hunger was assuaged by study.

While the opening four strophes are marked by a tension arising from a deliberate restraint of tone—an attempt to maintain a measure of distance—the tone of the following stanzas is increasingly reverential and grief-stricken. The poet's voice begins to reach a pitch of high intensity when he invokes the "hundred-thirty" sparkling faces of the hungry children and their laughter in response to a story by Sholem Aleichem. The reader's perception of the poet's intensity derives mostly from a double system of references, one that imposes a form of collusion between the poet and reader, both of whom know the fate of Mire and her pupils. The angst that this tragic irony generates is most eloquently conveyed in the image of the teacher counting the numbers of her "treasure," prefiguring the lament in the following strophe, "O, much better not to count!— / During the night twenty were cut down by a knife."

Sutzkever, whose child was poisoned by the Germans, seems to identify his child with Mire's orphans, an identification that is audible in the tone and lexicon with which he refers to them. In speaking about them, it is as if he were speaking to them, caressing and loving them, trying to shield them from pain and lurking death. His lament is, therefore, expressed in words used when addressing children: "In came Teacher Gerstein, there will be song / The chorus above the gates must resound. / It's ringing: 'Not Far is Spring.' "Several stanzas later, in a reference to the stage-setting prepared for the holidays, when only forty children are left, there appear these evocative lines, again as if spoken to the children:

"The stage is aglow with a sun, and a garden, / One can actually bathe in the stream."

Although heartbreaking, some of the iconography of suffering that follows is somewhat sentimental, a characteristic that occasionally creeps into Sutzkever's work. The most salient example of this is the lachrymose image of Mire searching for her blind mother in a cellar (ninth strophe). Nonetheless, it must be noted that Mire is neither a poetic invention nor a disembodied legend, but rather a real woman of flesh and blood, a teacher whose love for and devotion to the orphans was, indeed, legendary. Moreover, the somewhat stock-figure of her mother is alleged to be real as well. And real also, according to allegations, is the fact that the blind woman tried in vain to escape deportation by hiding out in a cellar. Nonetheless, "in poetry a credible impossibility is to be chosen before an incredible [or poetically awkward, one might add] possibility."[21]

The dignity of the preceding image, however, tends to neutralize the last one, throwing both into sharp relief. In alluding to the grief that the teacher and, in fact, all the adults suffered when they helplessly watched the terror or murder of children, the poet transforms ordinary words into enigmatic constellations. Thus Mire's skin becomes a "window pane in the stain of dusk," a transmutation produced by her realization that "during the night twenty [children] were cut down by a knife." The shock of this image conveys nuances of suffering so unspeakable that only its surreality can attempt to express the teacher's anguish.

Although this conceit may sound awkward in English, the original Yiddish is of singular power, suggesting pain so ineffable that it cannot be contained within consciousness alone, but has an impact on the viscera as well. Using a form of the grotesque, Sutzkever implies that the violence of the impact causes Mire's skin to become translucent, revealing the battered inner organs. Hence the stains of dusk on the window pane. In this organic unity, the grotesque has a metaphysical connotation, for the unity is only apparent and derives from things other than themselves. In the same way, when the poet uses the word "knife" as a metaphor for the demise of the children in the pits of Ponary or gas chambers elsewhere, the thing in itself, the knife, is clearly something other than its thingness.

Sutzkever's avoidance of naming the actual instrument of death or the enemy derives from a sustained determination, as mentioned in the preceding chapter, not to defile the sacrosanct memory of the murdered Jews. Ruth R. Wisse interprets this phenomenon as:

> special acts of aggression, annihilating the foe by denying him existence. The Germans are subjected to almost total linguistic extinction: they appear, when at all, stripped of human form and abstracted into instruments of death—the noose, the knife, the boot, the time of slaughter. Just as the "I" of the poem emphasizes his own triumphant presence, so he eliminates the actual enemy by sustained neglect.[22]

Moreover, the abstraction of the instruments of death is intended both to translate the unspeakable into the logos of speech and to raise it to a transcendental level. This vehicle makes the tragedy, if not more bearable, then at least more utterable.

Since the poetic universe of "The Teacher Mire" is organic, the images of murder are interconnected, revealing in the middle as in the conclusion of the poem similar abstractions of the instruments of death. Thus in the closing strophe, the precise weapon with which Mire, the children, and all the other Jews were killed is not mentioned—possibly, too, because a deliberate darkness shrouded the death of those who were deported or who disappeared into some other void. Instead, an "axe that cleaved the mind" is the symbol of annihilation. This image suggests and, at once, eschews the unutterable, while it evokes a sense of holy darkness that is richly orchestrated in the closing images: "Mire is a flower and the little children—bees. / And grayed has the flower, wilted her core / But tomorrow in the dew she will blossom once more."

Sutzkever's evasion of the thing-in-itself, the death of Mire and her hundred thirty charges, is revealed once more in surreal images. The surreal derives from the poet's use of a flower and identifying its place in nature with the unexpected. The flower into which Mire has been transmuted after her death has turned "gray," a hue generally not associated with wilted flowers. Such symbolic associations take their energy from a perception of singularity in connection with the object with which they are equated. Although intended as a reflection of the people and their morale, the teacher and children are presented in their uniqueness and, therefore, singled out for apotheosis. This is articulated in the inherent transcendentality of a flower that has "grayed" yet has not died, for "tomorrow in the dew she will blossom once more." Mire and the children, transformed into bees, are, therefore, immortal, not only because they have fulfilled their tragic mission in death, but also, and perhaps more importantly, because their mission presupposes the pollenization of posterity, as the imagery of a flower and bees implies.

Since Mire and her children are representative of the Jews in the ghetto, all the victims are apotheosized. For as the poet also suggests in the image of the undaunted old Jews, "in phyllactries like crowns," they fought back with everything they had. Most of the time, the most available and hence most effective weapon was their spiritual resilience—an ancient paradigm in which the Jews are well practiced. It is this that kept their souls from dying. The network of images of love so desperately unwavering and study and creativity so persistently growing in the ruins of the people's lives *and* buildings are structured to convey the value of that archetypal ethos. In the absence of any other more viable means (an issue that is more comprehensively discussed in the following chapter), the alternative was despair, the stunned surrender of those who could no longer endure.

Although not all the death or other imagery in this poem is transcendental, every allusion to the protagonists is reverential and encomiastic. For Mire and the children personify moral fortitude without the example of which no survival would have been possible, even if they themselves were in the end killed. Such a reading of the poem arises from the ambivalence inherent in the closing images, which suggest not only the spiritual pollenization of distant posterity, but of the immediate environment as well. In this elegaic record of the beginning and end of the Vilna ghetto, Sutzkever's desire is to inform, to instruct. This didacticism, coupled as it is with a creative mind, generates specific selections of characters and events. By means of these the poet eulogizes, while he conveys both an immediacy of perception and a determination to guide. The specific historical selections, the logic that governs them, and the mode of representation are all designed to throw light on the courage of individual acts of moral resistance. At the same time, as an interpretive mediator, the poet provides a model to be emulated by others in the ghetto.

Thus, the poet singles out those patterns that are most common, those that create an atmosphere in which the children find a bulwark against despair. These include the readings of the tragicomic but inspiring tales of Sholem Aleichem, the more sophisticated works of Perets, another masterful Yiddish writer, or the heroic story of Hirsh Lekert. Lekert, a member of the Jewish Labor Bund in Vilna, attempted to assassinate the governor for having subjected a group of workers participating in a May Day demonstration to a humiliating whipping. Although Lekert failed and was hanged, his heroic attempt became legend among the Jews and was intended to cheer the hearts of the dejected children.

These and other examples—notably the songs of hope and defiance or the teacher's theatrical entrepreneurship—demonstrate the ways in which Mire was able to harness the ebbing energies of both her children and her own. But the external events are like a nightmare that closes in on the controlling intelligence of the poet who selects them, since for him personally they are "the axe [that] had cleaved the mind," the beckoning of insanity. Because of its syntactical position, this appositive is both an allusion to the murder of Mire and the children and to the poet's state of mind. Although his anguish and the battle with madness might be controlled by the artifact of the poem, and though like many poems in the Holocaust "The Teacher Mire" is a verbal barricade against moral disintegration, in the end, it is also an expression of faith that the terrible reality will come to an end and that individuals like Mire and her charges will live in the yet to be born—in other Just Ones like them. If nothing else, his hope—however tentative, secularized, and tragic—is a vision of redemption, only a vision. That such a vision is more likely to be granted to those in the abyss than to those who contemplate it from a distance is not surprising, for without it, as the cliché would have it, survival is impossible. On a more empirical level, those who plumb the heart of evil are not only closer to its source but also to those pulsations of decency and compassion that make the two extremes stand in sharp relief against the background of each. It is this possibility of decency, as Mire's actions reveal and Sutzkever's poem articulates, that is often the wellspring of hope.

Isaiah Spiegel and Shmerke Kaczerginski: The Irony of Consolation

The apotheosis of the murdered children in "The Teacher Mire" reminds us that—whether personal or communal, cultural or national, religious or moral—the struggle to survive posits the child as the ultimate goal and, indeed, apogee of that exertion. For

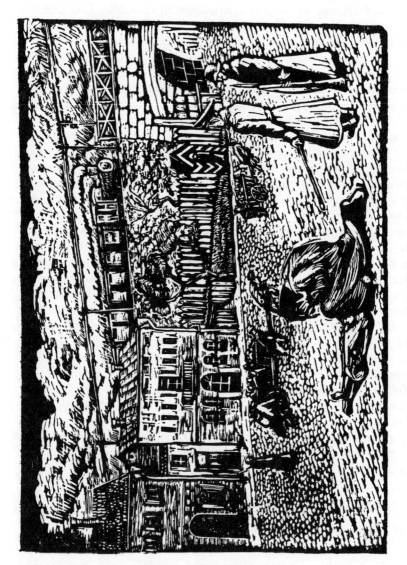

Jonas Stern, "Roundup of Children." (Etching)

as a bridge to the future and an extension of the self, the child is usually the referent and normative source of meaning in that struggle. In the extreme impossibilities of the Holocaust, the child was the first target of destruction, as Yitzhak Katzenelson repeatedly laments in his monumental *The Song of the Murdered Jewish People*:

They, the first to perish were the children, abandoned orphans,
The world's best, the black earth's brightest.
These children from the orphanages might have been our comfort.
From these sad, mute, bleak voices our new dawn might have
    risen.[23]

The hope of individual or collective survival through the child, and, in fact, the attempt to protect the child's life for its own sake were both obliterated with a sweeping finality. Parents like Katzenelson or such surrogate parents as Mire could, at best, do little more for their children than to die in joint embrace with them—often a gratuitously forbidden option.

The substance and pain of shorn parental protectiveness are most cogently expressed in lullabies to the murdered or about to be murdered children. Prominent in the corpus of ghetto poetry, this genre at once reflects and subverts traditional Yiddish lullabies. These, as Dov Noy's study indicates, are distinguished by specific rhetorical and structural conventions.[24] The infant is directly addressed by the singer, and the song identifies its explicit function, which is to put the child to sleep. The construction is generally triadic, including "three [rhymed] stanzas, often with a refrain; three acting characters; three steps of 'gradatio.' Three are the members of the nuclear family—singing mother, lulled child, (absent) father or his substitute."[25]

In most lullabies, the mother mentions the absence of the father, but the sexual implications and her articulation of resentment at having been abandoned or neglected are less evident in the Yiddish than in the universal lullaby. The singer's projections of the infant's achievements are for a distant rather than an immediate future. Both in this and in expectations of socio-economic success and spiritual values, the Yiddish lullaby also differs from its universal counterpart. The supernatural, the fabulous, and the miraculous elements that inform the universal cradle song are demythologized in the Yiddish and replaced by the extraordinary and the unusual. Finally, the lullaby, occupying a prominent place in the body of Yiddish poetry, belongs either to the *art song* or to the *folk song*. The former is perpetuated in writing, or has been published by an identified author. The author and composer of the latter have fallen into oblivion, because time and space have subjected their work to a process of folklorization.

The ghetto lullabies are, essentially, self-conscious art songs. Adhering, as they do, to the canons of their antecedents, they are, nonetheless, deliberate antitheses of traditional lullabies. Caught in unspeakable situations and rendered totally helpless, the distraught imagination of the potentially soothing and sleep-inducing voice of the singer is capable only of abusive ironies and parodies of itself, producing, at best, phantasmagoric forms of lamentations that would normally startle rather than lull a child to sleep. As in the more conventional lullaby, the singer of the ghetto rendition has a dual audience: the adult singer, engaged in a form of internal monologue, and the infant whom he or she is trying to lull to sleep (and the sooner it ceases to listen, the better). Whether or not these songs were actually sung to infants or children in the ghetto is perhaps less important than the fact that the children were inured to the ironies and parodies by the onslaught of catastrophes. Often master ironists themselves, they were quick to discern the secret parody hidden not so much in the lyrics, since these were obvious, as in the old and familiar melodies of lulling consolations to which the disjunctive words were set.

An example of this disjunction are two lullabies by Isaiah Spiegel, "Makh Tsu di Eygelekh" (Close Your Precious Eyes) and "Nit Keyn Rozhinkes, un Nit Keyn Mandlen" (Neither Raisins Nor Almonds), the latter a bitter inversion of the famous "Rozhinkes und Mandlen" (Raisins and Almonds).

Makh Tsu di Eygelekh

Makh tsu di eygelekh,
Ot kumen feygelekh
Un krayzn do arum
Tsukopns fun dayn vig.
Dos pekl in der hant,
Dos hoyz iz ash un brand;
Mir lozn zikh, mayn kind,
Zukhn glik.

Di velt hot Got farmakht,
Un umetum iz nakht,

Zi vart oyf undz
Mit shoyder un mit shrek,
Mir shteyen beyde do
In shverer, shverer sho
Un veysn nit vuhin
S'firt der veg.

Tsuzing:

Makh tsu di eygelekh . . .

Men hot undz naket bloyz
Faryogt fun undzer hoyz,
In fintsternish
Getribn undz in feld,
Un shturem, hogl, vint
Hot undz bagleyt, mayn kind,
Bagleyt undz inem opgrunt
Fun der velt.

Makh tsu di eygelekh . . . [26]

❑❑❑

Close Your Precious Eyes

Close your precious eyes,
Birds are flying nigh,
And circle all around
Aflutter above your crib.
A bundle ready in hand,
The house by fire rent.
We are off, my child,
To seek good luck.

God has shut our world so bright
And everywhere is dark, dark night,
And waits for us right here
With horror and with fear.
We are both standing there
In this dreadful, dreadful hour,
Not knowing where
The road will lead.

Refrain:

Close your precious eyes. . . .

Naked, of everything bereft
Chased, our homes we left,
In the pitch of night
Pursued into the field,
And storm, hail, and wind,
My child, escorted us
To the fathomless void.

Close your precious eyes. . . .

This lullaby adheres to all the rhetorical and structural elements of the genre, including the triadic construction; the direct addressing of the child; the identification of the song's function; the refrain; the rhyme scheme; the extraordinary and the unusual. But while in the classical lullaby the future greatness of the infant is a prominent characteristic, here it is conspicuously absent. Nullified too is the word "father." Further, while in the classical lullaby the extraordinary and the unusual are largely a product of the singer's literary imagination, here they are real. It is this reality that produces a visceral shudder and that sets the poem in sharp relief against the backdrop of its precursors, however tragic the content sometimes may have been.

Spiegel wrote this song both after the death of his little daughter, Eva, in the Lodz ghetto, and after the deportations of thousands of other children to death centers. The proffering of consolation is, therefore, its opposite—devoid of coherence because of the sinister subtext. This irreconcilable paradox demolishes the intent of the lullaby, subverting language and meaning, signifier and signified, and producing a dirge of bitter parody. The poet's child, much like the other children, is dead, though in a crib, around which birds flutter, and in a house destroyed by the conflagration. Both parent and dead child are about to embark on a journey to seek good fortune, as they and the rest of the Jews face the inevitable void.

"Neither Raisins Nor Almonds," is a somewhat more circumspect subversion of consolation:

Nit Keyn Rozhinkes un Nit Keyn Mandlen

Nit keyn rozhinkes un nit keyn mandlen,
Der tate iz nit geforn handlen,

Lulinke mayn zun,
Lulinke mayn zun.
Er hot farlozt undz un avek,
Vu di velt hot nor an ek,
Lulinke mayn zun,
Lulinke may zun.

S'shrayen soves, s'voyen velf,
Got, derbarem zikh un helf,
Lulinke may zun,
Lulinke mayn zun.
Ergets shteyt er un er vakht,
Mandlen, rozhinkes a sakh,
Lulinke mayn zun,
Lulinke mayn zun.

Kumen r'vet oyf zikher shoyn,
Zen dikh, kind, mayn eyntsik kroyn,
Lulinke may zun,
Lulinke, mayn zun.[27]

❏ ❏ ❏

Neither Raisins Nor Almonds

Neither raisins nor almonds,
You father left not for to sell them.
Go to sleep my son,
Go to sleep my son.
He has forsaken us bereft
For the unknown world he left,
Go to sleep my son,
Go to sleep my son.

Owls are shrieking, wolves are howling,
Dear, dear God, help us, the entreating,
Go to sleep my son,
Go to sleep my son.
Somewhere he is watching over us,
Lots of almonds and raisins he surely has,
Go to sleep my son,
Go to sleep my son.

He is sure to come back soon
For to see you, my precious one,

Go to sleep my son,
Go to sleep my son.

Much like "Close Your Precious Eyes," this cradle song re-
flects the conventions of the classical lullaby. The added feature is
the "father," who, reflecting the standards of the traditional lull-
aby, is absent but expected to return with gifts. And much like
"Close Your Precious Eyes," "Neither Raisins Nor Almonds" is
probably intended for Spiegel's daughter, yet it is addressed to a
son. The metonymic use of son for daughter is an attempt to en-
code the paradigmatic nature of the poet's and his child's personal
tragedies. For this figure symbolizes the mass destruction of chil-
dren of both genders and suggests the grief of all their parents,
even as they themselves are facing death. And yet the subversion
of solace is at once less resonant and more cynical in "Neither
Raisins Nor Almond" than in "Close Your Precious Eyes." On the
one hand, raisins and almonds are no longer to be had, for the fa-
ther has left not to sell them, as he had done in the past, but has
forsaken the family for such unknown worlds as the implied death
centers. On the other hand, the grieving voice of the singer assures
the child that the dead father, who is watching over the family
(much like the birds hovering over the crib of the dead child in
"Close Your Precious Eyes"), will return with gifts of almonds and
raisins.

Coupled with this note of solace is a covert, because guilty,
indictment of the father. The accusation is implied in the verbs
"forsaken" and "left" ("he has forsaken us bereft / for the un-
known world he left"). Although the singer may know the invol-
untary itinerary of the errant father, and though she or he may
agonize over the meaning of his voyage, it was commonplace for
those left behind to feel "forsaken" by the deported members of
the family and to be penitent for harboring such feelings. That this
is not an unusual response of most survivors of destruction or
death does not obviate the shock of the implication.

In the end one wonders for whom the lullabies were intended
and for what purpose. Whom does the grieving parent mean to
console? The murdered child who could not be protected? The yet
to be killed children to whom these cradle songs were probably not
sung (for who could sing such songs to living children)? Himself
and other grieving and helpless parents? These issues become par-
ticularly cogent in view of the fact that both poems, set to music

by Dov Beygelson, were performed at the opening of the ghetto's cultural center. The interesting thing is that the Jewish elder of the Lodz ghetto, H. Rumkowski,[28] whose eccentric and perhaps not quite sane leadership won him notorious immortality, banned the songs, because they openly addressed the Jewish tragedy and the German terror.[29] Nonetheless, the Jews continued to sing them, ignoring the edict and thus articulating their defiance. Hence the songs were as much an offering of consolation—even if bitter and parodic—and a form of lamentation as an expression of resistance.

Another attenuated endeavor to proffer consolation to the child, whose tentative security, like that of his protectors, was being rapidly dismantled, is Shmerke Kaczerginski's "Shtiler, Shtiler."[30] Kaczerginski wrote this poem to the musical composition of the eleven-year-old Alek Volkovisky. Both lyrics and music were produced in the Vilna ghetto and performed in April 1943 at a concert sponsored by the Judenrat.[31] One can only imagine the anxiety of hope with which the adult population hovered over the children, at this late date in the systematic destruction, and the anguish with which a mature poet set his poem to the music of a child.

The first stanza of this tripartite cradle song opens with an exhortation to silence not because speech may defile or desacralize the tragedy, but rather the fiend, because he is a fiend, will not understand it:

Shtiler, Shtiler

Shtiler, shtiler, lomir shvaygn,
Kvorim vaksn do.
S'hobn zey farflantst di sonim;
Grinen zey tsum blo.
S'firn vegn tsu Ponar tsu,
S'firt keyn veg tsurik,
Iz der tate vu farshvundn
Un mit im dos glik.
Shtiler kind mayn, vey nit oytser,
S'helft nit kayn geveyn,
Undzer umglik veln sonim
Say vi nit farshteyn.
S'hobn breges oykh di yamen,
S'hobn tfises oykhet tsamen,
Nor tsu undzer payn

Kayn bisl shayn,
Kayn bisl shayn.

◻ ◻ ◻

Hush, Hush

Hush, hush, let's be silent,
Graves are growing high,
The enemy has planted them;
Green, they reach blue sky.
All roads are leading to Ponary,
No road is leading back,
And your father vanished too
And with him our luck.
Hush, hush, don't cry precious,
Weep my child no more.
The depth of our tragedy
The enemies ignore.
Oceans have had always shores
And fences prisons had,
But to our anguish
There is no end,
There is no end.

The indictment of the fiend, who does not understand, would seem an awkward redundancy had it not been for the fact that the poet does not even consider the possibility of a compassionate friend outside the ghettos and camps. This deliberate figure of preterition makes emphatic the deadly isolation of the Jews. Indeed, the very omission suggests that, because of its indifference, the impervious world outside is also perceived as an enemy. And, by implication, so is the larger part of the openly anti-Semitic gentile population of both Poland and Lithuania. (Both countries had a claim on Vilna and the city belonged alternately to both.)

Moreover, the admonition to silence is intended to remind the Jews that they must be careful, for Nazi laws forbid the naming of facts. This includes the prohibition to identify the murderers, their brutality, and the specific places (among others, the notorious Ponary) where mass killings are being carried out. Indeed, as Kaczerginski writes, the verse "all roads are leading to Ponary" (s'firn vegn tsu Ponar tsu) had to be changed to "all roads are leading there now" *(s'firn vegn itst ahintsu).*[32] Yet the poet tries to cast out the phantoms of terror and grief as the mass graves are quickly multiplying. He also offers a song of silence to the tentatively living children and parents in order to lull, as H. Leivick puts it, their pain to sleep.[33]

The narrative of despair that informs the first stanza amplifies the following one, emphasizing the repeated beginnings of anguish and dread and their fugitive pauses. Fleeting are also the tropes of solace, for they are inevitably obliterated by the juxtaposition of abundant spring in the romantic landscape of Poland and Lithuania with the endless darkness that envelopes the condemned people:

> *Friling oyfn land gekumen,—*
> *Un undz harbst gebrakht,*
> *Iz der tog haynt ful mit blumen,—*
> *Undz zet nor di nakht.*
> *Goldikt shoyn der harbst oyf shtamen,—*
> *Blit in undz der tsar;*
> *Blaybt faryosemt vu a mame;*
> *S'kind geyt oyf Ponar.*
> *Vi di Vilye a geshmidte—*
> *T'oykh geyokt in payn,—*
> *Tsiyen kryes ayz durch Lite*
> *Itst in yam arayn.*
> *Svert der khoyshekh vu tserunen,*
> *Fun der fintster laykhtn zunen*
> *Rayter kum geshvind,—*
> *Dikh ruft dayn kind,*
> *Dikh ruft dayn kind.*

❑ ❑ ❑

Spring's descended on the land,
Fall's been ushered in for us.
And the mornings brim with flowers
Night's enveloped us.
Stalks aglitter with fall's gold hues,
We are full of pain;
A mother has been orphaned somewhere;
Her child sent to Ponary.
Like Vilia when restrained
And burdened flows in pain,
Ice floes cover Lithuania

Moving out to sea.
Somewhere darkness is breaking up
Sun rays seeping through the clouds
Rider, quickly come
Your child calls,
Your child calls.

The central image of these lines is the mother whose child is sent to Ponary. The intensity of her anguish and her truncated status as a parent and protector of her child are carried in the emblem of her orphanhood. It is by such metonymic figures that Kaczerginski pits the image of the impotent parent against the impotent orphan, equating both and developing the theme and strengthening the fact that parents could do no more for their children than children for their parents or themselves. Since no one will help either one, the singer significantly turns for deliverance not to God but to a horseman ("rider"), exhorting this mythic figure of redemption to heed the call of his child.

The final strophe reiterates the imperative of silence, while it interweaves tropes of despair with threads of encouragement, solace, and hope, adumbrated in the second stanza. The image of the ice-restrained Vilia (a river with a majestic history and mythosymbolic significance for the population of both Poland and Lithuania) is an obvious symbol of life. It is transformed in this stanza into gushing springs that, while flooding the hearts of the walled-in Jews with sorrow and terror, will in the end fill them with the relief of deliverance:

Shtiler, shtiler, s'kveln kvaln
Undz in harts arum,
Biz der toyer vet nit faln
Zayn mir muzn shtum.
Frey nit, kind, zikh s'iz dayn shmeykhl
Itst far undz farat,
Zen dem friling zol der soyne
Vi in harbst a blat.
Zol der kval zikh ruyik flisn,
Shtiler zay un hof . . .
Mit der frayhayt kumt der tate,
Sholf zhe, kind mayn, shlof.
Vi di Vilye a bafrayte,
Vi di beymer grin-banayte

Laykht bald frayhats-likht
Oyf dayn gezikht,
Oyf dayn gezikht.

❑ ❑ ❑

Hush, Hush, springs are gushing,
Flooding our hearts,
While the gates are not yet falling,
We must all be mute.
Don't rejoice, child, for your smile
Is still forbidden us,
Let the fiend see next spring
In the autumn leaves.
Let the springs flow serenely,
While you must hush and hope . . .
For with your freedom, little one,
Your father will return.
Sleep my child, then sleep.
Like the liberated Vilia,
Like the trees renewed and green,
Freedom is bound to shine
Upon your face,
Upon your face.

The solace is copious and deliberate. The singer's assurances that both freedom and the child's father will some day return is a vision of the future—an element that characterizes the classical lullaby. But the normative standards of this vision have been subverted. Reflecting the impossibilities of the present moment, the singer's expectations of the infant's coming of age, maturity, wedding, and spiritual or material achievements have been deliberately avoided. That the future—however uncertain and undefined—is mentioned at all is a measure of both the poet's tentative optimism and his attempt to offer comfort. Yet as deliberate as Kaczerginski's amplification of solace might be, and much as his song and the performance of it at a cultural event are a measure of moral resistance, the brutal mockery of hope is the subtext that dominates this as well as Spiegel's work. Perhaps it is this fact that caused both poets to immortalize the individual child and individual parent by transforming them into allegorical figures, cast into emblems that absorb into themselves the rest of the condemned community. Thus the individual parent, whether orphaned, grieving, or vanished, stands for all the parents, and the orphaned or dead child for all the children.

PART THREE

Issues of Resistance

Vey undz! Mir kenen, yo mir kenen zikh antkegn shteln oykh un aykh derkhargenen, mir oykh! Mir oykh!
Mir kenen, ober dos vos ir hot keyn mol nisht gekent un vet nit kenen keyn mol oyf der erd—
Nit hargenen a tsveytn! Nit oysrotn a folk vayl er iz verloz, vos hoybt umzist di oygn in der hoykh.
Ir kent nit nit derhargenen, ir zindike fun der natur, ir muzt's, eybike ir fokher mit der shverd.

□ □ □

Woe unto us! We are able. We can resist and even kill you. We, too!
We too!
But we can do what you never could and never will—not kill!
Not exterminate a helpless people who raise their eyes in vain on high.
You cannot keep from killing. You're born criminals. You must wave the sword forever.

Yitzhak Katzenenlson
The Song of the Murdered Jewish People

Chapter Five

Poetics of Exhortation

The Jews of prewar Poland had little economic power and nominal access to Poland's political infrastructure. Indeed, they were even barred from the civil service. Hence, as Lucy Dawidowicz writes, "Jewish politics were both symbolic and visionary with morality and messianism substituting for political and economic power."[1] Nonetheless, in the near millennium of their presence in Poland, the Jews developed a complex parapolitical structure and created a rich culture and literature. Both the political ferment and the cultural-literary imagination were shaped by religious fundamentalism and humanist enlightenment. This produced an ideology whose purpose it was to support all aspects of Jewish tradition and to seek equity and sanction for Jews as citizens in a hostile, sometimes murderous, world.

The measure of legitimacy that the Jews were able to carve out for themselves was obliterated by the Nazi occupation of Poland. All political parties as well as cultural and religious life were outlawed. Nonetheless, those organizations that managed to go underground defiantly continued, maintaining an intricate political network. Often the poets, whose voices resonated with cadences of timeless seers and prophets, were the spiritual backbone of the cells of these organizations. Emanuel Ringelblum, the noted historian and chronicler of the Warsaw ghetto (just as Zivia Lubetkin, one of the leaders of the Warsaw ghetto uprising) extolls the poets for providing sorely needed guidance, counsel, and leadership with regard to both spiritual and armed resistance.[2] Thus, the poets are praised not only for the cathartic value of their writing, but for its evocative political power as well. The latter was especially significant, for it often infused the people with a spirit of rebellion and played a significant role in motivating the disenfranchised to join the organized political units in those revolts that occurred during the Holocaust.

As a defense against helplessness, political poetry was largely hortatory, calling for rebellion and revenge. In this it differed from the literary tradition that lamented the pogroms and reflected the pragmatism of accommodation and appeasement in a world in which Jews had little recourse to civil rights and law in general. Whereas in the past a policy of appeasement was associated with survival of the religion and the community, in the present crisis many people realized its bankruptcy. Hence the other distinctive characteristics of political poetry in the Holocaust are their ideological repudiation of acquiescence as a vehicle of survival and their intense national spirit. These phenomena mark both Yiddish and Polish-Jewish poetry, as well as the work of those poets who before the war were either influenced by religious lore or who moved between religion and secularism coupled, as it frequently was, with cosmopolitanism and radicalism.

Like all poetry in the Holocaust, political poetry reflects the changing perceptions of the poets whose sensibilities were besieged by the events. Inasmuch as each ghetto and, above all, each concentration camp was a separate organism with little or no contact with other places, different hierarchies of human relations prevailed. Even political responses to the unfolding events were subject to such variables as topography, geography, and, most of all, to the attitude of the non-Jewish population in the surrounding areas. The Jews of Vilna, for example, found it easier either to form their own units or to join other partisan groups in the nearby forests than did the Jews of Warsaw. The reasons include the closer proximity of Vilna to the dense forests and the willingness of the Russians to support or accept Jews into the Russian-sponsored resistance brigades. The partisans in the forests near Warsaw were largely members of the Polish Armja Krajowa (A.K.; Home Army). Because of their unmitigated anti-Semitism, more often than not, they murdered those Jews who managed to get to the forests and who wanted to participate in resistance activities. Perhaps these are some of the reasons for the larger number of resistance poems written in the Vilna ghetto and the surrounding forests than in other parts of Poland. On the other hand, this greater productivity may be more apparent than real and ultimately due to the accident that more work from Vilna has survived.

Early and Later Political Poetry

An example of early political poetry is Abraham Sutzkever's "A Shtim fun Harts" (The Heart's Voice). Written in Vilna a few weeks before the ghetto was established, September 6, 1941, this poem is a fierce exhortation to armed resistance both as an act of honor and as a vehicle of survival, views that were to undergo progressive transmutations. Although Sutzkever never abandoned his vision of Jewish revolt, his motives for it were protean and reflected the rapidly changing reality.

A Shtim fun Harts

> A shtim fun harts bafelt mir: gloyb
> In shoyn farshvekhtn vort gerekhtshaft.
> Der vayter yoyrish fun a leyb
> Muz vidershpenikn zayn knekhtshaft.
>
> S'iz do a gang. Es ligt zayn tsil
> In vildn urvald fun zikorn.
> S'iz oykh faran aza batsil,
> Vos trogt dem sam fun toyznt yorn.
>
> Un zukhstu far dayn payn a zin—
> Farvandl zikh in ir antpleker,
> Un her vi zeydes vekn zin
> Vi shturemheck in bronz fun gleker.
>
> S'iz do a gang, iz kleter, shprayz
> Koyf oys dem doyrosdikn shtroykhl.
> Der toyt iz moykhl yeder grayz,
> Nor zayn a knekht iz er nit moykhl.[3]

❑ ❑ ❑

The Heart's Voice

The heart's voice commands: believe
In the already desecrated word of justice.
The distant heir of the lion
Must rebel against slavery.

There is a course. Its destination
Is the wild, primeval forest of memory.

There is also a baccilus
That carries its poison for a thousand years.

And if you seek a reason for your anguish—
Transform yourself into its revelation,
And hear how grandfathers waken sons
Like storm-thrusts cleaving the bronze of bells.

There is a course. Ascend, then, stride,
Free yourself of the long lasting stigma.
Death forgives every error,
Only slavishness it forgives not.

The restrained external organization of the poem—disposed
as it is in four four-line strophes, each marked by an iambic meter
and an a b a b rhyme scheme—stands in sharp relief against the
fiery inner content. Rooted in liturgical, anagogically allusive lan-
guage, this rallying call to armed resistance invokes the biblical
past as a mnemonic of both Jewish courage and faith in order and
justice. It is, moreover, an adumbration of the admonitory voice of
God that is transmitted not through revelation, but rather, in keep-
ing with Sutzkever's fundamental secularism, through the collec-
tive heart of Jewish consciousness—one that reverberates in the
heart of the poet.

The telescopic contraction of polar events—one marking the
birth of Judaic civilization, the other its imminent destruction—
heightens the resonance of the voice's summons to retrieve from
the "primeval forest of memory" the courage that the twentieth-
century counterparts of the biblical Jews desperately need. To am-
plify the hortatory voice of the heart, the poet invokes the name
of Judah. When Judah was anointed lion by his father Jacob, the
latter prophesied: "Thine hand shall be on the neck of thine ene-
mies" (Genesis 49:8). Although "distant," the "heirs of the lion,"
Sutzkever implies, are bound by the same archetypal prophecy
and, hence, obligation.

The note of hope in ultimate redemption expressed in the
trope, "believe / in the already desecrated word . . . of justice," is
ubiquitous in the poetry of this as well as that of other poets in
the Holocaust. The uniqueness of Sutzkever's injunction to believe
in justice lies in the implied link between justice and armed revolt
against present "slavery" rather than justice that comes as a result
of suffering and martyrdom. Jewish orthodoxy makes emphatic the

latter: the primacy of Kiddush Hashem (martyrdom in the name of God) mostly through acts associated with fearless pacifism. Sutzkever rejects this imperative, directing his fiercest anger "against the sin of patiently dying . . . ," as Ruth Wisse writes. Wisse further notes that Sutzkever "struggles against his own despair, but against the faint spirit of the Jews he lashes out in militant verse of almost prophetic resonance."[4] Consequently, in "The Heart's Voice," he urges his people to purge themselves of the conciliatory ethos that especially dominated the diaspora, "a baccilus that carries its poison for a thousand years." It is this ethos, Sutzkever suggests, that is causally linked to the cyclical reenactment of the tragic Jewish history. To extricate themselves from this fate, the Jews must recognize their own complicity in it, as the line "And if you seek a reason for your anguish, transform yourself into its revelation," suggests.

The closing verses of the poem, "Death forgives every error / Only slavishness it forgives not," while obviously an admonition, are paradoxically also a subtle recantation of this solemn reproach. For these words are ambivalent, signaling not only the public, censorious, and warning voice of the poet, but his private and intuitive self as well. And it is this lyric self that yearns to forgive what it knows to be easily forgivable. This self is deeply and lovingly rooted in the peaceful theodicy and ethos of its people. It also knows with a profound sensibility of feelings and experience that in a world of endless persecutions, the "error" of acquiescence has often been an example of pragmatism—one that required moral courage and was, in the final analysis, a vehicle of Jewish continuity. Hence, Sutzkever's bitter diatribe against his people seems to spring less from his perception of Jewish faintheartness than from his own sense of despair.

But Sutzkever's despair is always laced with hope. It is this that prompts him to adjure his people to regain the martial grandeur of their biblical ancestors and to repudiate the hallowed pacifism of the last thousand years. Although desacralized by history, it is the very voice of God—the God of an "eye-for-an-eye"—that resonates in the collective heart of the poet, demanding that his chosen people return to the authority of heroic biblical paradigms. Thus Sutzkever seems to believe that armed resistance in the ghettos would not only redeem the honor of the Jews, but it would also save Jewish lives—a notion he was forced, in the end, to abandon.

Sutzkever's ambivalence, his deep love and compassion for and his passionate anger at his people, is further orchestrated in a later poem, "Tsum Yortog fun Ghetto Teater" (To the Anniversary of the Ghetto Theater), dated December 31, 1942:

Tsum Yortog fun Ghetto Teater

A.

. . . *Mir hobn aleyn zikh farmoyert*
Un lebn bezunder.
Nit shmeykhlt arayn fun der fray, nit bedoyert—
Far undz ken afile der toyt zikh tsebliyen in vunder.

Vi kenen mir zayn den tsuzamen
In derselber mesibe?
Di sine tsu unds vet vi mayz aykh farsamen—
Undzere vundn vet heyln di libe.

Un biz vanen der droysn iz ayer—
Iz undzer di ghetto, do veln mir lign
Un knetn fun getlikhn harts a bafrayer
Un shleyfn a nigun . . .

B.

Shpilt aktyorn Yiddishe balatet un farmoyert,
Ven dos lebn kortshet zikh vi ongekhapte hor,
Ven oyf shteyner zidn royte tropns fun di nontste,
Un di geslekh varfn zikh vi oyfes nit-derkoylete,
Un kenen zikh nit oyfhoybn, avekflien, antrinen . . .
Shpilt khaveyrim! Zol zikh dakhtn: an amolik shtetl
Un me pravet khasene oyf harbstikn bes-eylemin
Mit gezang un volekhn un tantsndike likht,
Freylekh in a karahod arum der khosn-kale!
Shpilt! Un zol aroysklinghen fun ayer moyl dos Yiddish,
Reyn un loyter vi der gayst fun a geshokhtn kind,
Harb un hilkhik vi dos kol fun undzer biks pulver,
Vos vet morgn-ibermorgn
Shpiln fun di dekher . . .

Un ir, fargapte, umetike fidlers,
Vos bay nakht
Flegt ir zikh aroysganvenen in loyerdikn droysn,

Sharn zikh farbay di vent,
Arumgeyn di patroln,
Tsukrikhn tsu ayer alter khorevdiker heym,
Un oysgrobn fun dr'erd ayere fidlen
Ayngeflantste erev ayer opmarsh do aher—
Shpilt ir oykh!
Un knaypt oroys di same tifste tener!
Zoln zey zikh trogn iber ayere gebeynen
Un farvoglen vayt avu es finklt nokh a Yid . . .
Vu a harts nokh tsaplt in dervartung oyf a psure.
Zoln zey zikh trogn iber felder, iber frontn,
Rayn un loyter vi der gayst fun a gashokhtn kind.
Harb un hilkhik vi dos kol fun undzer biks un pulver,
Vos vet morgn-ibermorgn
shpiln fun di dekher. . . . [5]

❑ ❑ ❑

To the Anniversary of the Ghetto Theater

A.

We alone have immured ourselves
And live in isolation.
Nothing of the free world smiles upon us
Nothing commiserates—
For us, even death can flower in wonder.

How then can we be united
In the same community?
Hatred toward us will poison you like mice—
Our wounds love alone will heal.

And as long as the outside is yours,
Ours is the ghetto; here shall we lie
And from the divine heart knead a redeemer
And polish a tune. . . .

B.

Play, Jewish actors ragged and walled-in,
When life shrinks like hair on fire,
When red drops of the closest kin sizzle on stones,

When the streets thrash like not quite slaughtered poultry
That can neither raise itself, fly away, nor disappear . . .
Play friends! Let's pretend: an old shtetl and wedding
Festivities on the autumnal cemetery
With song and lively dance and dancing lights,
A merry circle around the bride and groom!
Play! and let the Yiddish ring from your lips,
Clear and resonant like the spirit of a slaughtered child,
Resounding and strong like the charge of our gun powder
That will tomorrow, the day after tomorrow,
Play from the rooftops. . . .

And you, you bewildered and spiritless fiddlers,
Who used to sneak out at night
Into the lurking outdoors,
Creeping against the walls,
To patrol the area,
Crawling to the ruins of your old homes
To dig up from the earth fiddles
You planted before you were made to come here—
You, too, play!
And let loose the most profound tunes!
Let them be carried over your remains
And roam far, where a Jew still twinkles,
Where a heart still flutters in anticipation of a message.
Let them be carried over fields, over frontlines.
Clear and resonant like the spirit of a slaughtered child,
Resounding and strong like the charge from our gun powder,
That will tomorrow, the day after tomorrow
Play from the rooftops. . . .

This poem distills with utmost precision the alternations in
Sutzkever's perceptions of the present tyranny and the bewildering
changes that it ushered in. "We alone have immured ourselves /
And live in isolation" is an echo of the scolding accusations in
"The Heart's Voice." But in "To the Anniversary," the poet's re-
cantation of his invectives is achieved with great alacrity and di-
rectness. Whereas in the former poem, it is the intuitive rather
than the rational self of the poet that rushes to the rescue of the
people it accuses and maligns, in the latter poem it is the inte-
grated consciousness that seems surprised by its diatribe. Thus the
poet asks in pensive tones: "How can we be united in the same

community?" This question produces a sudden epiphany—namely, that the wretched ground of history has forever buried the hope of human fraternity and with it the vision of equity and sanction for Jews as citizens in the countries in which they were born. Hence the bitter retort, "Hatred toward us will poison you like mice." Interestingly, this invocation of revenge does not call for the involvement of Jews in killing or bloodshed, a preterition that deconstructs the hortatory demand of armed resistance. In this too, Sutzkever reveals his intuitive abhorrence of violence that informs the ethos of his people.

In the mythic world of Genesis, invoked in "The Heart's Voice," word and deed coincide, and naming is being. Thus Judah is leonine when anointed lion, and, by extension, so is the Jewish people. In the Holocaust, word and deed also coincide, but the archetypal myth has been displaced by a modern one. What is implied rather than explicitly stated in "To the Anniversary" is that the process of naming and being causes the namer to transform the named into an *Ungeziefer* to be expelled from the human community and exterminated in gas chambers. It is then not the Jews who have "immured" themselves, as Sutzkever initially charges, but rather the Germans and their collaborators who have hurled the Jews into ghettos and concentration camps where they are being systematically killed. That "Nothing from the free world smiles upon us / Nothing commiserates" is hardly the fate Jews elected for themselves. This is the poet's crystalline realization of a knowledge he possessed anyway. Perhaps the very process of writing "To the Anniversary of the Ghetto Theater" helps him to distill his conflicting emotions. For in the end, he directs his invective against the murderers rather than the victims.

Although Sutzkever's fury is intense and his despair profound, the latter is not absolute. For the memory of the integrity of Jewish Vilna causes him to affirm that which made Jewish continuity possible and which he vilified in "The Heart's Voice": "Our wounds love alone will heal." The third stanza of "To the Anniversary of the Ghetto Theater" orchestrates this affirmation: "And as long as the outside is yours / Ours is the ghetto, here shall we lie / And from the divine heart knead a redeemer / And polish a tune."

The redeemer is not the providential Messiah, but rather the collective will of the people to transcend, as in the past, the inferno into which it has now been catapulted. In the present catastrophe, this quest can be attained, Sutzkever believes, by a conscious reconciliation of the spiritual energy associated with the diaspora and the renewed spirit of political rebellion and armed resistance articulated in the biblical paradigms.

The two stanzas that follow, constituting the second part of the poem, by their very length (fourteen and eighteen lines, respectively), stand in opposition to the initial three four-line strophes of the first part. The inordinate length of the second part seems less planned by the poet than spontaneously arising from the occasion. Reflecting unhampered emotions, the poet's ardent words—augmented by a rapid iambic meter, multiple line sentences, some marked by enjambments that further amplify the urgency of his exhortations—impel the "ragged and walled-in" actors and musicians to commemorate the first anniverasry of the ghetto theater with song and music. This they must do to keep their individual and collective souls alive. For that reason, the images of violence and death that are invoked during the ceremony are metaphoric and indirect, in essence a form of periphrasis. For Sutzkever uses language as a mode of defense. His reluctance to name the actual form of death—whether it be in the pits of Ponary or gas chambers elsewhere—is intended to protect the sensibilities of the audience and performers alike.

Nonetheless, such surreal metaphors of death as "Life shrinks like hair on fire / . . . red drops of our closest kin sizzle on the stones / and the little streets thrash like poultry not quite slaughtered, / and can neither raise themselves, fly away nor disappear" convey not only the violence with which the Jews were murdered, but also the helplessness of their situation. Yet Sutzkever urges them to carry on. Even those "fiddlers" who are dispirited must now exhume the fiddles that they had "planted" in the ruins of their homes, so that they, too, may play, "And let loose the most profound tones!" These tones, the poet commands, must "be carried over your remains, / "And roam far, where a Jew still twinkles . . . / Where a heart still flutters in anticipation of a message. / Let them be carried over fields, over frontlines, / Clear and resonant like the spirit of a slaughtered child, / Resounding and strong like the charge of our guns and powder / That will tomorrow, the day after tomorrow / Play from the rooftops."

These lines reveal the tireless affirmation of Yiddish life, love of the Yiddish language, the tradition of hope, the cultural activities, including theater, in such pits of darkness as the Vilna ghetto. Like an ancient prophet, Sutzkever urges the ragged and starving actors, singers, musicians, and their audience to fight back with all the weapons they have, with their stubborn song that must be "carried over their remains" to reach those remote places in the world "where a Jew still twinkles."

These words of desperate exaltation arise from the suspicion that most of European Jewry had already been destroyed. Yet the pulse of hope to establish a nexus with those Jews who are still alive in "some remote places" continues to beat. For this nexus, Sutzkever intimates, is a vehicle of assertion of the indomitable unity of Israel—a unity that is, incidentally, both aggadically (theologically) and halakahically (canons of Jewish law) ordained and articulated in some of the liturgy. Although Sutzkever is unlikely to have been interested in the theological commands, the secular implications of Jewish unity were obviously an integral part of his consciousness.

In the present nightmare, Sutzkever seeks to invest the pacifism of this universal Jewish solidarity with a solidarity in arms. For it is precisely this tradition of unity that will carry the immortal tune of the "spirit of the slaughtered child" and convey to the hearts that "flutter in anticipation of a message" that some Jews are still alive in the land of death; that they are fired with a will to fight back; that they desperately need weapons.

The affective significance of these lines is embodied in both the image of a "slaughtered child" and a vision of bullets "that will tomorrow, the day after tomorrow / Play from the rooftops." The substantive, the "slaughtered child," is a synecdoche that suggests the martyrdom of the Jewish people. The deliberate figure conjures up images of autos-da-fé and other sacrificial altars, including the present chimneys, on which hosts of innocent Jews were laid. That the poet implies ritual murder is conveyed by the symbolic use of "slaughtered" (*geshokhtn*) rather than the more neutral word "killed." The vision of bullets—bullets that will soon resist Nazi barbarism—is a vision of both desperate trust in the courage of the Jewish people and desperate hope that help will come from abroad. That the latter evaporated with the smoke of the Jews is a tragic fact of history. The former, however, was translated into numerous instances of underground resistance, proliferating in such wildernesses as Narotch and Rudnicka forests near Vilna. Indeed, Sutzkever himself played an important role as a partisan in the Narotch forests.

"To the Anniversary of the Ghetto Theater" reveals a sensibility that is more charitably disposed to the "failure" of the Jews to engage in military resistance than does "The Heart's Voice."

Perhaps a deeper understanding of the unusual peril facing the Jews and the unparalleled limitations closing in upon them subdued Sutzkever's anger and modulated his tone of voice. While his anger and despair never abated and his determination to fight back never faltered, his exhortations to do so were tempered by a realization of the unique problems that armed resistance presented to the Jews. When he wrote "To the Anniversary" and the subsequent political poems, he was a year or two older and himself probably crushed by the weight of the ghetto walls.

Nonetheless, "The Heart's Voice" is important not only because of the honesty of youthful exasperation or the nobility of the vision and dignity of images, but also because it illuminates one of the levels of human consciousness in its relation to the unfolding tragedy.

It is also noteworthy that perhaps more than any other of Sutzkever's poems, "The Heart's Voice" takes its analogue from Chaim Nachman Bialik's (1873–1934) seminal poem, "In the City of Slaughter." The Hebrew work, written in 1903 in response to the bloody Kishinev pogrom, is a fiery call to rebellion against Jewish history and Jewish fate. Bialik, like his follower Sutzkever, bitterly chastises his people for their acquiescence in the face of atrocity, and in God's own name calls for rebellion and revenge:

> Why do they pray? Why do they lift their hands?
> Where is their fist? Where is the thunderbolt
> That will settle accounts for all the generations,
> And lay the world in ruins, tear down the heavens,
> And overturn My Throne.[6]

And like Sutzkever's, Bialik's poem, having failed to provide a strategy for action, is in the end a wail of anguish. It is significant that "The City of Slaughter" closes with these words of despair:

> And now enough! Flee, man, now flee forever!
> Flee to the desert, and there go mad!
> Tear your soul into a thousand pieces,
> And fling your heart to the wild dogs,
> And let your tear fall upon stones,
> And your cry be swallowed by the storm.[7]

Apparently each poet, in the nightmare of his peculiar experience, allows his lyric self to intimate the truth that it intuitively knows—namely, that the Jews are a dispersed people with an uncompromising identity and religion, and that they are beleaguered by Christian enmity. Still, the power of "The City of Slaughter" was such that it motivated the formation of numerous Jewish self-defense groups (Zelbshuts) in various parts of Eastern Europe, merging with other political grass-roots movements during the Holocaust.

Death with Dignity, without Victory in Life

Before the waves of mass deportations and killings, the self-defense groups, often inspired by the poets' visions, constituted a phalanx whose program reflected prewar values—namely, the determination to defend and sustain not only the physical but also the moral and cultural life of the people. While these organizations were to become the backbone of armed resistance, their early activities involved the founding of or participation in a multitude of other parapolitical entities, essentially self-help societies that proliferated in various ghettos. Such ghettos as Warsaw or Vilna, possibly because of their size and density of population, provided the most fertile soil for a whole spectrum of political and quasi-political organizations. In the Warsaw ghetto, these organizations included the Anti-Fascist Bloc whose stated program was not only to form self-defense cadres, but also to enlist the forces of international and local resistance movements in order to secure Jewish, national, as well as social liberation (in hindsight, a quixotic vision). Another combat unit, Jewish Combat Forces (Żydowska Organizacja Bojowa, ŻOB), being more realistic and having as its constituent members various Zionist and socialist organizations, staged the Warsaw ghetto uprising. In the Vilna ghetto, the various Zionist and other political movements became the nucleus that was later to form the United Partisans Organization (Fareynikte Partizaner Organizatsye, FPO). It carried on armed resistance in the Rudnicka and Narotch forests.

The first reports of mass gassing of Jews, brought by escaped witnesses, were met with incredulity by the Jewish population. Blinded by a tradition of faith in the inherent decency of humanity, the Jews could not believe that a nation rooted in the bedrock of Western civilization would produce Auschwitz, the *Arschloch der Welt*, as the Germans aptly dubbed this place. But then, the rest of the world could not credit any German brutality in the occupied territories. Indeed, as Hannah Arendt writes in *The Origins of Totalitarianism,* the Nazis counted both on the improbability of their colossal crime and the world's inability to believe the reports that might be brought to its attention. "Hitler circulated millions of copies of his book in which he stated that to be successful, a lie must be enormous—which did not prevent people from believing him as, similarly, the Nazi's proclamations, repeated *ad nauseum* that the Jews would be exterminated like bad bugs (i.e., with poison gas) prevented anybody from *not* believing them."[8]

The issue of armed resistance, though seriously advanced by the underground, was initially rejected by many Jews because of the savage Nazi reprisals. The collective responsibility of the entire Jewish community for a single German life curtailed the urge for revenge even on the part of the boldest activists. The turning point was the growing awareness that there was no hope of survival. Devitalized by starvation, economic blockades, epidemic disease, and terror, the Jews of Warsaw were the first in all of Nazidom to stage an act of armed resistance. This event was to become the best known, though by no means the only act of Jewish rebellion. Singling out the Warsaw ghetto, Alexander Donat writes that these uprisings "without hope of victory in life" were unparalleled:

> There can be no struggle without hope. Why does the man unjustly condemned to death fail to turn on his guards as he is led to the gallows? Why did the three thousand Turkish prisoners Napoleon ordered drowned put up no resistance? Why did fifty thousand French Huguenots permit themselves to be slaughtered in a single night by the French Catholics? And what of the Armenians? There is no precedent for the eventual uprising in the Warsaw Ghetto, because it was undertaken solely for death with dignity and without the slightest hope of victory in life.[9]

The existential and metaphysical implications of "death with dignity and without the slightest hope of victory" are themes that inform Władysław Szlengel's poem, "Kontratak" (Counterattack). Coupled with these is the theme of revenge as a vehicle of reclamation of Jewish honor—obviously a concern shared by many Jews in the Holocaust. Inspired by an insurrection that took place in the Warsaw ghetto on January 18, 1943, "Counterattack" provides not only an account of this revolt, but also projects a prophetic vision of the Warsaw ghetto uprising that was to take place in April:

Kontratak

Spokojnie szli do wagonów,
Jakby im wszystko zbrzydło,
Piesko patrzyli szaulisom w oczy—
Bydło!
Cieszyli się śliczni oficerkowie,
Że nic nie działa im na nerwy
Że idą tępym marszem hordy,
—I tylko dla werwy
Trzaskały pejcze:
W mordy!
Tłum milcząc padał na placu,
Nim się w wagonie rozełkał,
Sączyli krew i łzy w piaczysty grunt,
A "panowie"
na trupy
od niechcenia
[rzucali]
pudełka—
    "Warum sind Juno rund."
Aż w ten dzień,
Gdy na uśpione sztymungiem miasto
Wpadli o świcie, jak hieny z porannej mgły,
Wtedy zbudziło sie bydło
I
obnarzyło kły . . .
Na ulicy Miłej padł pierwszy strzał.
Żandarm się zachwiał w bramie,
Spojrzał zdziwiony—chwilę stał,
Pomacał roztrzaskane ramię—
Nie wierzył.
Coś tu nie jest w porządku,
Tak wszystko szło gładko i w prost,
Z łaski i protekcji
Cofnięto go z drogi na Ost
(Miał kilka dni satisfakcji),
Aby odpoczął w Warszawie,
Gnając to bydło w akcji,

I aby oczyścić ten chlew,
A tu
Na Miłej ulicy KREW . . .
Żandarm sie cofnął z bramy
I zaklął "—Naprawdę krwawię,
A tu już szczękały brauningi
Na Niskiej,
> *Na Dzikiej,*
>> *Na Pawiej.*
Na krętych schodach, gdzie matkę starą
Ciągnieto za włosy na dół,
Leży esesman Handtke.
Bardzo dziwnie się nadął,
Jakby nie strawił śmierci,
Jakby go zdławił ten bunt.
Zacharkał się krwawą śliną
W pudełko—'Juno sind rund,"
Rund, rund.
Pył wdeptać złoconym szlifem,
Okrągło wszystko się toczy,
Leży błękitny żandarmi uniform
Na zaplutych schodach
Żydowskiej Pawiej ulicy
I nie wie,
Że u Szultza i Toebbensa
Kule pląsają się w radosnym rozśpiewie,
BUNT MIĘSA,
BUNT MIĘSA,
BUNT MIĘSA!
Mięso pluje przez okno granatem.
Mięso charczy szkarłatnym płomieniem
I zrębów życia sie czepia!
Hej! Jak radośnie strzela się w slepia!
TU JEST FRONT, PANICZYKI!
FRONT—PANOWIE DEKOWNIKI!
HIER
TRINKT MAN MEHR KEIN BIER,
HIER
HIER HAT MAN MEHR KEIN MUT,
BLUT,
BLUT,
BLUT.

Zdejmować rękawiczki z jasnej, gładkiej skóry,
Położyć pejcze—dać hełmy na głowy—
Jutro komunikat dać prasowy:
"Wbiliśmy się klinem w blok Toebbensa."
Bunt mięsa.
BUNT MIĘSA,
ŚPIEW MIĘSA!
Słysz niemiecki Boże,
Jak modlą się Żydzi w dzikich domach,
Trzymając w ręku łom czy zierdź.
Prosimy Cię, Boże, o walkę krwawą.
Błagamy Cię o gwałtowną smierć.
Niech nasze oczy przed skonaniem
Nie widzą jak sie wloką szyny,
Ale daj dłoniom celność, Panie,
Aby się skrwawił mundur siny,
Daj nam zobaczyć, zanim gardła
Zawrze ostatni, głuchy jęk,
W tych butnych dłoniach, w łapach z pejczem
Zwyczajny nasz człowieczy lęk.
Jak purpurowe krwiste kwiaty,
Z Niskiej i z Miłej, z Muranowa,
Wykwita płomień z naszych luf.
To wiosna nasza! To kontratak!
To wino walki uderza do głów!
To nasze lasy partyzanckie,
Zaułki Dzikiej i Ostrowskiej.
Drżą nam na persiach numerki "blokowe",
Nasze medale wojny żydowskiej.
Krzyk czterech liter błyska czerwienią,
Jak taran bije slowo: BUNT. . . .
. . . .
A na ulicy krwią się oblepia
Zdeptana paczka:
"JUNO SIND RUND!"[10]

❑ ❑ ❑

Counterattack

Peacefully they walked to the train,
Sick and tired of the daily battle,
Doggedly gaze into the brutal eyes did

The cattle.
The handsome officers gloated
That they are bothered by nothing,
That with a dull step the hordes are marching,
And only for diversion
The whips cracked,
Slashing their faces!
The throng in silence sank to the ground,
Before it dissolved in sobs in cattle cars,
Their blood and tears,
Trickling into the sandy ground,
And the *Herrenvolk*
Carelessly tossed
little boxes
on the corpses—
    "Warum sind Juno rund."
Then, on that day,
When on the *Stimmung* lulled city
They pounced like hyenas in dawn's early mist,
Then the cattle awakened
And
Bared its teeth . . .
On Miła Street the first shot was heard,
A gendarme staggered at the gate,
He stared surprised—stood still for a moment,
Patted his shattered arm—
Didn't believe it.
Something is not right,
Everything went so smooth and straight,
As a favor, because of special influence,
He was turned back from the Eastern Front
(Had a few satisfying days),
Rested in Warsaw,
Driving this cattle in an *Aktion*,
And cleaning up this pigsty,
But here,
On Miła street, BLOOD . . .
The gendarme pulled back from the gate
And swore: I'm really bleeding,
But here Braunings were barking
On Niska,
    On Dzika,

On Pawia.
On the crooked stairway,
Where an old mother
Was dragged by the hair,
Lies SS-man Handtke,
Strangely puffed up,
As if he couldn't digest death,
As if he choked on the revolt.
He belched, spitting up blood
Into the little box—'*Juno sind rund,*
Rund, rund.
Golden epaulets crush the dust,
Everything spins around,
The sky-blue uniform lies
On the spittle-covered stairs
Of the Jewish Pawia Street
And doesn't know
That at Schultz and Toebbens
Bullets whirl in a joyous song,
REVOLT OF THE MEAT,
REVOLT OF THE MEAT,
REVOLT OF THE MEAT!
Meat spits grenades out the windows.
Meat belches out scarlet flames
And clings to the edges of life!
Hey! What joy to shoot in the eye!
This is the front, my Lords!
Hier
Trinkt man mehr kein Bier,
Hier hat man mehr kein Mut,
BLUT,
BLUT,
BLUT!
Peal off the fair, smooth, leather gloves,
Put your whips aside and helmets on.
Tomorrow issue a press release:
"Penetrated the lines of Toebbens' block.
REVOLT OF THE MEAT,
REVOLT OF THE MEAT,
SONG OF THE MEAT!
Hear, O German God,
How the Jews, in the "wild" houses pray,

Clenching in the fist a stick, a stone.
We beg you, O God, for a bloody battle,
We implore you for a violent death.
Let our eyes not see, before we expire,
The stretch of the train tracks,
But let the precise aim of our hand, O Lord,
Stain their livid uniforms with blood,
Let us see, before the mute groan
Shreds our throats,
Our simple human fear in their
Haughty hands, in their whip-wielding paws.
From Niska, Miła, and Muranowska Streets,
Like scarlet flowers of blood,
Sprout the flames of our gunbarrels.
This is our Spring! Our Counterattack!
The intoxication of our battle!
These are our partisan forests:
The alleys of Dzika and Ostrowska Streets.
"Block" numbers quiver on breasts,
Medals of the Jewish war.
The cry of six letters flashes in red,
Like a battering ram bellows the word: REVOLT. . . .
. . . .
And on the street, the bloodied,
Trampled packet:
JUNO SIND RUND.

"Counterattack," like most of Szlengel's poetry, is marked by
both corrosive irony and colloquial language. These characteristics
he shares with *Skamander*, an interwar literary movement of
young Polish poets who, rejecting causes and sharing certain sim-
ilarities with the Russian Acmeists, showed in their verses a pre-
dilection for irony, satire, and colloquialisms. But Szlengel's irony
is a reductio ad absurdum of the *Skamander* paradigm. It is thus
that he repeatedly shows the glaring absurdity inherent in the ap-
plication of prewar literary standards to occupation literature. The
violence of his world is such that it obviates any rational argu-
ment in support of aesthetic considerations, a notion, as noted in
the preceding chapter, that Przyboś and Różewicz came to share
with Szlengel somewhat later.

"Counterattack" projects a vision of a world that has been
stood on its head and has reduced human beings to cattle and fur-

ther to meat, displacing them to the lowest rung on the "Great Chain of Being" ladder. This realization and the violent grief arising from it, are mirrored in the structure of the poem. Its 112 lines, unhampered by any strophic architectonics, seem to fall in a torrent, getting ahead of the poet himself who apparently neither can nor will leash his volatile emotions. His technique, clearly dictated by the occasion, tends to evoke a sense of copiousness, augmenting the power of his feelings. This is further amplified by the metallic sound of the poem's rhythms and the uneven, often oblique, rhyme scheme.

Written in the late stages of the ghetto—after the January 1943 rebellion which temporarily stopped the newly resumed deportations—this poetic mimesis reflects the mood of those people who came face to face with the final knowledge. It is of this that Alexander Donat speaks, noting that there is no hope of survival and that, therefore, armed resistance must be undertaken "solely for death with dignity and without the slightest hope of victory in life." This knowledge was granted the Jews of Warsaw despite their initial degradation, a perception that marks the opening lines of the poem and is narrated by a persona who presents the events from the point of view of both the bestial Germans and their bovinized victims.

While gloating that nothing unnerves the hordes of Jews passively marching to the cattle cars, the "handsome [German] officers" are, nonetheless, bored with the unchanging scenario. To introduce a measure of excitement to the routine, they slash the faces of the condemned with their cracking whips. Like an eye of a camera, the focus suddenly shifts to the helpless "throng . . . before it dissolves in sobs in the cattle car." These montagelike frames project a picture of a world turned not only upside-down but also inside-out: a hell brought to the surface of the earth. In this secular inferno, before being brought to gas chambers, the people are gratuitously whipped, shot at, and throttled in cattle cars. The chaos of this antiworld, as Szlengel intimates, is such that it voids the Nazis of humanity; it empties them of the last vestiges of empathy and compassion, and transmutes them into a demonic order of *Übermenschen*. Because of this metamorphosis, they perceive the enclosed world from their position. Hence they see their victims as cattle on their way to the slaughter house.

In "Counterattack" Szlengel comprehends metaphorically the manifestations of this process, revealing the transformation of both the aggressor and the victim. As Szlengel sees it, the victim, too, is not impervious to the processes of dehumanization. Thus in Sartrean terms, "the gaze of the other" determines the self-perception of the gazed upon. Reflecting the collective consciousness of his people, the poet is a kind *eiron*, a suffering knower, who is partially guilty because he has hidden the secret of their shame: their present bovinization as well as general degradation as *pharmaki*, the scapegoats led to the altars of history.

Like Sutzkever, Szlengel despairs, and the psychic energy of his despair shifts its concentration from the victimizer to the victim in a kind of alternating cathexis. Thus like Sutzkever, Szlengel regards the condemned culpable, ignoring the viability of the various forms of spiritual resistance (discussed in the foregoing chapter) that marked the Jewish response to the Nazi assault. It is for this reason that he merely adumbrates the self-possession with which they met their death. "The throng in silence sank to the ground." Yet in "Co Czytałem Umarłym" (This I Read to the Dead), the poet pays homage to the dignity of their self-possession in face of the terror and anguish confronting them. *"Najbardziej męczyło to, że wiedzieli co ich czeka, że wyjechali z koszmarnym bagażem prawdziwych czy nie prawdziwych wiadomości o sposobie zabijania."*[11] (The most painful was the fact that they knew what awaits them, that they left with the nightmarish baggage of authentic or unauthentic information about the methods of killing.)

But in "Counterattack," the Jews are praised not so much for their spiritual integrity as for the armed rebellion with which they were and will be able to transcend the Nazi attempt to debase them. The encomium lauds the bovine, starving, ragged, and inexperienced ghetto fighters who proved their mettle in the January insurrection against the armed from head to foot SS Goliath. It further prophesies the revolt that was to take place in April: "Then, on that day / When on the *Stimmung* lulled city / like hyenas they pounced at dawn's early mist, / Then the cattle awakened / And bared its teeth."

The succeeding lines reflect the results of the unfolding battle and make emphatic the fact that in certain respects the invincible Goliath is not totally bereft of human attributes. He is afraid when attacked, he bleeds when shot, he dies when killed. Although he finds it hard to believe, he shares these basic human characteristics with the bovine Jews. Thus, incredulous that a Jewish bullet shattered his arm, an SS man, who because of political favoritism came from the Eastern front to the Warsaw ghetto for a respite and a few days of distraction by rounding up "the cattle in an *Aktion*," perceives the unexpected Jewish bullet as the very cause of the sudden disruption of the basic cosmic unity. "Something is not right," he proclaims surprised. Far greater is the shock of another German who lies dying at the bottom of the stairs "down which an old mother had been pulled by her hair."

As the poem unfolds, Szlengel's irony becomes progressively more corrosive—a tone that is in direct proportion to his belief that the fighting Jews have tipped the balance of the day. The narrative voice, marked as it is by a split point of view, evokes, in the successive lines, an image of reflecting mirrors in which the Nazified perception of the world and the Jew is reflected in the Jewish mirror in an ironic tour de force. Thus the block letters anaphora, "REVOLT OF THE MEAT, / REVOLT OF THE MEAT, / REVOLT OF THE MEAT!" And so while the SS are stunned by the Jewish rebellion and, hence, the sudden disruption of the cosmic order, the "cattle," reduced even further to "meat," have finally shown to the Nazis and the world, but above all to themselves, what that "meat" can do: "Meat spits grenades out the windows. / Meat belches out scarlet flames / And clings to the edges of life! / Hey! What joy to shoot in the eye!"

Both the irony and fury reach a cumulative climax in the poem's closing lines. In fierce yet simple ghetto slang, the poet lays bare the desperate exaltation and hopeless grandeur of the fighting Jews, while he prays in mock prostration to the German God. German self-divinization was commonplace in the Holocaust. Displacing the traditional concept of God with the image of a Germanic Aryan, the SS flaunted their divinity, especially when they bullied and tortured pious old Jews, insinuating that the God of the Jews is either impotent or indifferent to their agony and supplications for deliverance.

In his execrations, the poet invokes the "wild" houses—tenements in the ghetto that were emptied of their inhabitants during bloody *Aktions*. In the interludes, these buildings were transformed into temporary sanctuaries for those Jews who were unable to secure work permits. Without these coveted pieces of paper, no Jew could be assigned to any of the "blocks"—German slave factories in the ghetto, including those of Schultz and Toebbens. These persons were not allowed to be in the ghetto and, hence, not allowed to live.

Inspired by the January insurrection and anticipating another "Counterattack," Szlengel foresaw the "wild" asylums as the sacred ground on which the "meat," clinging "to the edges of life," would be transformed into fierce resistance units. In his visionary anticipation of "this Jewish war," the poet entertains no delusions of survival. Such quixotic possibilities could not be expected of an exhausted and walled-in remnant, whom the outside world refused to help. Hence, he longs for a violent death—one that will signal the dignity of the fearless battle the Jews have staged. This will preempt "the stretch of the train tracks" leading to Treblinka and, above all, satisfy the craving of the fighters and other Jews to "see before the mute groan shreds . . . [their] throats, / . . . [their] simple human fear in the haughty hands, in [the] whip-wielding paws" of the Germans. Invoking a formulation typical of martial prayers, Szlengel writes, "We beg you, O God, for a bloody battle, / We implore you for a violent death." Thus, it is not only his fierce rejection of a protracted death via train tracks leading to gas chambers, but also an impassioned prayer of an undaunted partisan determined not to die before he kills the enemy.

The more impassioned the poet's vision of the revolt, the darker and richer become the conceits. Such romantic and surrealistic images as "flames," "like scarlet blood-flowers' sprouting from "gun barrels," or as street alleys transforming themselves into "partisan forests" tend to transport the reader from the expository to the imaginative effect of the poem. The poet who seems to have a clear vision of what he describes—namely, the "intoxication" of the arriving Jewish spring with its surreal forests and flowers—creates a nexus of empathy between himself and the reader. For the reader sees what the poet imagines and exalts in Szlengel's realized vision.

Szlengel's prophetic hymn in anticipation of the April revolt, a vision prompted by the first Jewish shots fired during the January insurrection, finds some echoes in Yitzhak Katzenelson Yiddish poem *The Song of the Murdered Jewish People*. In canto XIII, entitled "With Halutzim," Katzenelson also invokes the January rebellion as the beginning of the Warsaw ghetto uprising. Unveiling both his confusion and elation at the realization that the Halutzim are firing at the Germans, the poet bewails the dearth of weapons, a fact that prevents him from joining the fighters:

There was nothing for me—yet for me there was everything!
    Though too late.
No, no! Never too late! The last Jew who kills a murderer saves his
    people.

Even a murdered people can be saved. Save! I said to them.
I encouraged them and myself. I spoke and wished them success.[12]

Although *The Song of the Murdered Jewish People* is essentially a jeremiad that laments the destruction of the Jews, it is nonetheless informed by concerns of resistance and passivity as well as the nature and the manner of Jewish death that profoundly distressed and confounded Sutzkever, Szlengel, and others during and since the Holocaust. Emanuel Ringelblum, and later Zivia Lubetkin, Marek Edelman, Alexander Donat, Yuri Suhl, and a host of others provided cogent arguments in defense of the beleaguered and forgotten Jews, whose alleged passivity was more apparent than real, for they fought back with all they had.

Chapter Six

Word into Deed

Many poets came of age during the unfolding apocalypse, not only inspiring and exhorting the people to rebellion, but actually participating it. In so doing, they transformed word into deed. For Abraham Sutzkever, who was a leading partisan, this provided the historical anchor that he sought in "The Heart's Voice," fixing the Jewish response to aggression in the biblical paradigm, "an eye for an eye." Whereas in the past, the traditional domain of poetry among European Jews was the synagogue, among such gun-wielding poets as Sutzkever and others, like Shmerke Kaczerginski, the domain of poetry was the front line of underground resistance.

Universalism and Particularism

Two examples of such poems are Kaczerginski's "Partizaner Marsh" (March of the Partisans) (August 1943) and Sutzkever's "Bagleytlid Baym Avekgeyn in Vald" (Song at the Departure to the Forest) (September 10, 1943). The two works were produced within a few weeks of each other, when each of the poets set out for the forest with a contingent of partisans. Mediated by opposing ideologies, the poems reveal two rather typical aspects in the spectrum of political responses to the catastrophe. Kaczerginski's poem reveals a universalist vision that locates hope in the fundamental fraternity of communism. Redemption both Jewish and gentile will come, according to this writer, through the integrated efforts

of the world's working classes. In fact, it is this solidarity alone
that will defeat the Nazis. Sutzkever's "Song at the Departure to
the Forest," on the other hand, lays bare, as does all of his work,
his identification with Jewish particularism. Cognizant of the
deadly isolation of the Jews, the poet believes that Jewish redemp-
tion will come only through the mystical, though secular, link be-
tween the prostrated ghetto Jews and their upright biblical
ancestors.

"March of the Partisans" is an artless poem, written in folk-
bardic language, devoid of rhetorical embellishments and extrane-
ous metaphors:

Partizaner Marsh

Der veg is shver, mir veysn
Der kamf nit laykht, kayn shpil.
A partizan zayn lebn leygt in shlakht,
Far groysn frayhayt tsil.

Tsuzing

—Hey F.P.O.!
—Mir zaynen do!
Mutik un drayste tsum shlakht,
Partizaner nokh haynt
Geyen shlogn dem faynt,
Inem kamf far an arbeter makht.

Es zaynen fest di glider,
Gemusklt in shtol un in blay,
Mir geyen bloyz oyf haynt funem ghetto aroys—
Kidey morgn aykh tsu brengen di fray!

Hey F.P.O.! . . .

Baym blut fun shvester, brider,
Mir shvern tsu kemfn biz van—
Mit Hitlers yeder glid baputst vet zayn,
Di vafn fun partizan.

Hey F.P.O.! . . . [1]

❑❑❑

March of the Partisans

The road is difficult, we know,
The combat not easy, no game.
A partisan lays down his life in battle,
For great freedom's sake.

Refrain

Hey F.P.O.!
We are here!
Bold, daring, and ready for battle.
This very day the partisans
Will defeat the fiend,
In the struggle for workers' power.

The limbs are strong,
Muscles of steel and lead,
We are leaving the ghetto today
In order to bring you freedom tomorrow.

Hey F.P.O.! . . .

Upon the blood of our sisters and brothers,
We vow to fight until
Hitler's every limb will adorn
The weapons of the partisans.

Hey! F.P.O.! . . .

This simple martial hymn uses all the standard topoi associated with this genre. Thus, to inspire courage and fortitude, the poet lists the formidable obstacles facing the partisans: the difficult road, the bloody battles, and the mandate to destroy the enemy. The visionary Marxist ideology is the poem's only salient feature, calling for partisans to lay down their lives in the name of both universal freedom and "worker's power."

"Partisan March" was written in August 1943, after the uprising and destruction of the Warsaw ghetto and the obliteration of most other ghettos—Vilna to be officially liquidated in September, a few weeks later. By this time thousands of Jews had already been killed and buried in the mass graves of Ponary, only ten kilometers from Vilna, while the allies and the world stood by indifferently. Kaczerginski must have realized by then the total isolation of the Jews, and he must have known that they could not count on the support of the outside world. One would, therefore, expect that his sense of bitterness would be so complete as to cause him to disdain the world and reject the view of working-class solidarity. Apparently his faith was not crushed nor was his trust in the Soviet Union totally destroyed.

Indeed Russia was to prove the last bastion of hope for the beleaguered Jewish partisans. The Soviet Union, unlike such Polish independence organizations as "The Home Army" *(Armja Krajowa)*, was willing to help Jewish partisans defeat their common enemy. Consequently, those Jewish combatants who could somehow obtain weapons—a Soviet prerequisite for joining partisan units—were incorporated into supervised partisan brigades. However, since many Jewish partisans, although fiercely determined to fight the Nazis, could not obtain the required firearms, their presence among the fighting battalions was challenged by Soviet authorities. A case in point is Major General Klimov who was flown in from Moscow to survey the partisan movement in White Russia. Kaczerginski, himself, assumed the responsibility of explaining to Klimov the insurmountable difficulties that Jews encountered in obtaining weapons.[2] More vulnerable to attack than their armed counterpart, the majority of weaponless Jews suffered heavy casualties in the forests. However, where weapons posed no problem, the Jewish brigades, on the whole, were able to join the various united battalions in a relentless campaign against German installations.[3] Quixotic a vision as it may have been, Kaczerginski's faith found an anchor, however grudging, in Soviet pragmatism.

Unlike Kaczerginski, Sutzkever sought in the ideology of Jewish particularism a vehicle for ending the role of the Jew as victim of history. That a feat of such gargantuan proportions might be accomplished by a people engulfed in the Holocaust—when powerful and sovereign nations in Europe collapsed under a less formidable assault—Sutzkever's poetic self apparently did not permit itself to doubt. His vision may have been partially shaped by his despair and by his participation in Jewish resistance. Hence not a helpless victim, he was able to translate the exalted dream of "The Heart's Voice" into the reality of combat and revenge. In "Song at the Departure to the Forest," he, therefore, speaks with the authority of experience about the emergence "of future sons" who are atavistically and metaphysically linked to the heroic Maccabees:

Bagleytlid Baym Avekgeyn in Vald

Vakst aroys, ir heldn—feste ayngeshparte yungen,
Vakst aroys, ir tsukunftzin, un zayt der velt bavust.
Gor der viln funem folk, in untererd farshlungen,
Kleyet zikh—a lavendiker shtram in ayer brust.

Oyb es hot farzhavert in der voglenish dos ayzn,
Faylt fun im arop di nekhtns un im shlayft atsind.
Keyn mol iz nit shpet dem folks nekome tsu bavayzn,
Oystsukoyfn mit gever di doyrosdike zin.

S'hobn shtet farvandlt zikh in shteynerne fareter,
Tsugeshmidt tsu zindike griber ayer gang.
Hobn velder aykh bagrist mit zingendike bleter:
—Kumt tsu undz, ir tayere, un laytert dem ferlang.

Loyb tsu aykh, ir nay-gezalbte gvuredike geyer,
Ayer fus hot opgeshtupt dem lokerdikn rand.
S'hot in aykh a glants geton der rum fun Maccabeyer,
Vi mit yorn tsvay toysnt tsurik in eygn land.

Shtendik zenen do tsu dr'erd geboygene un mide.
Vey dem knekht in hofenenug oyf rakhmim—by a knekht.
Vi di Maccabeyer blozt funander di miride,
Zol der kovet oyf loykhtn in shverdikn gefekht![4]

❑ ❑ ❑

Song at the Departure to the Forest

Sprout forth, you heroes—strong, stubborn lads,
Sprout forth, you future sons, and become known in the world.
The entire will of the people has been swallowed by the earth,
But a lavalike surge is shaping itself in your breast.

If the sword has rusted in uncertainties,
File away from it its yesterdays and polish its today.
It is never too late to show the people's vengeance,
To redeem the long lasting sin with weapons.

Cities have been transfigured into betrayers of stone,
Chained to sinful graves your path.
Forests, therefore, greeted you with singing leaves:
Come to us, dear ones, and refine your demand.

Be praised, you newly anointed strong questers,
Your foot has pushed back the lurking brink.
The glory of the Maccabees has suddenly shone within you,
Just as it did two thousand years ago in our own land.

There are always those who stoop to the earth and the tired.
Woe to the slave who hopes for mercy from a slave.
Like the Maccabees spread all over the rebellion,
Let our honor shine again in the fencing sword.

In the typical Sutzkeverian tension between stately form and
dynamic content, this poem invokes the authority of ancient par-
adigms to rouse awareness in the fighting Jew that, standing alone,
he must seek both spiritual and physical strength in the memory
of heroic Jewish archetypes. It is from this mythic consciousness
that the heroic deeds of the partisans will "sprout forth," as the
numinous image, "Vakst aroys ir tsukunftzin" (literally, "sprout
from the earth, you future sons") suggests. Although "the entire
will of the people has been swallowed by the earth," the partisans
can reforge themselves by means of the transcendental "lavalike
surge" that erupts from the soil of biblical reality. And it is this
historical anima that will inspire the partisans to remove from
their swords "the rust of [yesterday's] uncertainties" and to redeem
"the long lasting sin" with newly polished weapons.

The tension of these lines is embodied in the ambiguous sub-
stantive, "the long lasting sin." This iconograph suggests two
meanings—namely, the sin of Jewish passivity and the sin of the
endless chain of crimes visited upon the Jews. That the second
meaning carries more weight is signaled by the sudden shift of
tone and imagery in the third strophe. While the two preceding
and the two following strophes are marked by a haughty tone, the
pivotal third one echoes with cadences of unmistakable Jewish ex-
haustion. This weariness derives from the implacable hatred to-
ward Jews that has culminated in the present catastrophe. The
dual image of cities that "have been transfigured into betrayers of
stone" and that have "chained to sinful graves your path," suggests
that Jewish destiny, notably the present cataclysm, has resulted

from "sins" connected with that hatred and persecution rather than with the Jewish ethos.

Since most of civilized urban Europe and especially the cities of Poland have become a Jewish "grave," the handful of beleaguered Jewish resistance fighters must turn to Poland's primordial forests to "refine their demand." This means that they must affirm the right of Jews to share this planet with other peoples, to defend that right by waging a war of resistance, however futile it may be at this time of unmitigated tyranny, and thus to redeem Jewish honor.

The desolate image of the city, the traditional asylum of Jews escaping from the pogroms of small shtetls and villages, is intensified by an ironic invocation of nature, the romantic source of solace to human suffering in general and to Sutzkever in particular. The irony is heightened by the hyperbaton, "hobn velder" (begin did forests) instead of the more natural syntax, "velder hobn" (forests began), and earlier, "s'hobn shtet" (begin did cities) instead of "shtet hobn" (cities began). This coupled with the falling spondaic rhythm of the verses intensifies the tone of extreme weariness signaled by the subtle irony.

The final images of the poem unite catastrophe and redemption, drawing to themselves once more the mystical vision of Jewish past and present. The synthesis of this dialectic is a new progeny, "the newly anointed mighty questers," the "future sons" of both the glorious Maccabees and the exhausted, decimated modern Jews, whose swords must resurrect Jewish honor.

Where to Obtain Weapons? How?

Interestingly, the virtually insurmountable difficulties in obtaining the necessary weapons in order to translate a vision of resistance into cold reality is passed over by Sutzkever in this as well as most of his other political poetry. Only one mythopoetic work, "Di Blayene Platn fun Roms Drukeray" (The Lead Plates of the Rom Press), imagines the ways in which the Jews might have been able to secure weapons:

Di Blayene Platn fun Roms Drukeray

Mir hobn vi finger geshtrekte durkh gratn
Tsu fangen di likhtike luft fun der fray—

Durkh nakht zikh getsoygn, tsu nemen di platn,
Di blayene platn fun Rom's drukeray.
Mir, troymer, badarfn itst vern soldatn
Un shmeltsn oyf koyln dem gayst funem blay.

Un mir hobn vider geefnt dem shtempl
Tsu epes a heymisher eybiker heyl.
Mit shotns bapantsert, bay shayn fun a lepml—
Gegosn di oysyes—a tseyl nokh a tseyl,
Azoy vi di zeydes a mol inem templ
In gildene yom-tov-menoyres—dem oyl.

Dos blay hot geloykhtn baym oysgisn koyln,
Makhshoves—tsegangen an os nokh an os.
A shure fun Bovl, a shure fun Poyln,
Gezotn, gefleytst in der zelbiker mos.
Di Yiddishe gvure, in verter farhoyln,
Muz oyfraysn itster di velt mit a shos!

Un ver s'hot in ghetto gezen dos kle-zayen
Farklamert in heldishe Yiddishe hent—
Gezen hot er ranglen zikh Yerushalaim,
Dos faln fun yene granitene vent;
Farnumen di verter, farshmoltsn in blayen,
Un zeyere shtimen in hartsn derkent.[5]

❑ ❑ ❑

The Lead Plates of the Rom Press

Like fingers stretching through bars
To grasp the luminous air of freedom,
We moved through the night to sieze the plates,
The lead plates of the Rom Press.
We, dreamers, must now become soldiers
And into bullets melt down the soul of the lead.

And again we broke open the seal
Of a familiar, eternal cave.
In the cover of shadows, by the glow of a lamp,
We poured the letters one by one,
Just as in the temple, long ago, our grandfathers
poured oil into golden holiday-menorahs.

Forged into bullets, letter after melted letter,
The lead was luminous with thought.
A verse from Babylon, a verse from Poland,
Boiling, gushing each like the other.
Jewish might hidden in the word
With bullets must now blow up the world!

And those in the ghetto who saw the weapons
Clenched in heroic Jewish hands,
Saw Jerusalem struggling,
The destruction of those granite walls;
Sensing the meaning of the molten words,
In the heart recognizing their voice.

Dated September 12, 1943, this highly polished poem with its tight construction and perfect rhyme scheme (a b a b a b; c d c d c d; etc,) had apparently been revised more than once. The compulsion that motivated these changes is similar to the one that moved Sutzkever to rewrite such poems as "The First Night in the Ghetto" or "The Circus." The shock of awareness that most of Poland's and, indeed, Europe's Jews had been and were still being destroyed in February 1943, allegedly the date of the poem's first draft, apparently caused the poet to recoil from having cast in other poems aspersions on the memory of the dead and dying. Moreover, Sutzkever was somewhat older and wiser, crushed by the weight of reality, when he reread or later submitted for publication poems marked by censorious tones and accusatory language. He seems to have been particularly loath to indulge in any form of criticism after he had time to assimilate the truth of the utter helplessness of the Jews. Perhaps the dawning of this awareness caused him to imagine what the Jews might have done if the evil that engulfed them had been less extreme.

It is for this reason that, like Sutzkever's other hortatory poetry, "The Lead Plates of the Rom Press" locates a link between the heroic past and the present. Hence images of contemporary events coalesce with historically, liturgically, and anagogically allusive language. And it is also for this reason that central to the poem—though intimated rather than explicitly stated—is the insurmountable problem the Jews faced in staging any act of armed resistance. Obviously, resistance was at best a formidable task in all the Nazi occupied countries; however, whereas the non-Jewish underground was militarily and morally supported by the population of their respective countries and by their governments in exile, the Jews of Poland had to face not only the Germans but the largely hostile Poles as well. Subject to anti-Semitism even before the racist doctrines promulgated in Nuremberg, during the war, the Jews were exposed to ever increasing Polish enmity toward them. There were, of course, righteous Poles who agonized over the Jewish catastrophe and Polish anti-Semitism, and who risked their own lives to help the trapped Jews; but they constituted a very small minority. The tragedy that this fact reveals is that non-Jews could have helped, but very few chose to do so. On balance more Jews were denounced to the Nazis than were saved.

A case in point is the two Polish independence organizations: *Armja Ludowa* (AL; People's Army) and *Armja Krajowa* (AK; Home Army). The rather weak Socialist AL accepted into its ranks those Jews who made it to the forests. On the other hand, the official and more powerful AK—notably its right wing division *Narodowe siły zbrojne* (National Armed Forces)—with few individual exceptions, was known to murder Jews during and even after the war.[6] Thus when ŻOB (Jewish Combat Forces), whose total Warsaw ghetto arsenal in July 1942 was one pistol, appealed for arms, the AK—which was supervised by the Polish emigre government centered in London—refused, according to Itzhak Zukerman, to comply with the plea.[7] "As late as January 1943," writes Ber Mark:

> The commander-in-chief of A.K., 'Grot' (General Stefan Rowecki), wrote secretly to London that the 'Jewish Communist' circles in the [Warsaw] ghetto (meaning the Fighting Organization) wanted weapons, but he was not sure that they could make use of them, and perhaps they should not be given any. Later the A.K. did provide some arms, but by that time the insurgents had taken to manufacturing their own or buying them from German and Italian marauders at outlandish prices.[8]

For the ghetto insurgents who figure in Sutzkever's poem, manufacturing of weapons was more likely in an imagined rather than in the real world. Apparently, the Germans had their own ideas about making use of the lead plates in the Roms Printing Press and excellent means of carrying out their plans. According to testimony of former members of the FPO,[9] the best that most partisans could do was to buy or steal firearms. Generally, peasants who quickly learned to exploit the desperate situation by charging exorbitant prices were the purveyors of these weapons. Since many of them were in disrepair, the Jewish underground learned to repair them or to replace faulty parts. Purloining of firearms occurred in such places, among others, as the Wilcza Lapa Hospital, a former Polish railroad employee facility on the outskirts of Vilna. The Germans appropriated it for their wounded soldiers who came in train convoys from the Eastern front. A forced work detail of Vilna Jews, serving as menials, undressing or otherwise having access to the soldiers, pilfered as many small arms as they could get their hands onto and hide on their own bodies or in bundles they smuggled into the ghetto. This practice proved particularly fruitful when the number of wounded soldiers swelled and the Jews, who tended them, were forced to work late hours. Because the Jews were often returned to the ghetto in trucks, frisking and general security were more lax during these late hours and the smuggling of weapons into the ghetto less dangerous.[10]

The world in which Sutzkever's insurgents operate is transcendental, more mythical than real. However, as David G. Roskies writes, "no one will fault the poet" for his poetic reshaping of history, "for writing a midrash on Jewish heroism which remains true to the spirit of the fighters."[11] In this mythic realm, the youthful combatants actually do what Sutzkever (and perhaps others) hoped they might have done had it been possible; they manufacture their own arms by breaking into one of the greatest Jewish publishing houses in Eastern Europe, stealing and recasting lead plates into bullets.

Characteristically, Sutzkever's technique of commemorating this imagined event interweaves poetry of bold statement with enigmatic constellations of words that erupt into singular images or dissolve into mystical utterances. The simile, "like fingers stretching through bars / To grasp the luminous air of freedom," suggests despair and, above all, determination so absolute that it produces a state of disembodiment, a dissolution of selfhood. These adroit fingers are the metamorphosed Jewish "dreamers" who, in their protean state, are further transformed into "soldiers" who must "melt down the soul of the lead" into "bullets." These images, recalling hieroglyphic notations, resonate with layers of meaning. "Dreamers" is an allusion, among other things, to the shapers of diaspora culture with its essential pacifism, love of scholarship, and devotion to the study and interpretation of the Holy Scriptures. "Dreamers" conjures up images of generations of Talmudic scholars, midrashic writers, and other commentators, reverentially exploring the mystical meanings of such theosophic doctrines as the Zohar or the Cabala. These "dreamers" must now strike a blow at the very "soul" of diaspora culture. For not only must they become "soldiers," but they also have to initiate an act of sacrilegious significance: the transformation of rows of sacrosanct letters into bullets. Thus the coveted literary record of the diaspora, immortalized in "A verse from Babylon [the inception of diaspora culture], a verse from Poland" and imprinted in the very soul of the lead plates, must be destroyed to defend the honor, if not the survival, of that culture.

These pensive words lay bare, once more, Sutzkever's deep reverence for the distinctive diaspora ethos. And it is with a sense of deep grief that he notes the necessity to give up these cherished values: "Jewish might rooted in the word / In a salvo of bullets must now blow up the world."

The second and fourth strophes are an attempt to ameliorate this deep sense of tragedy by linking it with ancient ones, notably with the attempt of the Greeks to Hellenize and thus destroy Judaism in 198 B.C.E. However, the Jews repelled the enforced assimilation by staging a guerilla rebellion led by Judah the Maccabee (the Hebrew word for "hammer"). In 164 B.C.E., when the Jews recaptured Jerusalem, they purged the temple of the pagan defilement and rededicated it to Jehovah. This victory is commemorated as Hanukkah, the feast of lights. Sutzkever, who like the other dreamers-turned-soldiers, carries the memory of this event in his heart, invokes the name of the Maccabees in a 1945 revision of the poem[12] and generates symbols to link the past and present. Hence the mystical network of words in the second strophe: "And again we broke open the seal / Of the strangely familiar, eternal cave." The "seal" suggests the separation of past and present, while the "cave" denotes the "heart" where the transcendental memory of Jerusalem is lodged. And so, the newly anointed soldiers of Sutzkever's poem pour the molten verses into bullets just as their grandfathers, the Maccabees, poured "oil into the golden holiday-menorah" with which they purged the temple of all idols.

The closing lines of the poem are a subtle attempt to justify the metamorphosis of the Jews, the dreamers-turned-soldiers, as well as the transformation of rows of type into bullets. This justification is couched in the evocation of a mystical link between the fighting Polish Jew and the ancient defenders of the falling "granite walls" of the temple in Jerusalem. Thus, whoever might on ethical or religious grounds question the reforging of the sacrosanct letters into bullets (probably the poet himself) will comprehend the moral efficacy "of the molten words, / and in his heart recognize their voice"—the voice of struggling Jerusalem.

The difficulties in connection with obtaining or producing weapons prevailed not only in the ghettos of Vilna and Warsaw, but obviously in every ghetto and certainly more so in concentration camps. Nonetheless, there were rebellions in numerous places, including Cracow, Czestochowa, Bendzin, Bialystok, Auschwitz, Sobibor, and Treblinka—the most tenacious and heroic of which, as Itzhak Zukerman (one of the leaders of the Warsaw ghetto uprising) writes, having been "fought by the Bialystok ŻOB."[13] These acts of desperation were intended to determine not the manner of Jewish life—this was no longer possible—but rather a manner of Jewish death. In the silence of the universe in which neither God nor humankind took much note of the dying Jews, some of them, having fought back with everything they had—as their poetry testifies—died silent and sometimes heroic in their silence, resigned and somehow dignified in their resignation. Others died fighting with Molotov cocktails or whatever weaponry they could manufacture, steal, or buy.

Chapter Seven

S.O.S.

Both the predicament of the Jews and the general indifference of the world to it are evoked in a slim anthology of poetry entitled *Z Otchłani* (Out of the Abyss). Published in 1944 and containing the work of such poets as Czesław Miłosz (destined to become the Nobel laureate for literature), Mieczysław Jastruń (a much respected poet in postwar Poland), and Jan Kott (who was to become an eminent Shakespearean scholar and literary critic), this anthology was microfilmed and secretly sent to London and later to New York by the National Jewish Committee (*Żydowski komitet narodowy*). This collection of poetry on the Jewish catastrophe is a living testament to the vital, albeit futile, role poetry played in the Holocaust. For as late as 1944, the poets, both Jewish and Christian, tried to secure help by rousing the conscience and moral indignation in their readers abroad.

Jakób Apenszlak, the New York editor of *Out of the Abyss*, comments that *"wiersze te stanowią rewelacje nie tylko ze względu na okoliczności, w jakich powstały.... Mowią nam więęej o tym, co czuli, co myśleli, jak przejmowali ciosy rąk zezwierzęconych Niemców niewolonicy ghett, skazańcy zepchnięci na dno upokorzenia i mąk cielesnych, niż suche zestawienia faktów i sprawozdania z terenu martyrologji."*[1] (These poems are not only a revelation of the conditions under which they were created.... More eloquent than chronicles of facts and reports from the annals of martyrdom, these poems unveil what the slaves of the ghettos—the condemned, the humiliated, subjected to physical punishment—felt and thought, how they responded to the blows of the bestial Germans.)

Józef Wittlin, also in New York at this time, writes, "*Ręka drży, język zasycha, dech zamiera—gdy czytamy te wiersze. Wstyd pali oczy, co przesuwają się po czarnych, żałobnych żędach tych pięknych a gorzkich stróf. Wstyd oczom, że czytają te śpiewne relikwie zagłady i bochaterstwa, że czytają i nie ślepną.*"[2] (The hand trembles, language dries up, breath dies when we read these poems. Shame stings our eyes as they cross the black, funereal verses of the beautiful and bitter strophes. Shamed are the eyes that read the songlike reliquaries of destruction, that read and are not struck blind.)

Czesław Miłosz and Mieczysław Jastruń
Indifference, the Nemesis of Humanity

That no political action would result from the moral revulsion and anguish of the few readers abroad, poets like Miłosz, Kott, and Jastruń may have suspected in 1944 after most of the Polish Jews had already been killed. Nonetheless, Miłosz's "Campo di Fiori" and Jastruń's "Tu także jak w Jerusalem" (Here Too as in Jerusalem) are a last-ditch attempt to prod the conscience of those who might yet be able to help.

Although both poets have their poetic roots in the mellifluous language of Polish romanticism, both "Campo dei Fiori" and "Here too as in Jerusalem" are marked by language characteristic of restrained reporting rendered by an objective observer. It is this aesthetic of emotional self-control, more than any other stylistic compulsion, that produces an unsettling aura of the commonplace. This shift is not unusual for Miłosz; indeed, he is famous for his multidimensional poetic sensibility and his gift for speaking with many voices. These characteristics are in part attributed to the breadth and depth of his experiences. Born in Lithuania in 1911, he had lived in different parts of Tsarist Russia, Estonia, and Poland, frequently leaving and later returning to the same place, and always open to the culture that distinguished the place where he lived. Moreover, he had close ties with numerous literary movements in Poland, often determining their development. During the German occupation he lived in Warsaw, where he was editor of an underground anthology of poetry, *Pieśń niepodległa* (The Independent Song). In 1951 he left Poland, lived in Paris until 1960, and since that time he has lived in the United States, where he has taught Polish literature at Berkeley.

The brutality of the German invasion of Poland in 1939 caused Miłosz (like many other Polish poets mentioned in this study) to call into question the very purpose and morality of art. The savagery that he witnessed challenged the humanistic principles and faith that are associated with poetry. He argues:

> The act of writing a poem is an act of faith; yet if the screams of the tortured are audible in the poet's room, is not his activity an offense to human suffering? And if the next hour may bring his death and the destruction of his manuscript, should the poet engage in such a pastime?[3]

He resolved this moral dilemma by an unequivocal answer, as Alexander M. Schenker writes in his introduction to Miłosz's *Utwory poetyckie* (Poetry): "If the world is in pieces, it is the artist's duty to glue these pieces together, to oppose the forces of destruction with his own creative powers."[4] In this Miłosz draws close to Abraham Sutzkever, but unlike the latter, Miłosz invests his poetic language and prosody with increasing terseness, directness, nakedness, and simplicity. Together with such poets as Przyboś (discussed in the second chapter) and Jastruń, Miłosz left an indelible mark on postwar Polish poetry.

Jastruń, a Jew, born in 1903, reveals in his mature poetry an independent poetic spirit, although his early poetry shows strong Skamander influences (see preceding chapters). His major work is meditative, concerned, among other things, with the human relationship to time. The author of a biography of Mickiewicz, which has been translated into many languages, he is also an essayist and literary critic much respected in his native Poland, where he died several years ago. During the war, he was in hiding on the "Aryan side" of Warsaw. Nonetheless, he managed to produce a body of poetry, *Godzina strzeżona* (The Defended Hour), published in 1944.

Miłosz, a righteous Christian, reflects in "Campo dei Fiori" his deep anguish in the face of the Jewish catastrophe and the ignominy of the Poles and, by symbolic extension, of the silent world. Jastruń, a Jew, stands outside this guilty history. It is noteworthy, however, that both Miłosz's poem and Jastruń's "Here too as in Jerusalem," like all the poetry in *Out of the Abyss*, eschews such words as Jew, Pole, or German. Józef Wittlin interprets this phenomenon in Manichean terms. "*To znaczy, że dla poetów ghetta, potworna sprawa między Żydami a Niemcami jest już sprawą ludzkóśoi. I nie jest to już nawet tragedja TEJ wojny. To*

*jakaś gigantyczna walka żywiołów swiatła z żywiołami ciemno-
ści, walka dobra i zła, rozgrywająca się na płaszczyżnie wiecz-
ności.''*[5] (This means that for the ghetto poets, the monstrous con-
frontation between the Jews and Germans is an issue confronting
all humanity. And it is not just a tragedy of *this* war. This is a kind
of gigantic struggle between the principles of light and darkness, a
struggle between good and evil, enacted on the stage of eternity.)

Campo di Fiori (Miłosz)

*W Rzymie, na Campo di Fiori
Kosze oliwek i cytryn,
Bruk okrywały winem
I odłamkami kwiatów.
Różowe owoce morza
Sypią na stoły przekupnie,
Naręcza ciężkich winogron
Spadają na puch brzoskwini.*

*Tu, na tym własnie placu
Spalono Giordana Bruna
Kat plomień stosu zażegnał
W kole ciekawiej gawiedzi.
A ledwie płomień przygasnął,
Znów pełne były tawerny
Kosze oliwek i cytryn
Nieśli przekupnie na głowach.*

*Wspomniałem Campo di Fiori
W Warszawie, przy karuzeli
W wiosenny wieczór pogodny,
Przy dźwiękach skocznej muzyki.
Salwy za murem ghetta
Głuszyła skoczna melodja
I wzlatywały pary
Wysoko w pogodne niebo.*

*Czasem wiatr z domów płonących
Przewiewał czarne latawce,
Chwytali skrawki w powietrzu
Jadący na karuzeli.*

Rozwiewał suknie dziewczynom
Wiatr od tych domów płonących,
Śmiały się tłumy wesołe
Wczas pięknej warszawskiej Niedzieli.

Morał ktoś może wyczyta,
Że lud warszawski czy rzymski
Handluje, bawi się, kocha
Mijając męczeńskie stosy.
Inny ktoś może wyczyta
O rzeczy ludzkich mijaniu,
O zapomnieniu co rośnie
Nim jeszcze płomien przygasnął.

Ja jednak wtedy myślałem
O samotności ginących,
O tym, że kiedy Giordano
Wstępował na rusztowanie,
Nie było w ludzkim języku
Ani jednego wyrazu,
Aby coś zdołał powiedzieć
Ludzkości, która zostaje.

Już biegli wychylać wino
Sprzedawać białe rozgwiazdy—
Kosze oliwek i cytryn
Nieśli w wesołym gwarze.
I był już od nich odległy,
Jakby minęły wieki,
A oni czekają chwilę
Na jego odlat w pożarze.

A ci, ginący samotni,
Już zapomnieni od świata,
Język nasz stał się im obcy
Jak język dawnej planety.
I wszystko będzie legendą.
A wtedy po wielu latach
Na wielkim Campo di Fiori
Bunt wznieci słowo poety.[6]

❑ ❑ ❑

Campo dei Fiori

In Rome, on Campo dei Fiori,
baskets of olives and lemons
cobbles spattered with wine
and the wreckage of flowers.
Vendors cover the trestles
with rose-pink fish;
armfuls of dark grapes
heaped on peach-down.

On this same square
they burned Giordano Bruno.
Henchmen kindled the pyre
close-pressed by the mob.
Before the flames had died
the taverns were full again,
baskets of olives and lemons
again on the vendors' shoulders.

I thought of Campo dei Fiori
In Warsaw by the sky-carrousel
one clear spring evening
to the strains of a carnival tune.
The bright melody drowned
the salvos from the ghetto wall,
and couples were flying
High in the blue sky.

At times wind from the burning
would drift dark kites along
and riders on the carrousel
caught petals in midair.
That same hot wind
blew open the skirts of the girls
and the crowds were laughing
on the beautiful Warsaw Sunday.

Someone will read a moral
that the people of Rome and Warsaw
haggle, laugh, make love

as they pass by martyrs' pyres.
Someone else will read
of the passing of things human,
of the oblivion
born before the flames have died.

But that day I thought only
of the loneliness of the dying,
of how, when Giordano
climbed to his burning
he could not find
in any human tongue
words for mankind,
mankind who live on.

Already they were back at their wine
or peddled their white starfish,
baskets of olives and lemons
they had shouldered to the fair,
and he already distanced
as if centuries had passed
while they paused just a moment
for his flying in the fire.

Those dying here, the lonely
forgotten by the world,
our tongue becomes for them
the language of an ancient planet.
Until, when all is legend
and many years have passed,
on a new Campo dei Fiori
rage will kindle at a poet's word.[7]

Tu także jak w Jerusalem (Jastruń)

Tu także jak w Jerusalem
Jest posępny mur płaczu.
Ci którzy pod nim stali,
Już go nie zobaczą.

Pusta noc, pusty dom, głuchy gmach.
Stąd ich wywleczono.

Została ciemność i strach
I wnęcza—śmierci łono.

Domy w kamiennym pochodzie
Pod nie ubłaganym niebem,
Jakby szły za pogrzebem
Tysiące rodzin.

Chrześcijanie, rzuceni lwom,
Wiedzieli za co konają,
A wy—Oto pusty wasz dom,
Ogień ślepy właściciel zajął.

Nie żucił nikt dobrej ziemi
Na ten masowy grób—
Milczeniem pozdrowieni,
Wolni od zdrady słów!

Gdyście ustami, jak rany,
Pragnący wołali wody,
Do pociągów odrutowanych
Nikt wody nie podał.

Uciekła ziemia z pod wyklętych,
Zapadła się w dymy kolei
Warszawa, gdy w szybach pięter
Słońce wołało, że dnieje.[8]

❑❑❑

Here Too as in Jerusalem

Here too as in Jerusalem
There is the somber Wailing Wall.
Those who stood near it
Will see it no more.

Empty night, empty building, deaf edifice.
From here they were dragged.
Darkness and terror remained,
And the interior—the womb of death.

Buildings in a stony procession,
Under an unappeased sky,

As if thousands of families
Following a funeral.

Christians, thrown to the wolves,
Knew why they were perishing,
But you?—Here is your empty house,
Fire, a blind proprietor, occupies it.

No one cast the good earth
Onto that mass grave—
Greeted by silence,
Free of treacherous words.

When with mouths like wounds,
Parched, you called for water,
No one brought water
To the sealed trains.

The earth fled under the condemned,
Warsaw fell in the smoke of the trains
And in the windows of the buildings
The sun announced dawn.

At the center of each poem is the terrifying realization that the nemesis of humanity is indifference. As an interpretive witness, Miłosz records the hallucinatory juxtaposition between the gun salvos of the immured Jews fighting in the Warsaw ghetto uprising and the sounds of a gay tune rising from the carrousel poised at the outer edge of the inferno. The incongruous proximity of the death rattle of the ghetto (which had finally been subdued by German artillery and by incendiary bombs, reducing the entire ghetto to a wasteland of cinders and rubble) and the gay laughter of the reveling Poles causes the poet to invoke the memory of the execution of the sixteenth-century philosopher Giordano Bruno at Campo dei Fiori. The symbolic significance of this bridging of historical and contemporary events lies in the parallel fate of the philosopher and the Jews. Both were victims of intolerance, a crime that sanctions the murder of one person just as readily as that of millions. Significantly, Giordano Bruno—much like the Jews of his own century—was betrayed to the Inquisition and executed at the stake. He was charged with heresy for his belief in the infinite nature of the universe, his defense of the Copernican system, and his interest in Neoplatonism and Pantheism.

Implied in the parallel fate of the Jews and Giordano Bruno is a general indictment of Christianity, which, having fostered intolerance, culminated in the Nuremberg doctrines. But Poland, a devoutly Christian nation, is specifically accused by a Polish Christian himself, appalled that his compatriots have actively or passively betrayed the Jews to the deadliest inquisition yet: the stake of the ghettos and concentration camps.

Caught in the nightmare of history, Jastruń recedes into a more distant past than does Miłosz. Like Sutzkever, his coreligionist, Jastruń invokes the myth of Jewish continuum, casting a bridge between the Wailing Wall and the wall of the Warsaw ghetto. It is noteworthy that the Wailing Wall has been a symbol not only of grief at the destruction of the temple and dispersion of the Jews, but also that of hope—hope expressed in the eternal Jewish affirmation: "Next Year in Jerusalem." The wall of the Warsaw ghetto, however, signals the final unloosening of the darkest energies of evil that are obliterating the very possibility of such affirmations. The bitter irony of the image of the dual walls—uniting and separating ancient and modern Jews—derives from the fact that while the ancient Jews were cast out of their land and scattered in the world, their descendents, the modern Jews, are cast out of the world, their "smoke blown out of the chimney of history . . . / their grave dug in the air . . . / Between heaven and earth" as "Funeral," another of Jastruń's elegies, in *Out of the Abyss* laments.

Both Miłosz and Jastruń agonize over the single, unvaried constant in human evolution: the seesaw of cruelty and murder, intolerance and indifference. In the past as in the present, Miłosz shows, the rabble's response to a single victim or several million has been the same: the bystanders "haggle, laugh, make love, / as they pass by martyrs' pyres," unable to find a single expression in the human language to protest the carnage. The chill of this juxtaposition is exacerbated by the fact that it is, after all, not one person but rather several hundred largely unarmed, fighting Jews who are dying behind the ghetto walls and thousands of others who are perishing in Treblinka and Maidanek. The analogy, therefore, signals not only similar responses of a rabble separated by time and space; it also reminds us of the difference between the immorality of a culture hundreds of years ago, which witnessed the execution of individual victims with gleeful tolerance, and the savagery of the twentieth century, which tolerates the obliteration of millions of people with the same indifference. The poem's subdued language, discursive logic, and reflectiveness point to the moral that the dying Jews have already been "forgotten by the world," causing human language to ring foreign to them, like "the language of an ancient planet." In his prescience the poet prophesies that, like Bruno, the terrible reality of contemporary Jewry will soon become but a legend, nullified by history.

In Jastruń's poem, human indifference is translated into images of silence—silence so absolute that only "buildings in a stony procession / Under an unappeased sky" bear witness to the conflagration in the ghetto. Jastruń's world is bereft of God and divested of human witnesses who might be willing to see and much less to "cast the good earth / onto the mass graves." The concatenation of the poem's images evokes a sense of cosmic silence so absolute that it actually resonates in the consciousness of the reader. Images of empty houses consumed by fire, "a blind proprietor"; surreal iconographs of "mouths like wounds," whose cry for water is silenced by the deafness of those who would not hear; "buildings in a stony [funereal] procession"; the sun announcing dawn in the windows of empty buildings crowd the imagery of the earth fleeing "under the condemned," as the Warsaw ghetto collapses in the implied admixture of smoke rising from the burning buildings, the trains, and the crematoria chimneys. Paradoxically, the solitary consolation is silence, for only silence is "free of treacherous words."

Miłosz's poetic universe, on the other hand, explodes in a cacophony of sounds and kinetic energy. The vulgar jingle of a carrousel; raucous laughter of the rabble; couples flying "high in the cloudless sky"; wind-born cinders like "dark kites" rising over the ghetto walls; girl's skirts blown open by the hot wind—all these denotations of indifference drown out the "salvos from the ghetto wall."

The pictorial power of "Campo dei Fiori" and "Here too as in Jerusalem," coupled as it is with tones of inconsolable, if objectively expressed grief suggests the poets' disquieting suspicion that the edifices and, in fact, the very foundations of Western civilization are going up with the smoke of the Jews. For civilization and its determinants, the poets seem to imply, are a stream of events generated by antecedent and contemporaneous processes. It is this that produces a continuum within which accepted and established beliefs, customs, and laws are transmitted from one generation to the next, from one culture to another. The progression of events from the earliest beginnings of Western civilization to the Wailing Wall, to Giordano Bruno, to the wall of the Warsaw ghetto and the merry carrousel outside it—all these had established such a continuum: an archetype against which future bloodlettings will be measured and included within the purview of the acceptable and permissible. In paralleling Giordano Bruno and the Jews, or in linking the Wailing Wall with the wall of the ghetto, the poets reflect their deep apprehension that Western civilization has, in the end, been a dismal failure.

Yet despite their despair, both poets, like most of the writers in the Holocaust, continued to write. Indeed, unlike those bystanders who passively watch "martyrs' pyres" or who even take the trouble to justify their own indifference by such clichés as the transiency of human life (fifth strophe), Miłosz vows, in the closing lines of his poem, to breathe into the cinders of the immolated word the resonance of protest. But anguish and irony mark this solemn promise; for he knows that standing with but a few who share his alarm, his voice will, at best, be heard in times to come, when the events he is witnessing will be but a legend. Perhaps then, after "many years have passed / on a new Campo dei Fiori / rage will kindle a poet's word." If nothing else, the awareness of impotence contained in this promise is an expression both of Miłosz's moral integrity and of his sense of empathy for and solidarity with the fighting and perishing Warsaw ghetto Jews.

A Jew of the New Testament

"Campo dei Fiori" and Miłosz's other wartime poetry were officially published after the war in a volume entitled *Ocalenie* (Salvation) in 1945. Among the poems included in this volume, perhaps the most eloquent and the most germane to this discussion, is the surrealistic "Biedny Chrześcijanin patrzy na ghetto" (A Poor Christian Looks at the Ghetto). In it Miłosz provides a chilling formulation of the turmoil he, a solitary Christian neighbor, experiences as he watches the destruction of the Warsaw ghetto. The poet's despair, his political and moral isolation, and his frustration and impotence, reach the highest emotional pitch in the closing three stanzas of the poem:

Powoli, drążąc tunel, posuwa się strażnik-kret
Z małą czerwoną latarką przypiętą na czole.
Dotyka ciał pogrzebanych, liczy, przedziera się dalej,
Rozróżnia ludzki popiół po tęczujacym oparze,
Popiół każdego człowieka po innej barwie tęczy.
Pszczoły obudowują czerwony ślad,
Mrówki obudowują miejsce po moim ciele.

Boję się, tak się boje strażnika-kreta.
Jego powieka obrzmiała jak u patriarchy,
Który siadywał dużo w blasku świec
Czytając wielką księge gatunku.

Cóż poweim mu, ja, Żyd Nowego Testamentu,
Czekając od dwóch tysięcy lat na powrót Jezusa?
Moje rozbite ciało wyda mnie między pomocników śmierci:
Nieobrzezanych.[9]

◻◻◻

Slowly, boring a tunnel, a guardian mole makes his way,
With a small red lamp fastened to his forehead.
He touches burned bodies, counts them, pushes on,
He distinguishes human ashes by their luminous vapor,
The ashes of each man by a different part of the spectrum.
Bees build around a red trace.
Ants build around the place left by my body.

I am afraid, so afraid of the guardian mole.
He has swollen eyelids, like a patriarch
Who sat much in the light of the candles
Reading the great book of the species.

What will I tell him, I, a Jew of the New Testament
Waiting two thousand years for the second coming of Jesus?
My broken body will deliver me to his sight
And he will count me among the helpers of death:
The uncircumcised.[10]

Miłosz takes an image of a subterranean animal, a mole, and
identifies its existence in nature with the unexpected: a Jew mak-

ing his way in the subterranean world of the Warsaw ghetto
bunkers and sewers. Such images of human reductivity, antici-
pated in Kafka's *Metamorphosis*, appear in other Holocaust poems,
in Szlengel's "Counterattack," for example, in which human be-
ings are reduced to cattle. Unlike the mole in nature, the human
mole, using the sewers as an avenue of escape from the burning
ghetto, encounters in his impossible world improbable substances:
"human ashes" distinguished from other essences "by their lumi-
nous vapor, / The ashes of each man by a different part of the
spectrum."

The surreal landscape of this poem suggests the mythical, a
world made timeless by what Mircea Eliade calls "transhuman
revelations,"[11] thought to express the absolute truth that took
place at the dawn of time. Miłosz, the artist as mediator of experi-
ences as primal (if unparalleled) as those that make for mythology,
interprets the *truth* he sees as the dawn of a new time. The unfold-
ing history is to him the only valid revelation of reality. Moreover,
his close proximity to the events and the immediacy of his ex-
periences overwhelm his emotions. And "when a poet is over-
whelmed by strong emotions," writes Miłosz, "his form tends to
become more simple and more direct."[12] Yet the word constella-
tions of "A Poor Christian Looks at the Burning Ghetto" rise like
a barricade between the poet and reader, much like the barriers
between archaic myths and their uninitiated, modern reader.

Obviously, Miłosz is direct, even if the truth he narrates is
unutterable and the images he projects seem surreal. Hence, what
the "mole," the protagonist of his poem, actually encounters in his
subterranean sojourn is a sewer strewn with corpses of badly
burned Jews who jumped out the windows of flaming buildings
and who died of their burns while attempting to reach the "Aryan
side" of Warsaw. Indeed, so badly burned are they that they form
an undifferentiated mass of ash; and only the human "mole,"
guided in the darkness by a cyclopean eye, "a small red lamp fas-
tened to his forehead," can distinguish one body from another by
their "luminous vapor, . . . by a different part of the spectrum."

Significantly, the poet is afraid of the "mole." For being Jew-
ish, he is the "guardian mole," the source and keeper of the
Torah, "the book of the species," and the giver of the New Testa-
ment. The poem's pervasive sense of angst arises from the implied
causal relationship between the poet as Christian, "the uncircum-
cised Jew of the New Testament," and the destruction of his reli-
gious ancestor to whose safekeeping "the book of the species,"

hence the very underpinning of Christianity, has been entrusted. The mood of unease builds to cumulative distress when the reader realizes the sense of guilt and impotence experienced by a person who single-handedly refuses to be absorbed into cosmic indifference. The poet's metaphysical and existential isolation and his guilty (because he is Christian) relationship to the Jews are expressed in these evocative insect images:

> Bees build around a red trace.
> Ants build around the place left by my body.

So dispensable is the "guardian mole," so futile his religious legacy, that nothing but insects build around the red trace left by his red lamp. And so insignificant is the poet's solitary human attempt that nothing but a useless trace, as futile as the memory of the Jews, will remain for posterity. And so, despite his conscience and his protest, articulated in his poetry, Miłosz is afraid that "waiting two thousand years for the second coming of Jesus," he will be counted "among the helpers of death."

Miłosz did not wait for the second coming of Christ, nor did he allow his grief to paralyze his moral sensibility. His personal protest, a vow he makes in "Campo di Fiori," is ubiquitous in his writing; for grounded in religion, humanism, and politics, his work reflects his determination to preserve and create human values. Nor is his apprehension that the Jewish tragedy will be but a legend, a sentimental utterance to be casually forgotten. In his *Zniewolony umysł* (Captive Mind), published in 1953, Miłosz warns against this, providing a mandate for and challenge to writers to guard against any tendency to co-opt the landscape of slaughter and project onto it extra-Holocaust concerns (erotic, existential, aesthetic, etc.) or to misappropriate it for political or any other ideologies. Aware that verisimilitude of the Holocaust is impossible and the details, because not analogous, are difficult to assimilate, the poet asks not to superimpose images onto this tragedy that do not derive from it.[13]

The concerns articulated by Miłosz are very timely and draw particularly close to those of Elie Wiesel who is deeply disturbed by the wild profusion of myths generated by the mass media. These include fictionalized and vulgarized accounts of the Holocaust; abstractions of theories; misinterpretations of survivors' testimonies; and a plethora of Nazi gutter historiography. All of these attempt to explain, exploit, or deny the Holocaust. This is not to suggest that the causes and effects of the tragedy are not the proper and necessary subject of inquiry. One would only hope that writers, film makers, philosophers, social scientists, and others would reflect Wiesel's and Miłosz's concerns and would heed their mandate for faithful presentations of facts.

Epilogue

Birthday

Joy and laughter
What a lovely day
Bobus turned three
Let's celebrate

Yet another year
We have all survived
To celebrate his birthday
And laud and clement skies

This was years ago—
All that's left is pain. . . .

from *Painful Echoes . . .*
the Holocaust diary of Dr. Luba Krugman Gurdus

Of the literature produced in the Holocaust and saved in milk tins or other hermetically sealed containers and unearthed after the war, George Steiner says:

These books and documents . . . are not for "review." Not unless "review" signifies, as perhaps it should in these instances, "a seeing-again," over and over. As in some Borghes fable, the only decent "review" of the *Warsaw Diary* or Elie Wiesel's *Night* would be to re-copy the book, line by line,

pausing at the names of the dead and the names of the chil-
dren as the orthodox scribe pauses, when recopying the Bible,
at the hallowed name of God.[1]

Would this mandate suffice? I think not, even if I share Stein-
er's wish to honor, indeed, to consecrate, the very names of those
who died in the Holocaust and whose manuscripts were so care-
fully resurrected after the war. Perhaps the obscurity of many writ-
ers—notably of the poets who wrote in languages not easily
accessible to scholars—is a result of our failure to "review" their
work and, hence, to encourage even the viewing of it. It is for this
reason that the forgotten bards may have died twice. Surely, Alvin
Rosenfeld's thesis of "double dying" might apply as much to them
as to survivors writing *post factum*. The latter, Rosenfeld cogently
argues, are "beset by a double burden . . . that of recollection,
which is painful enough, but also that of psychic restoration and
moral reconciliation, which may be simply impossible."[2]

Clearly, like those who survived, the writers in the Holo-
caust have bequeathed a legacy of their epoch to posterity; their
writing, notably their poetry, has vivified the complex spectrum of
human responses to wretchedness and agony. But because the con-
textualizing process was contemporaneous with unfolding events,
their work is marked by an authority of a special kind. Unlike the
reflective nature of post Holocaust writing—significant as it is—
poetry in the Holocaust is informed by an authenticity and,
hence, truth that resides in the contiguity of events and human
responses to them.

I undertook this study to reanimate the poetry in the Holo-
caust, to rediscover its unmediated truths. To that end I sought the
most suitable method of analysis and found it in textual explica-
tion. For the close scrutiny imposed by this critical approach is a
form of "perspectivism" that allows the work of art to be evalu-
ated within its own context and its own time: in short, it allows
the poetry to speak its own truths. These reveal that the poetry in
the Holocaust provides existential correlatives to both the histori-
an's objective chronicling of fact and the various forms of post Ho-
locaust writings. As a form of mimetic art it unveils a spectrum of
personal and communal perceptions and responses to unfolding
events. It shows that despite the traditional pacifism of Judaism,
the Jews were not passive, for they fought back with all they had.
They were the first in all occupied Europe to rise in armed revolt
against the Germans. They created an underground culture and in-

genious support systems without which survival would have been impossible. While there was a crisis of faith, they continued to affirm life and Jewish traditional values, of which writing poetry is but one example. And it is not that they wrote secretly at the risk of life, but that they wrote at all, exhorting the people to armed rebellion (even when it was impossible), to spiritual resistance, and moral conduct. That manuscripts were saved together with other records—those of Emanuel Ringelblum, for example—renders them both sacred and a valuable record from which generalizations and stratagems for the prevention of future catastrophes might be culled.

If I have learned anything from the truths expressed in the subject of this study, it is this: the very need to "brace" my feelings, as it were, in order to maintain an aesthetic distance and objectivity with respect to the poetry and my analysis of it, allowed me to gain a sense of objectivity with regard to my memories and perceptions of my personal experiences in the Holocaust. When I embarked on this work, I sought neither an inward journey to reanimate the past nor catharsis that would lay demons to rest. The former was not necessary, the latter impossible. Yet I have gleaned a clearness of understanding that I lacked before. What significance this crystallization (or distillation) may have for others, I do not know; but I offer it in the form of autobiographical reflections that—while provoked by the poetry—may, in the end, be only obliquely related to the subject of this book.

A Woman I See with a Girl's Eyes

I

I was a child in Warsaw when the capital was occupied by the Germans and the ghetto sealed off; and during the ghetto uprising and my subsequent incarceration in Maidanek, Skarzysko, and Czestochowa, I was an adolescent. Obviously, the nearly six-year ordeal in these places—not to mention postwar pogroms in Poland and DP camps in Germany—exerted a claim both on the girl I had been and on the woman I was to become. Yet, the atrocities that I experienced were not unusual in the unusual landscape of ghettos and concentration camps, of smokestacks and mass graves. As a woman, I still see with a girl's eyes one or another event as it spontaneously surfaces in the daily tumult of life or when I deliberately summon it. But the meaning of certain events and the responses they elicited become clearer when I feel their texture as a woman, when I surrender to their motion and let it move through me.

As a girl in the ghetto and camps, I knew certain truths that only the immediacy of experience could yield. A woman, I still know many of these truths. But total recall is neither always possible nor perhaps even desirable, for contrary to contemporary psychology, to remember certain events might be worse than the vacuous spaces memory both recoils from and strains to fill. Moreover, to isolate an experience is, in the end, to submit it to refractions of the distorted prism of time. And yet the truths that I now know are no less valid than those I knew as a girl. For standing at a distance from the intensity of the events, I have the advantage of seeing them bifocally—as a girl and as a woman.

As a girl, I had to survive, to survive not only physically but spiritually as well. This truth is one that is granted the woman that I am. For I know now that my soul too had to be kept alive. And I further know that it was the struggle to retain my sense of selfhood and system of values relatively intact even under the most brutal conditions that kept absolute despair or madness at bay and helped me to endure. Although I lived these truths in the ghetto and camps, I am not certain that I remember being conscious of them. However, I do know that even as a child—or perhaps because I was a child—I saw with a clarity that I never possessed before, or since, the difference between good and evil, between right and wrong. There were those who were murdering us, and there were such persons as Janusz Korczak,[3] whom I often saw in the ghetto with his retinue of orphans. Nonetheless, my cognitive faculties were those of a girl in an extreme situation. Most of the time, therefore, I had neither the energy and leisure nor wisdom and experience to explore the meaning of life nor even that of survival. Yet I must have known that there was meaning in both, although I would have been at a loss to define it. If I were pressed for a definition, my bewildered response no doubt would have been: "I want to live." Everything in me cried out in defense of my life. My whole being throbbed with not wanting to die, just as it throbs in most victims.

Perhaps in me beat the pulse of my people who for two millennia struggled to affirm the simple right to a place on this little globule in the cosmic vastness. Perhaps, it is for this reason that I wanted to live not only for myself, but also for my father who died in Maidanek a few days after we were deported to that camp during the Warsaw Ghetto Uprising. I think that the mandate to live for him guided my behavior in a more compelling way than I realized as a girl. I further think that, to the extent that I could exert any control over my existence, this necessity was the very meaning that kept me going when giving up would often have been easier and more sensible.

I had yet another imperative, another reason for not succumbing to the blackness that engulfed us. I wanted to live for my mother and sister, just as they wanted to live for me. For the three of us constituted a kind of phalanx, one organism with one abiding purpose—to be there for each other, to live or die together. This sense of oneness was all that was left of our world. All around us were violence, death, and grief. Our only defense was our love. In our mutual devotion, we were each other's refuge and keeper, balance and hope. In this, we were more fortunate than most of the others whose entire families had already been killed. Our unusual luck as well as our devotion to each other earned us the appellation, "the mother and the two children." Some of our survivor friends who knew us in the camps still refer to us in these terms.

Our love for one another was expressed in myriads of ways: when we deloused each other in tender silence or with promises of better times to come; when we quibbled because my mother insisted on giving my sister and me more than a spoon of her soup of which we did not want to deprive her ("arguments" that provoked the Kapo of our barrack to banish us to a punitive one); when we buttressed the ruins of our world with dreams. These dreams were no longer of returning to life as it was in the past, for my father and most of our relatives had already been killed and our home in Warsaw reduced to rubble. Our dreams were of a place in some undefined world, for no easily imagined world seemed either safe or attainable. There was nothing heroic or noble in these and other fantasies, most of which involved finding our cousins who fled to the Soviet Union when the Germans entered Warsaw. I offer no excuses for them. I make no apologies for the dearth of dreams of revenge, escape, deeds of valor—though they did occasionally surface—nor for the triteness of reveries of sumptuous meals. But as a woman, I know that these imaginings, like our love, were defenses against despair. It is for this reason that they were commonplace in the ghettos and camps.

II

The tendrils of my memory have coiled, at this very moment, around a specific event: a selection in Maidanek. It was an unusual selection, different from the daily crack-of-dawn selections or the random ones at the gates of the camp when the work details returned to the camp grounds. During both these selections, notably the morning ones, great numbers of us were dispatched to the gas chambers and ovens of Maidanek. The selection I am referring to was a midday one, and like all such events it determined our fate. That afternoon I was picked with a group of women to be transferred to another camp. We were to be the second contingent of women to leave Maidanek alive between May and August 1943. The first group was sent to Auschwitz, and few, if any, survived.

I was relatively optimistic, because the German civilian who chose us appeared to be less brutal than the SS guards and assured us that we were being sent to Skarzysko, a labor camp. But despair quickly subdued my tentative hopefulness. Despite our daily efforts not to be separated, my mother and sister were both assigned to another work detail that fateful day and would not, therefore, be included in this transport. Wild with worry, I turned to the Polish Kapo of our punitive barrack. Although her sadism was notorious, she responded to my pleas, and, like a lowly demon, she scribbled in my mother's and sister's identification numbers in her book of tentative life.

At the same time, unknown to me, my mother and sister traded places with two women who were included in the transport to Skarzysko, for all four thought that the group was bound for the gas chamber, not another camp. Careful to shield me from their terrible suspicion and determined not to let me die alone, my mother and sister kept this to themselves. I learned about the secret life-death barter only recently when, during one of our "remembrances of things past," I invited my sister to read this chapter. She was mystified that in the course of the forty-three years since the end of the war, I did not learn about this "transaction." So was I. Apparently this issue never came up in our inexhaustible remembrances.

There was not much more for either one of us to say. Neither one of us knows what our joint reminiscences are yet to unveil. But we do know that the separation that all three of us bewailed that day and my naiveté or optimism as well as my mother's and sister's terror that I may die without their comforting presence helped to save our lives (though the memory of the two women who most likely perished in the gas chambers of Maidanek is intolerable, even if they thought that trading places would save their lives). The irony of this episode is that during the final selection, before being herded into the trains for Skarzysko, I was relegated to the gas chamber while my mother and sister were shoved toward life. Horrified, my mother cried out to the SS man, the dispenser of life and death: *"Das ist mein Kind,"* and some atavistic emotion in him responded to my mother's anguish. He let me live.

It is not only that the three of us were ready to die for each other. We wanted to live for each other, a feat often more difficult to accomplish. We had a tacit, perhaps even inchoate, agreement not to allow one of us to die in solitary terror—the way my father died in the gas chambers of Maidanek—or to live in total aloneness. We took this mandate for granted. It was our choice, a measure of unuttered victory, contingent, nonetheless, on the will or whim of the killers, who often deliberately separated families even in death.

Another surfacing recollection—a form of "involuntary memory"—brings into sharp relief certain events in Skarzysko. When I was infected in that camp with typhus and my left cheek and entire neck no longer had any skin, because they were completely covered with suppurating sores, and I was put in the notorious "hospital," which few left alive, it was my mother's and sister's love and parts of their rations that saved me. Only the woman with "galloping consumption" (in the camps, a widespread form of tuberculosis that ended in death within a few days of the onset of the disease), who in her feverish delirium often fell off her bunk crushingly landing on me, caused me to think: "This is enough. I cannot go on." But I did, because my mother and sister gave me parts of their rations, and hunger caused parts of my mother's body to swell. Her legs were covered with running sores, just as were my little sister's, whose courage still awes me. She was the intrepid one. Despite grave danger—an immediate bullet in the head—she was the one who sapped boiling liquid soap, a waste product, from certain machines in the ammunition factory in Skarzysko.

Once, we crept into the factory lavatory to wash our hair and, in terror of being discovered, I forgot to add cold water to the hot suds, the only soap available to us. I poured the scalding liquid over my sister's head. The scabies and mange with which her scalp had already been covered were multiplied by blisters caused by the burning suds. My terrible mistake condemned my little sister to further anguish, for the condition of her scalp targeted her for shears that were to shave her hair, a cherished possession, because it made one look more human and less likely to be killed—we thought. For weeks she devised ingenious strategems, half sleeping, half sitting vigil after a hard shift's labor, in order to outwit the Kapo who wanted to perform the indignity. Actually, the Kapo's intentions were far from evil. She thought that my sister's ravaged scalp would have a better chance of healing without hair in which a multitude of lice nested. In the end the Kapo relented. For she, like most everyone in the three-barrack complex in Skarzysko that housed the women from Maidanek, was moved by this thirteen-year-old's terror and determination.

Another time at dawn, in subzero weather, after returning from our night shift at the ammunition factory, my sister poured out a "pushka" (a tin into which we urinated) behind our barrack, because the latrines were far away and the ground was covered with snow and ice. It was treacherous to walk in huge wooden clogs, feet wrapped in rags. The snow that accumulated under the clogs created a slippery seesaw. A patrolling Kapo, who was responsible for keeping the grounds of the rat-and-vermin-infested barracks "clean" and who spotted my sister, beat her within an inch of her life as I helplessly looked on. But my mother in her desperate eloquence and desperate boldness attacked the Kapo, warning him that her blood would not rest in the grave and that it would haunt him forever. During the next several selections the Kapo saved my life. At this point, I was too sick to work in the ammunition factory and, hence, not allowed to live. But my mother's and sister's love breathed life into me, and we all survived. My mother has since died. My sister and I are still, in some way, one organism. Perhaps this helped us to survive.

There were other reasons, some seemingly senseless, that kept me going. One was my effort not to give in lest I be shot in the snow, lest my blood melt the snow and turn it crimson. Why I dreaded this more than any other death, I do not know. Perhaps it was more acceptable than the gas chamber and thus more accessible to consciousness.

III

The wretched ground of history that was my experience was later to be known as the central event of our century and, perhaps, of all time. That this would be so, I knew as a girl. Yet on some precognitive, if profound level, I think I must have intuited that my most fundamental experience had been my home and the tradition into which I was born. Although I probably never consciously thought of it, I must have lived it, at least on some level, even in the darkest of pits.

Somehow I must have known who I was, even when I would not have known who I was had I seen a reflection of myself in a mirror: a spectral skeleton with shaved head and festering sores in which lice bred. Despite this metamorphosis, wracked by disease, and more dead than alive, the core of my selfhood somehow remained relatively intact. Somehow, on some fundamental level, even after a savage beating with an iron rod I received from Brigida, the notorious SS woman in Maidanek, I was my parents' child, and especially my sister's sister, for she witnessed this savagery, and her anguish, I knew, was greater than mine.

I was even more especially my father's daughter, for in the three- or four-day agony in the cattle train that carted us from the infamous Warsaw ghetto *Umschlagplatz* to Maidanek, he held my hand as I leaned against his love, which never faltered, and sought his protection, which he could no longer provide. After an SS man bayonet-whipped my gentle father, he still held my hand, just as he did when, laden with knapsacks and bundles, we were made to run from the train to the no-man's-land between fields four and five in Maidanek. Waiting for several days in this unsheltered place of limbo, we both drank water from the puddles, for there was no other to be had. And there he knew that he would die when he asked me, he who always took care of us, to take care of my mother and sister. So when I was made to sort out hair, eyeglasses, and other sundry human possessions into neat piles (for *Ordnung muss sein*) in a huge crater—an enormous cavity in an open field in Maidanek—I knew on some level, like ineluctable fate, who I was, who I had to be.

When I prayed in Skarzysko for angels to descend and to carry us away from the blood engorged gates that separated the ammunition factory, where we slaved, from the rat- and lice-infested camp, where we lived, I retained enough of who I had been to entreat the angels to brush with their terrible wings the brutal Ukrainian guards and make them recoil from their own deeds. For every Sabbath night, as we were marched to the camp, the guards enacted a ritual of beating and killing to the accompaniment of a recording of the Yiddish song, *Gut Vokh*, (have a good week) that in better times greeted the new week. With nauseating immediacy, I remember the bite of their nails and whips, the ice of their bayonets, and the howling dogs blood-licking the earth.

I also remember that I did not disintegrate when I witnessed particularly dreadful shootings, hangings, or beatings. Some affected me more than others. I remember a hanging, the first such brutality I witnessed. It involved two young women, perhaps girls not much older than I, who, having dared an escape, were hanged with great ceremony. The two, who knew hope's futile promise and who imparted it to us, swung from the gibbet for several days and nights for all women to see in the center of the women's camp in Maidanek.

Like most of those who in the end were killed, I never believed that I would die. Like many of the condemned whom I knew, I managed to retain this wild, groundless faith. And like them, I was enough myself even when I was beside myself with physical agony, terror, and grief. I retained a scrap of myself even when I saw the specters into which my mother and sister were metamorphosed and when I feared that the next selection would send us to the gas chamber. Nor did I forget who I was when I saw trucks full of naked, quivering rag-doll humans piled up high, fresh out of gas chambers and carted to the crematoria.

No matter how helpless I was rendered, I was enough myself to look upon the killers—or rather shrink from them—with the dread and contempt that is specifically reserved for ultimate evil: a Nazi and a Nazi cohort. That I always felt superior to them, however absolute my terror and helplessness, I knew as a girl. I do not recall feeling dehumanized, even if as a woman I understand the intended dehumanization when we were made to stand naked—my sister, I, and other girls in the blush of our budding breasts—as the German guards leered at us during the selections. But I will always remember our terror and our helplessness. And I will never forget their self-dehumanization, their self-degradation. They were beasts and we were human.

I also remember my mother's incantations: "We are more than human. And if we survive, and our truth is revealed and believed, others will want to touch us, for our suffering has sanctified us, rendered us inviolable." In her distraction my mother uttered at least one truth—namely, that we were more than human. Otherwise, our minds would have been unhinged now and most of us raving mad. Yet, most survivors lead vital and productive lives. That this is so might be all the more surprising, for our wounds have not really healed. Wounds like ours do not heal. Nor have we ceased to mourn. Grief like ours cannot be restoratively mourned. Yet we are not lacking in creative energy. Indeed, the strength that helped us to remain human and allowed us to reconstruct our lives in alien, often hostile, lands and that guided us through the trials and tragedies of normal life is the very strength that carried us through the catastrophe and later through pogroms and DP camps. Hence, as a woman, I want to remember with equal clarity the atrocities and the "more than human" quality of the condemned. I especially do not want to forget the "more than human" quality of those who went to the gas chambers with quiet dignity. I also do not want to forget those other victims who hurled their loud protestations, laments, and terror against the murderers and against those who acquiesced in silence or indifference.

As a woman, I wonder what effort we had to exert not to succumb to absolute despair and hopelessness. How did we resist the downward pull of a world ruled by *Übermenschen*? In fact, some of the atrocities that were my portion either to witness or personally to live through were so brutal, sadistic, and bizarre that I have yet to speak of them. Obviously, any determination not to fall apart was not enough to survive. For if it were so, others with moral and physical fortitude far greater than mine would have survived as well. It was largely randomness, the vagaries of chance, that shaped our destiny in this land of death. After all, six million of us were killed.

IV

When memory is either meticulously invoked or when it insinuates itself, I am sometimes able to garner one or another epiphany. The one that is most constant is the significance and vitality of prewar life: the tradition of optimism and hope, of study and perseverance, of communal responsibility and cooperation, and less abstractly, of simple love and decency that informed not only my nuclear but also my extended family. This is not to suggest that prewar life and conduct were always unimpeachable. Life in relatively backward, poor, and anti-Semitic Poland was far from being idyllic. The teeming Jewish quarters of Warsaw, where we lived, were not always an example of untainted moral probity. Nonetheless, this less than perfect world did not tip the values scale or shatter the resonance of tradition. When we found ourselves in the darkness and our world was rapidly reduced to ruins, the foundations and scaffoldings of prewar values provided support for the vast majority.

Yet, for many of us, prewar life often seems eclipsed or relegated to the rarely visited attic of memory—as if that life had no formative influence on our perceptions and responses. I think that the difficulty to focus on that period arises from the fact that our anguish is so fathomless and the atrocities we experienced so unspeakable that the events that preceded them are obscured. Perhaps also the memory of the lost world, precisely because it disappeared into a void, is grief too great to bear, sometimes as deep and as paralyzing as the memory of the barbarism that caused it to vanish. I am not sure. But I strain to recall that life, for, as a woman, I know that it sustained the morale of the girl in the ghetto and camps. It was the tradition that affirmed hope and sanctified life, even as we were sacrificed on the altars of history, that was my backbone and my underpinning.

For how else can I as a woman explain that in the Warsaw ghetto, before the rush of roundups, deportations, and other disasters, both my sister and I, like many other children, attended clandestine schools? Small groups of children met for classes every day either in one or another child's overcrowded residence or that of the teachers'. There were five children in our group and five teachers. Because education was forbidden, this act was sabotage, and the penalty was immediate death. But we defended our values— and thereby our morale—by rebelling with the only weapons available to us: our books hidden under our coats, pressing against hunger and fear as we walked to our "classes."

More often than not, I remember, my mother and other mothers stood guard at the window during the makeshift schools to look for the sudden appearance of the Germans and their Ukrainian and Lithuanian cohorts, who, armed from head to foot, frequently descended upon the ghetto like a dark, otherworldly devastation. If the monstrous invasion was spotted early enough, there was perhaps time to elude it. Our makeshift escape was a room, the door of which was concealed by a moveable wardrobe. The corresponding rooms in all the apartments above and below ours were similarly camouflaged. In the end, this sanctuary—having become particulary important after July 1942, the beginning of the mass deportations and the final liquidation of the ghetto—had to be abandoned, for another one like ours was uncovered and everyone in it shot.

By this time, our education and other spirit-sustaining activities had to be terminated. One of these was the children's theater in which my sister and I performed. In the Warsaw ghetto, there were several such theaters whose exclusive performers were children. Many of these fledgling actors were orphaned and most of the time hungry and frightened. Yet they dazzled the audience with their talent, virtuosity, and resilience—all fostered by dedicated teachers and professional actors who undertook to train the children and who actually directed some rather spectacular performances. There were, for example, two Polish-Jewish actors, Irena Oberska and Michał Znicz (both ultimately killed), whose fame, I was told in the ghetto, had been well established on the Polish stage and screen before the war. I am not sure whether or not they were actually involved in directing any of the children's theaters, but I remember that they attended our performances, encouraging us all and assuring some, including me, that because of our talent they would, after the war, train us to become famous actors. Such assurances were a gift of hope, a promise not only of a future but also of normalcy, of food, of happiness. These promises were a form of tentative redemption that sometimes managed to assuage the horror and the anguish. On a more practical level, some of those who either directed or who were otherwise involved in the children's theaters worked together with the tenement self-help associations, one of which my father headed. As a woman, I know that these acts, the sole form of rebellion available to us, sustained our morale.

In our family, before the roundups and other disasters and even during their interludes, nightly readings of Yiddish literature were undertaken by my father (something we never did before the war, for Polish was our dominant language). We children brought to these readings songs and poems we learned in the streets of the ghetto and in the theater or poems we wrote ourselves. And we wrote frequently, either individually or in collaboration with our friends. To the extent that it was possible and even when it was not, we strained for a modicum of prewar normalcy to meliorate the misery. Children are especially expert at this art of the imagination.

Nothing could come closer to eating than imagining eating when hunger, like an avalanche, threatened to sweep us out of existence. Nothing could come closer to being children—when the streets, lined with corpses of those who died of starvation or exposure, were a trap for roundups—than playing in the attics of the

Halina Olomucki, "Boy Selling Star of David Armbands in the Warsaw Ghetto." (Charcoal)

tenements in which we lived. Shortly after the ghetto was sealed off and curfew enforced, these attics (most apartment houses in Warsaw had one) became a honeycomb of pathways, an overground route of travel between one building and another in one block of apartments. These ingenious devices of movement, made possible by crude openings just large enough to crawl through in the adjoining walls of buildings, were hardly intended as playgrounds for children. Much like the famous sewer system used for clandestine movement, the attic streets—more limited in the distances they allowed one to travel—were used for various purposes, including the ghetto uprising in April 1943. Notwithstanding the serious purposes for which they were intended, for us (certainly until July 1942), the musty, full of cobwebs, attic roads were a playground of simple games as well as of soaring imagination. In a world of endless anguish, hunger, terror, epidemic disease, and death, all intended to destroy us even before the gas chamber or the mass grave, such moral energy on the part of children was a means of fighting back.

Several months before the uprising in the ghetto, my father built an underground bunker in collaboration with two men. The bunker was intended for three families, a total of twelve persons. The entrance to it was a made-to-swivel toilet bowl in our ground floor apartment, and it had two levels, the second several feet deeper underground. We were still optimistic enough to equip it with a burial place, and we even had some Molotov cocktails, a water pump, batteries, and food. We descended into that catacomb on the eve of the revolt to find to our surprise a band of partisans who used our vault as headquarters for our area of the ghetto (Nowolipki 45, the Hoffmann shop). Apparently, my father worked with the resistance, even if he did not join them in battle. He had tuberculosis and was no longer young (though much younger than I am now when he was killed in Maidanek a month later).

There was also a French teacher in our bunker. How she and many others found their way into it, I am not sure. We slept in shifts in this crowded netherworld, and my sister and I had our first French lessons. My sister and I were children and there were not enough weapons for us. So we studied French, simply because there was a French teacher in our bunker and because, as my father argued, this seemingly absurd activity in a disintegrating world sustained our morale and kept terror, even if only for a moment, at bay. Never seeming to falter in his hope that my sister and I would survive, he further thought that these lessons might prove useful to us in the future. I think as my father did, because they were as viable as any other available, or rather unavailable, weapon. For no one in the world, as is common knowledge, was willing to send us any armaments or offer any other help. The French lessons, indeed, did prove useful to me in my much later studies in the United States, for I remembered not only the bit of grammar I learned but also every moral nuance connected with these brief instructions.

In the chaos of Skarzysko, a copy of Goethe's *Faust* circulated among some of us. I read parts of it despite the hunger and rats that gnawed at us. In the rush of memory when I teach the work now, I realize that I did not understand it then or rather that my understanding of it was different. After all, I gave it a concentration camp reading and I was very young. Since the boundaries between text and interpretation are fluid, they are a function of who and where in history we are—a central canon of much contemporary philosophy and literary theory. Yet, the fact that many of us valued books and loved reading before, after, and even during the Holocaust, when this unexpected manna sometimes nourished the soul, is but one indication that the Holocaust did not change us or our basic system of values, even if we will never be the same.

V

In the ghettos, in hiding, among the partisans in the forests, historians were feverishly recording the unfolding catastrophe for posterity. As we know, poetry, the noblest of literary expressions, flourished in the ghettos and was even produced in the concentration camps. Indeed, in two of the three camps in which I was incarcerated, it was not unusual to see women huddled on the lower levels of the three-tier bunks composing songs. In our barrack in Skarzysko there was one girl, Gutka, who was particularly gifted. In fact, as fate would have it, she shared our barrack in Częstochowa as well, for we were shunted from camp to camp together. Although she was often fretful and easily provoked to anger, she was a *poet* and, therefore, much indulged and loved by most of us. When her imagination was unfettered and her songs of pain or succor rose like wings of ghosts in the naked plank-wall barrack, our imagination too was released. And so was our sense of humor and laughter however black both may have been.

The inevitable circuit of empathy and union that Gutka's imagination created often helped to unleash talent latent in many of us. So we joined her in new songs sung to old tunes—some sentimental, others banal, but all familiar to us. These ephemeral creations gilded the darkness of our lives and were, in general, a vehicle of spiritual sustenance. The intuitive purpose of such creativity was neither the song for itself nor even the poem as bearer of witness—since without writing material this was hardly possible—but rather the process. For it was the process that helped to keep the spirit from dying. Often, this activity was accompanied by idealized tales of prewar life. Such reminiscences of the lost world, though painful, were also healing, for they immortalized and sanctified the past, exorcising, even if only for an hour, the specter of starvation or the terror of the chimney. Moving backward in time, and breaking through the wall of pain, memory strained toward the life-sustaining belief in a return of the lost world.

What is further memorable is that, although they did not happen every day, these times of creativity were the ones when the spirit of readiness to help each other was most apparent. Of course, not everyone was engaged in creativity—a fact that reflects normal life. Nor did creativity necessarily foster mutual help. But it helped to mobilize coping mechanisms of which mutual help was an important part. L. Eitinger, a psychiatrist and survivor, like Viktor Frankl, writes:

> The group of people who were able to mobilize the most adequate coping mechanisms were those who, for one reason or another, could retain their personality and system of values more or less intact even under conditions of nearly complete social anomy. Those who were most fortunate in this respect were the persons who . . . could both show and practice interest in others, who could retain their values inside the camp at the same level as outside the camp.[4]

These forms of spiritual resistance—mutual help, recalling the past, and recording the present for posterity—have been in the tradition of the Jewish response to two millennia of persecution.

This is not to suggest that the demonism that ruled the chaos of the ghettos and camps did not destroy prewar standards of conduct. Indeed, it did. Yet most of the people whom I knew—largely women, for concentration camps were gender-segregated—retained a strong enough trace, a vital enough spark, of essential humanity to allow for the belief that the agony would end, that families would ultimately reunite. If nothing else, this faith alone—not to mention invocations of the past and projections for the future— was frequently enough to exert control over behavior.

Testimony of survivors often makes emphatic the primacy of morale, of bonding, and of mutual support. And when this testimony bewails obliterated prewar ethical standards, when it decries moral disintegration, we must understand such charges in relative terms. To be sure, there was in all the ghettos and camps a category of debased, degraded, and dehumanized wretches who, among other things, voluntarily carried out atrocious tasks to curry some favor with the Germans—or so they may have hoped. Some of the Jewish police in the Warsaw ghetto come to mind. That in their despair they hoped thus to save both their own lives and those of their families hardly vindicates them.

There were also Jewish Kapos in the camps who did not hesitate to abuse Jewish prisoners. I lack the charity, I do not have the nobility of heart to make excuses for them. Neither did others. When we were transported to Skarzysko, an old-timer Kapo in that camp attacked a dazed man guilty of some infraction. Appalled by the savagery and forgetting her own terror, my mother showered the Kapo with bitter invectives, attempting to remind him that he and his victim were both Jews. The Kapo responded to these moral remonstrations with a shower of blows to my mother's head and face.

Apparently, the infamy of this man followed him to Buchenwald, where he was executed by members of the camp's underground. It seems that they made no excuses for him either. Nonetheless, I take no pleasure in this poor devil's fate, for there might have been less extreme means of punishment.

Although there were such contemptuous wretches as this Kapo, the fact is that they constituted a small minority and that most people, certainly those whom I knew both in the ghetto and in the concentration camps, never willingly or knowingly committed any atrocities. What some fail to see is that for every despicable opportunist there was often someone like my mother.

At rock bottom, even such prisoners as the *Sonderkommandos* were not, necessarily, dehumanized—though they were forced to herd their own people into the gas chambers where they, too, ultimately died. After all, the moral choices of the *Sonderkommandos* were reduced to zero. And as Shakespeare has Paulina declare in *The Winter's Tale*, "It is an heretic that makes the fire,/

Not she which burns in't." It is the bestial Nazis who made the fire of Auschwitz, not they who were forced to feed it and then burn in it.

That the conditions on this far side of evil were at best subhuman need not be repeated. Prisoners were brutalized, terrified, starved, covered with vermin and sores, rendered totally helpless, and more, but most were anything but dehumanized. For dehumanization, as I understand it, means to be divested, among other things, of such characteristically human qualities as empathy, pity, and the ability to perceive and to honor the sacredness of life. To be dehumanized is, moreover, a function of volition, at least a measure of it, perhaps also of self-perception—a form of "I am what I think I am."

That most of those whom I knew retained their basic humanity is born out by the fact that few, very few, Jews had enough murder in their hearts—though the impulse might have been justified, and the opportunities were ample—to pick up weapons and indiscriminately murder Germans after liberation. Nonetheless, some of these very Jews planned and staged armed revolts in such places, among others, as the Warsaw ghetto, Auschwitz, Sobibor, and Treblinka without the slightest hope of survival.

VI

The trailing and groping roots of my recollections come to rest, at this moment, on several events connected with the foregoing reflections. In Maidanek, a concentration camp as barbaric as Auschwitz, though considerably smaller, in place of lavatories there were barrels behind the barracks into which the women relieved themselves. Many of us consciously and deliberately subdued our sense of modesty in a world bereft of the last vestiges of civilization and made bestial not by us. We suspended shame, not because we were rendered less human, but rather because it was wise and practical to do so.

In Skarżysko, in the "hospital" mentioned above, there was a man who, I think, was dying of galloping consumption. I saw him only once, though I knew that he was there even after I saw him. He had no clothes. He rose from his bunk and tottered to relieve himself in the barrels that in this place—the lowest pit of both camp and "hospital"—were located near my bunk. I was frightened by the ghostly apparition of the naked man, a hairless shade with sunken cheeks, dark eyes wild with fever, and pasty gray skeletal limbs against which his genitals appeared startingly large and bluish. It was the first time I saw a naked man. We were both helpless in our communal and personal hells.

As a girl, I felt not only dread toward but also pity for this *Mussulman* (an appellation given to those who gave up). Perhaps he had the same sentiments for me, or perhaps he was too sick to take note of anyone. I doubt that he survived. I owe my survival to my mother's and sister's devotion and perhaps, in this case, no less importantly to the fact that I was relegated to this dark fissure of the "hospital" barrack, for, having been infected with typhus and covered with scabies and a form of infectious scalp-mange, I became an untouchable. In fact, the guards were afraid to venture into this crevice of the barrack lest they be exposed to disease when they were weeding out the Mussulmen for the mass grave behind the "hospital." As a woman, I know that the naked man and I were not less human because we were forced into this wretched camp and because the only choice available to us was to feel.

In the ammunition factory of Skarzysko, there worked a Polish woman, a devout Catholic, who lived in town. I, a slave, sat next to her at the workbench where we both sorted bullet shells. My appearance filled her with disgust. I can understand the reason. But that she spat at me and my Jewishness as I involuntarily shook lice out of my hair—I still had hair at the time—when the itch was intolerable and the scratching inevitable, shows, I believe, that the woman was more degraded than I. She gave me neither soap nor compassion, neither bread nor pity, only her hate. My sorry appearance was hardly a function of personal choice or personal uncleanliness. Sometimes I assured her of this and reminded her that before my camp incarnation I used to be very clean, and my mother, in fact, used to be fastidiously clean. I explained to her—actually she knew it well—that we had no bathing facilities and that the barracks were infested with lice and rats. Most of the time my response to her was silence.

I knew one young woman, the daugher of a rabbi (a fact I hesitate to add, for she may sound like a stock figure). Her baby was born into the cesspool of the camp latrine. Lovely Lilka, laid waste and reduced to skeletal transparency, ate lice while she was pregnant. Some of us thought her mad. She was not. She was pregnant and very hungry. But she never stole anyone's bread. Apparently her *Lagerschwester* understood Lilka, for she never abandoned her even if she found Lilka's behavior repugnant.

Like Lilka and her *Lagerschwester*, practically all the women I knew managed to bond with another woman or two. Yes, our manners coarsened: we quarreled and fought, swore and cursed, abandoned modesty and became rapacious. Yes, we lost our fastidiousness and squeamishness: some of us even ate lice, and most everyone else greedily gnawed stinking horse bones if we were fortunate enough to find pieces of them in the meager portion of watery soup that was doled out to us as we pushed and shoved on the exasperating soup lines. But that in this land of death and anguish there was no consistent pattern of savagery, not to mention murder, among the victims is a source of great wonder to me. One need only consider the moral chaos in our present world of privilege and plenty.

Once, in the cover of darkness a man stole into our barrack to make love to a woman who expected him. Worried about the corruption of her children's innocence in this darkest of moral pits, my mother excoriated the couple, charging them with bestiality. Intimacy like this, she admonished them, is disgraceful in the presence of young girls. Although this was the only such incident we witnessed, occasional love trysts did occur at great risk to the lovers, for men and women were deliberately segregated and housed in different parts of the camp. Although as a girl I was shocked by the immodest conduct of the lovers, as a woman I consider the event tolerable, in fact, understandable. It seems to me that the mutual consent under which the lovers in my barrack met might have been an attempt to recapture a modicum of normalcy, an expression of natural human impulses and perhaps even longing for love. This is especially significant, since, as we all knew in the barrack, the nocturnal visitor—even if he might have brought the woman a ration of bread—was not a Kapo. He, therefore, did not belong to the class of the camp's privileged whose libido was not entirely enfeebled by starvation and the general horror of this place.

If the couple in my barrack was rendered less human, think of Kinemann—a German national and second in command in Skarzysko—who, for entertainment, forced Jewish men and women to copulate. How these men and women did it or pretended to do it, I do not know. But I do know that I never heard of any male prisoners in Skarzysko and Czestochowa raping women (all the prisoners in these camps were Jews). Perhaps they did not have the energy or, more likely, they were morally sound enough not to indulge in such baseness. The only rapes I knew about involved guards and the notorious SS director of Skarzysko, Herr Bertenschlager, who forced the prettiest Jewish girls into the woods and completed his orgy by shooting them.

In all the fathomless misery of this antiworld, only a blanket of ours was stolen by another prisoner. The theft was a great loss, for a blanket often served as an outer garment. We had neither coats nor underwear. My sole wardrobe in Skarzysko was a huge flannel housecoat, the back of which was rendered stiff by the menses of a woman to whom this garment belonged possibly before she was killed. Thereafter, an empty sacking of a straw mattress I shared with my mother and sister became my "cape." Admittedly, the theft was a great shock, for the thief was a Jew, and we continued to hold the belief that a Jew should not do such a thing to another Jew. One could argue that this theft is an example of the dehumanization of the victims. Although as a girl I thought the thief was a beast, as a woman, I do not see it this way—possibly because after the Holocaust everything seems permissible.

VII

Perhaps, in the end, reality is a function of our thoughts, of memory, of who and where in history we are and the relative point from which we perceive it. Perhaps, also, specific states of consciousness shape reality, provoking it to implode those recollections that are most pertinent to it. Memory is also selective, even if we do not summon specific events for scrutiny, even if recollections insinuate themselves assaulting sweet moments of life and ravaging their tranquility. Perhaps, further, memory does not always remember the sharpness of certain details, for the edges have been dulled by time and pain. Yet, these very processes cause certain events to stand in sharp relief against the backdrop of fading details. And then, remembrances require diverse kinds of understanding. Some are immediately accessible to consciousness and easily interpreted. Others cannot be fathomed at all.

Obviously, the memories that inform these pages are only a handful, not meant to be a comprehensive history of my experiences in the Holocaust. My concern is specific, and my intent is to highlight those forms of "passive" resistance that buttressed our morale and helped us to survive relatively whole even if, as mentioned earlier, we will never be the same.

In the end, the corpus of poetry—the subject of this book—is, I believe, the most eloquent support of the argument I posit in this epilogue. Indeed, as a woman, worried about the moral chaos of the world in which I live, I marvel—perhaps even immodestly—at the resilience of people who, among other forms of spiritual resitance, wrote poetry in the shadow of gas chambers. Such expressions of opposition are as compelling as any others. Clearly, they are as deserving of remembrance as the destruction and the agony of Europe's Jews.

Notes

Introduction

1. Henryk Grynberg, "The Holocaust in Polish Literature," *Notre Dame English Journal*, vol. 11, no. 2 (April, 1979): 115.

2. See, for example, David G. Roskies, *Against the Apocalypse: Responses to Catastrophy in Modern Jewish Culture* (Cambridge, Massachusetts and London, England: Harvard University Press, 1984), as well as his *The Literature of Destruction: Jewish Response to Catastrophe* (Philadelphia, New York, Jerusalem: The Jewish Publication Society, 1989), and Yechiel Szeintuch, "Yiddish and Hebrew Literature under the Nazi Rule in Eastern Europe" (Yitzhak Katzenelson's Last Bilingual Writings and the Ghetto Writings of A. Sutzkever and Y. Spiegel), Ph. D. dissertation (Jerusalem: Hebrew University, 1978) [in Hebrew].

3. David G. Roskies, "The Holocaust According to the Literary Critics," *Prooftexts: A Journal of Jewish Literary History*, vol. 1, no. 2, (May, 1981): 209–16.

4. Janusz Korczak, *Ghetto Diary*, trans. Jerzy Barbach and Barbara Krzywicka (Vedder) (New York: Holocaust Library, 1979), pp. 113–14.

5. Czesław Miłosz, *The Witness of Poetry* (Cambridge, Massachusetts, and London, England: Harvard University Press, 1983), pp. 3–4.

6. David Roskies, "The Pogrom Poem and the Literature of Destruction," *Notre Dame English Journal*, vol. 11, no. 2 (April 1979): 90.

7. Noah Rosenbloom, "The Threnodist and the Threnody of the Holocaust," *The Song of the Murdered Jewish People*, trans. Noah Rosenbloom (Israel: Beit Lohamei Haghettaot, 1980), p. 121.

8. Abraham Sutzkever, "Unter Dayne Vayse Shtern" (Under Your White Stars), *Yiddishe Gas* (Jewish Street) (New York: Farlag Matones, 1948), p. 39. Translation my own.

9. Ibid.

10. Irving Howe and Eliezer Greenberg, Introduction, *A Treasury of Yiddish Poetry*, ed. Irving Howe and Eliezer Greenberg (New York: Schoken Books, 1976), p. 52.

11. Jacob Glatstein, "Without Jews," ibid., pp. 331–32.

12. Kadia Molodowsky, "God of Mercy," ibid., pp. 289–90.

13. Quoted in Sidra De Koven Ezrahi's, *By Words Alone: The Holocaust in Literature* (Chicago: University of Chicago Press, 1980), p. 138.

14. Ibid., p. 143.

15. Nelly Sachs, "O the Chimneys," *O the Chimneys*, trans. Michael Hamburger, Christopher Holme, Ruth and Matthew Mead, and Michael Roloff (New York: Farrar, Strauss and Giroux, 1974), p. 3.

16. Paul Celan, "There Was Earth in Them," *Speech Grille and Selected Poems*, trans. Joachim Neugrochel (New York: Dutton, 1971), p. 173.

17. Chaim Kaplan, *The Warsaw Diary of Chaim Kaplan*, trans. Abraham Katsh (New York: Colliers, 1976).

18. Ibid., p. 79.

19. Irving Howe and Eliezer Greenberg, *A Treasury of Yiddish Poetry*, p. 15.

20. Yechiel Sheintuch, "The Work of Yitzhak Katzenelson," *The Jerusalem Qarterly*, no. 26 (Winter 1983): 49.

21. Ibid.

22. Władysław Szlengel, "Okno na Tamtą Stronę" (Window Facing the Other Side), *Co czytałem umarł* (This I Read to the Dead), ed. Irena Maciejewska (Warsaw: Państwowy Instytut Wydawniczy, 1979), pp. 59–60. Further references to Szlengel's poems are in this anthology. Translations my own.

23. Ibid.

24. Shmerke Kaczerginski, "Bamerkungen fun Zamler" Introduction, *Lider fun Ghettos un Lagern* (Ghetto and Concentration Camp Songs), ed. Shmerke Kaczerginski (New York: Shoulson Press, 1948), p. xi. Translation my own.

25. See "Z Otchłani" (Out of the Abyss, Introduction) *Pieśń ujdzie cało: Antologia wierszy o Żydach pod okupacją niemiecką* (The Song Shall Pass Unscathed: an Anthology of Poetry About Jews Under the German Occupation), ed. and intro. Michał M. Borwicz (Warsaw: Centralna żydowska komisja historyczna w Polsoe, 1947; Ruta Sakowska, *Ludzie z dzielnicy zamkniętej* (People in a Walled in Community) (Warsaw: Państwowe Wydawńictwo Naukowe, 1975); Zivia Lubetkin, *In the Days of Destruction and Revolt* (Israel: Ghetto Fighters House, 1981).

26. Czesław Miłosz, *The History of Polish Literature* (London: Collier and Macmillan, 1969), p. 80.

27. Szlengel, *Co czytałem umarłym* (This I Read to the Dead).

Chapter One

1. Irena Maciejewska, "Introduction" in Władysław Szlengel, *Co czytałem umarłym*, p. 6. Translation my own.

2. See Chapter 7, "Laughing Off the Trauma of History," Roskies, *Against the Apcalypse*, pp. 163–95.

3. Szlengel, "Telefon" (Telephone), *Co Czytałem Umarłym*, p. 61.

4. Ibid., pp. 63–64.

5. Ernest Cassirer, *An Essay on Man* (New Haven: Yale University Press, 1965), p. 9.

6. Robert Lifton, *Death in Life: Survivors of Hiroshima* (New York: Random House, 1967), p. 509.

7. Itzhak Yanasowicz, *Abraham Sutzkever: Zayn Lid un Zayn Proze* (Abraham Sutzkever: His Poetry and His Prose) (Tel-Aviv: Israel Book, 1981), p. 66. Translation my own.

8. Roskies, *Against the Apocalypse*, p. 252.

9. Ibid., p. 253.

10. Abraham Sutzkever, "Di Ershte Nakht in Ghetto" (The First Night in the Ghetto), *Di Ershte Nakht in Ghetto* (Israel: Di Goldene Keyt, 1979), pp. 10–11. Translation my own.

11. Sidra Dekoven Ezrahi, *By Words Alone: The Holocaust in Literature* (Chicago: University of Chicago Press, 1980), p. 21.

12. By "dramatic irony" I mean that irony which resides in the contrast between an idea expressed at a specific time and the significance of it perceived later or by persons other than the writer.

13. Chaim Kaplan, *The Warsaw Diary of Chaim Kaplan*, trans. Abraham Katsh (New York: Colliers, 1976), p. 79.

14. Lifton, *Death in Life*, p. 481.

15. For a more comprehensive discussion of Shekhina see Sidra Dekoven Ezrahi, *By Words Alone*, p. 136.

16. Ruth Wisse, "Introduction: The Ghetto Poems of Abraham Sutzkever," *Burnt Pearls: Ghetto Poems*, trans. Seymour Mayne (Oakville, Ontorio: Mosaic Press/ Valey Edition, 1981), p. 11.

Chapter Two

1. See Chapter 2, "The Liturgy of Destruction" and Chapter 4, "the Pogrom as Poem" in Roskies' *Against the Apocalypse*.

2. Irena Maciejewska, Introduction, *Co czytałem umarłym*, p. 17.

3. Szlengel, *Co czyłatem umałym*, pp. 37–38.

4. Szlengel, "Rzeczy" (Things), pp. 125–27.

5. See Lucy Dawidowicz, *The War Against the Jews: 1939–1945* (New York: Bantam Books, 1975), p. 419.

6. Chaim Kaplan, "Journal of the Warsaw Ghetto," *Commentary* (November 1965), pp. 42–45.

7. See the sartorial digression in Jonathan Swift's *A Tale of a Tub*.

8. Szlengel, "Rzeczy," p. 127.

9. Ibid., p. 127.

10. See my discussion of "Kontratak" (Counterattack) in Part 3, Chapter 1 of this work.

11. Szlengel, "Rzeczy," p. 128.

12. Abraham Sutzkever, "A Vogn Shikh" (A Cartload of Shoes), *Lider Fun Yam Hamoves* (Songs from the Dead Sea) (Tel-Aviv: World Federation of Bergen Belsen Associations, 1968), p. 23. Translations my own.

13. Jozef Bau, "Szpital obozowy" (Camp Hospital), *Pieśń ujdzie cało,* pp. 56–57. Translations my own.

14. Dante, *Inferno,* ed. and trans. John D. Sinclair (New York: Oxford University Press, 1961), p. 363.

15. Bau, "Głód" (Hunger), *Pieśń ujdzie cało,* p. 57.

16. Abraham Sutzkever, "Kerndlekh Veyts" (Grains of Wheat), *Yiddishe Gas,* pp. 32–33.

Chapter Three

1. Henryk Grynberg, "The Holocaust in Polish Literature," *Notre Dame English Journal,* vol. 11, no. 2 (April 1979): 115.

2. Borwicz, "Introduction," *Pieśń ujdzie cało,* p. 31.

3. Chaim Kaplan, *The Warsaw Diary of Chaim Kaplan,* p. 79.

4. Miłosz, *The History of Polish Literature,* p. 402.

5. Ibid.

6. Julian Przyboś, "Jestem pracownikiem słowa" (I Am a Craftsman of Words), *Pieśń ujdzie cało,* pp. 34–35.

7. Miłosz, *The History of Polish Literature,* p. 403.

8. Abraham Sutzkever, "Gezang funa Yiddishn Dikhter in 1943" (Chant of a Jewish Poet in 1943), *Lider fun Yam Hamoves,* p. 79.

9. Martin Buber, *Tales of Hasidim: The Later Masters* (New York: Schocken Books, 1948), p. 55.

10. Borwicz, Introduction, *Pieśń ujdzie cało,* p. 25–26.

11. Szlengel, "Już czas" (It's High Time), pp. 129–30.

12. Byron Sherwin, "Wiesel's Midrash," *Confronting the Holocaust: The Impact of Elie Wiesel,* ed. Alvin Rosenfeld and Irving Greenberg (Bloomington: Indiana University Press, 1978), p. 125.

13. Yitzhak Katzenelson, *The Song of the Murdered Jewish People,* trans. Noah H. Rosenbloom (Israel: Ghetto Fighters' House, 1980), pp. 53–55.

14. Ibid., p. 68.

Chapter Four

1. Zivia Lubetkin, *In the Days of Destruction and Revolt*, trans. Ishai Tubbin (Israel: Ghetto Fighters' House, 1981), p. 62.

2. Lucy Dawidowicz, *The War against the Jews*, p. 351.

3. Borwicz, Introduction, *Pieśń ujdzie cało*, p. 14.

4. Roskies makes a similar point in *Against the Apocalypse*, pp. 185–89.

5. Dawidowicz, *The War Against the Jews*, p. 291.

6. Ibid.

7. Both my sister and I briefly studied French with a young teacher who found her way into our bunker. The bunker, built by my father, was intended for twelve persons, but actually sheltered about fifty, including a brigade of ghetto fighters.

8. Szlengel, *Co czytałem umarłym*, pp. 49–50.

9. Ibid., p. 38.

10. Miłosz, *The Witness of Poetry*, p. 85.

11. Irena Maciejewska, "Introduction," *Co czytałem umarłym*, p. 27.

12. Ibid., pp. 25–26.

13. Quoted by Maciejewska, ibid., p. 26.

14. Lucjan Dobroszycki, "The Untold Story of the Lodz Ghetto," *New York Times Magazine* (New York: July 29, 1984).

15. Szlengel, "Posłowie" (Postscript), pp. 51–52.

16. Wisse, *Burnt Pearls*, p. 13.

17. Northrop Frye, *Anatomy of Criticism* (Princeton: Princeton University Press, 1957), pp. 294–96.

18. Abraham Sutzkever, "Di Lererin Mire" (The Teacher Mire), *Lider fun Yam Hamoves*, pp. 68–70.

19. Yitskhok Rudashewski, *The Diary of the Vilna Ghetto*, trans. Percy Matenko (Israel: Ghetto Fighters' House, 1973), pp. 29–30.

20. Ibid., p. 33.

21. See Aristotle's *The Poetics*.

22. Wisse, *Burnt Pearls*, p. 14.

23. Yitzhak Katzenelson, *Song of the Murdered Jewish People*, p. 40.

24. Dov Noy, "The Model of the Yiddish Lullaby," *Studies in Yiddish Literature and Folklore* (Jerusalem: Hebrew University of Jerusalem, 1986), Monograph Series 7, pp. 203–35.

25. Ibid.

26. Isiah Spiegel, "Makh tsu di Eygelekh" (Close Your Precious Eyes), *Lider Fun Ghettos un Lagern*, p. 92.

27. Isiah Spiegel, "Nit Keyn Rozhinkes un nit Keyn Mandlen" (Neither Raisins nor Almonds), *Lider Fun Ghettos un Lagern*, p. 93.

28. Rumkowski and Moses Merin of Sosnowiec were about the only two communal leaders who willingly joined the Judenrat. Each man perceived himself as a monarch and acted like a dictator, trying, notheless, to save as many lives as possible.

29. See editorial comment in *Lider Fun Ghettos un Lagern*, p. 93.

30. Sh. Kaczerginski, "Shtiler, Shtiler . . . ," *Lider Fun Ghettos un Lagern*, pp. 88–89.

31. Ibid.

32. Ibid, p. xvi.

33. H. Leivick, "Dos Folk Zingt Eybik" (The folk sings eternally), *Lider fun Ghettos un Lagern*, p. xxxiii.

Chapter Five

1. Dawidowicz, *The War Against the Jews*, p. 353.

2. Emanuel Ringelblum, *Notitsn fun Varshever Ghetto* (Notes from the Warsaw Ghetto) (Warsaw: Farlag Yiddish Buch, 1963, vol. 2), pp. 189–93.

3. Sutzkever, "Shtim fun Harts" (The Heart's Voice), *Yiddishe Gas*, p. 18.

4. Wisse, *Burnt Pearls*, p. 16.

5. Sutzkever, "Tsum Yortog Fun Ghetto Teater" (To the Anniversary of the Ghetto Theater), *Lider fun Yom Hamoves*, pp. 39–40.

6. Chaim Nachman Bialik, "In the Slaughter Town," *The Golden Peacock: A World Treasury of Yiddish Poetry*, ed. and trans. Joseph Leftwich (New York: Thomas Yoseloff, 1961), p. 56.

7. Ibid., p. 57.

8. Hannah Arendt, *The Origins of Totalitarianism* (New York: Harcourt, Brace, and World, 1951), p. 137.

9. Alexander Donat, *The Holocaust Kingdom* (New York: Holocaust Library, 1963), p. 104.

10. Władysław Szlengel, "Kontratak" (Counterattack), p. 137–40.

11. Szlengel, "Co czytałem umarłym," p. 17.

12. Katzenelson, *The Song of the Murdered Jewish People*, p. 75.

Chapter Six

1. Shmerke Kaczerginski, "Partizaner Marsh" (March of the Partisans), in *Lider fun Ghettos un Lagern*, p. 345.

2. For a more detailed discussion, see Lester Eckman and Chaim Lazar, *The Jewish Resistance* (New York: Shengold Publishers, 1977), pp. 40–42.

3. Ibid.

4. Sutzkever, "Bagleytlid Baym Avekgeyn in Vald" (Song at the Departure to the Forest), *Lider fun Yam Hamoves*, p. 93.

5. Sutzkever, "Di Blayene Platn Fun Roms Drukeray" (The Lead Plates of the Rom Press), ibid., p, 94.

6. This writer escaped a pogrom staged by the AK in Działoszyce and in Chorzów in 1945.

7. Itzhak Zukerman, "The Creation and Development of ŻOB," *A Holocaust Reader*, ed. and intro., Lucy Dawidowicz (New York: Berhman House, 1976), pp. 359–80.

8. Ber Mark, *Uprising in the Warsaw Ghetto*, trans. Gershon Freidlin (New York: Schocken Books, 1975), p. 7.

9. Information furnished, among others, by Sol Aaron, a partisan in the Rudnicka forests.

10. Ibid.

11. Roskies, *Against the Apocalypse*, p. 250.

12. Ibid.

13. Zukerman, *A Holocaust Reader*, p. 379.

Chapter Seven

1. Jakob Apenszlak, "Słowo wstępne" (Introduction), in *Z otch⁄ lani: Poezja ghetta z podziemia żydowskiego w Polsce* (Out of the Abyss: Ghetto Poetry of the Jewish Underground in Poland) (New York: Association of Friends of our Tribune, 1945), p. 5. Translations my own.

2. Jozef Witlin, "Pokłon poetom ghetta" (To the Ghetto Poets), *Z otchłani*, p. 8.

3. Miłosz, *The History of Polish Literature*, p. 458.

4. Alexander Schenker, "Introduction," in Czesław Miłosz, *Utwory poetrycki* (Poetry) (Ann Arbor: Michigan Slavic Publications, 1976), p. xvii.

5. Witlin, *Z otchłani*, p. 10.

6. Miłosz, "Campo di Fiori," ibid., p. 23–24.

7. Miłosz, "Campo Dei Fiori," *Collected Poems* (New York: Ecco Press, 1973), pp. 33–35.

8. Mieczysław Jastruń, "Tu także jak w Jeruzalem" (Here too as in Jersualem), *Z Otchłani*, p. 14.

9. Miłosz, "Biedny Chrzescijanin patrzy na ghetto" (A poor Christian looks at the ghetto), *Utwory poetyckie*, p. 100.

10. Miłosz, "A Poor Christian Looks at the Ghetto," *The History of Polish Literature*, pp. 459–60.

11. Mircea Eliade, *Myths, Dreams, and Mysteries*, trans. Philip Mairet (New York: Harper & Row, 1960), p. 23.

12. Miłocz, *The History of Polish Literature*, p. 459.

13. Miłosz, *Captive Mind*, trans. Jane Zielenko (New York: Knopf, 1953), p. 41.

Epilogue

1. George Steiner, *Language and Silence: Essays on Language, Literature, and the Inhuman* (New York: Atheneum, 1967), p. 168.

2. Alvin Rosenfeld, *A Double Dying: Reflections on Holocaust Literature* (Bloomington: Indiana University Press, 1980), p. 53.

3. Janusz Korczak, the beloved pediatrician, pedagogue, and writer, notably of books which taught Jewish and Catholic children religious and other forms of tolerance, was director of one of the most renowned orphanages in the Warsaw ghetto, *Dom sierot* (Orphan's Home). When the Germans ordered the children of the orphanage to march to the *Umschlagplatz* for deportation to the gas chambers of Treblinka, Korczak was at the head of the procession. Although efforts were made to rescue him, he refused to leave the children and perished with them in the death center.

4. Eitinger, "On Being a Psychiatrist and a Survivor," *Confronting the Holocaust: The Impact of Elie Wiesel,* ed. Alvin Rosenfeld and Irving Greenberg (Bloomington: Indiana University Press, 1978), p. 196.

Selected Bibliography

Aaron, Frieda W. "Poems." *Centerpoint: A Journal of Interdisciplinary Studies*, vol. 4, no. 1 (Fall 1980): 79–84.

————. "Poetry in the Holocaust." *Perspectives on the Holocaust*. Ed. Randolph A. Braham. Boston, The Hague, London: Kluwer Nijhoff Publishing, 1983.

————. "Poetry and Ideology in Extremis: Ghetto and Concentration Camp Poetry." *Comparative Poetics: Proceedings of the Xth Congress of the International Comparative Literature Association*. Ed. Claudio Guillen and Peggy Asher. New York: Garland Publishing, 1985.

————. "Yet the Song Continued: Polish and Yiddish Poetry in the Ghettos and Concentration Camps." *Remembering for the Future: The Impact of the Holocaust on the Contemporary World*. Oxford, New York, Beijing, Frankfurt: Pergamon Press, 1988.

————. "Yiddish and Polish Poetry in the Ghettos and Camps." *Modern Language Studies*, vol. 19, no. 1 (Winter 1989): 72–87.

Alexander, Edward. *The Resonance of Dust: Essays on Holocaust Literature*. Columbus: Ohio State University Press, 1979.

Apenszlak, Jacob. "Słowo wstępne" (Introduction). *Z otchłani: Poezja ghetta i podziemia żydowskiego w Polsce* (Out of the Abyss: Ghetto Poetry from the Jewish Underground in Poland). New York: Association of Friends of our Tribune, 1945.

Arendt, Hannah. *The Origins of Totalitarianism*. New York: Harcourt, Brace, and World, 1951.

Auerback, Rokhl. *Varshaver Tsavoes* (Warsaw Testaments). Tel-Aviv: Yisroel-Buch, 1974.

Bau, Jozef. "Głód" (Hunger). In *Pieśń ujdzie cało: Antologia wierszy o Żydach pod okupacją niemecką* (The Song Will Continue Unscathed: an Anthology of Poetry About Jews Under the German Occupation). Edited with an introduction by Michał Borwicz. Warsaw: Centralna Żydowska komisja historyczna w Polsce, 1947, p. 56.

————. "Szpital obozowy" (Camp Hospital). In *Pieśń ujdzie cało*, pp. 56–57.

Bialik, Chaim Nachman. "In the Slaughter Town." *The Golden Peacock: A Worldwide Treasury of Yiddish Poetry*. Ed. and trans. Joseph Leftwich. New York: Thomas Yoseloff, 1961.

Blumental, Nakhman. *Shmuesn Vegn der Yiddisher Literatur Unter der Daytsher Okupatsye* (On Yiddish Literature Under the German Occupation). Buenos Aires: Union Central Isrealita Polaca en la Argentina, 1966.

————. *Verter un Vertlekh Fun der Khurbn-Tkufe* (Big and Little Words in the Holocaust). Tel-Aviv: I. L. Peretz Publishing House, 1981.

Borwicz, Michał, M. *Literatura w obozie* (Literature in the Concentration Camp). Kraków: Centralna Żydowska Komisja Historyczna, 1946.

————. "Introduction." In *Pieśń ujdzie cało*. pp. 10–50.

————. *Pieśń ginących: Z dziejów tworczości żydów pod hitlerowską okupacją* (Song of the Dying: Jewish Creativity Under the German Occupation). Kraków, Łódz, Warszawa: Centralna Żydowska Komisja Historyczna, 1947.

————. *Ruch podziemny w ghettach i obozach: materiały i dokumenty* (Underground Movements in the Ghettos and Concentration Camps: Materials and Documents). Warszawa, Lódz, Kraków: Centralna Żydowska Komisja Historyczna, 1946.

Bosmijian, Hamida. *Metaphors of Evil: Contemporary German Literature and the Shadow of Nazism*. Iowa City: University of Iowa Press, 1979.

Bryks, Rachmil. *Ghetto Factory 76*. Trans. Theodor Primack and Eugen Kullman. New York: Bloch Publishing Co., 1967.

Buber, Martin. *Tales of Hasidim: The Later Masters*. New York: Schocken Books, 1948.

Camus, Albert. *The Rebel: An Essay on Man in Revolt*. Trans. Anthony Bower. New York: Knopf, 1957.

Cassirer, Ernest. *An Essay on Man.* New Haven: Yale University Press, 1965.

Celan, Paul. *Selected Poems.* Trans. Michael Hamburger and Christopher Middleton. Harmondsworth: Penguin, 1972.

————. *Speech-Grille and Selected Poems.* Trans. Joachim Neogrochel. New York: Dutton, 1971.

Czerniakow, Adam. *The Warsaw Diary of Adam Czerniakow: Prelude to Doom.* Ed. Raul Hilberg, Stanislaw Staron, and Jozef Kermish. Trans. Stanislaw Staron et al. New York: Stein and Day, 1979.

Dante. *Inferno.* Ed. and trans. John D. Sinclair. New York: Oxford University Press, 1961.

Dawidowicz, Lucy. *The War against the Jews: 1939–1945.* New York: Bantam Books, 1976.

————. *A Holocaust Reader.* New York: Behrman House, 1976.

Des Pres, Terrence. "The Dreaming Back." *Centerpoint,* vol. 4 (Fall, 1980): 13–18.

————. *The Survivor: An Anatomy of Life in the Death Camps.* New York: Oxford University Press, 1976.

Dobroszycki, Lucjan. *The Chronicle of the Lodz Ghetto.* Trans. Richard Lourie et al. New Haven and London: Yale University Press, 1984.

————. "The Untold Story of the Lodz Ghetto." *New York Times Magazine,* July 29, 1984.

Donat, Alexander. *The Holocaust Kingdom.* New York: Holocaust Library, 1963.

Edelman, Marek. *Getto Walczy* (The Ghetto Fights Back). Warsaw: Bund, 1945.

Eitinger, L. "On Being a Psychiatrist and a Survivor." *Confronting the Holocaust: The Impact of Elie Wiesel.* Ed. Alvin Rosenfeld and Irving Greenberg. Bloomington: Indiana University Press, 1978.

Eliade, Mircea. *Myths, Dream, and Mysteries.* Trans. Philip Mairet. New York: Harper & Row, 1960.

Fackenheim, Emil. *The Jewish Return to History: Reflections on the Age of Auschwitz and a New Jerusalem.* New York: Schocken Books, 1978.

Fickowski, Jerzy. *Odczytanie Popiołów: Wiersze* (A Reading of Ashes: Poems) London: Association of Jews of Polish Origin in Great Britain, 1979.

——— . *A Reading of Ashes.* Trans. Keith Bosley and Krystyna Wandycz. London: Menard Press, 1981.

Fine, Ellen S. "The Act of Listening." *Midstream.* August/September 1981, pp. 54–57.

——— . "The Journey Homeward: The Theme of the Town in the Works of Elie Wiesel." In *Responses to Elie Wiesel.* Edit. Harry James Cargas, pp. 231–58. New York: Persea Books, 1978.

——— . *Legacy of Night: The Literary Universe of Elie Wiesel.* Albany: State University of New York Press, 1982.

——— . "Literature as Resistance: Survival in the Camps." *Holocaust and Genocide Studies*, vol. 1 (1986): 79–89.

Friedlander, Albert H. Edit. *Out of the Whirlwind: A Reader of Holocaust Literature.* New York: Union of American Hebrew Congregations, 1968.

Fry, Northrop. *Anatomy of Criticism.* Princeton: Princeton University Press, 1957.

Fussel, Paul. *The Great War in Modern Memory.* New York: Oxford University Press, 1975.

Gelbard, Izabela (Czajka). *Pieśni załabne getta* (Ghetto Dirges). Katowice: Julian Wyderka, 1946.

Glatstein, Jacob. *Poems.* Trans. Etta Blum. Tel-Aviv: I. L. Peretz Publishing House, 1970.

——— . *The Selected Poems of Jacob Glatstein.* Trans. Ruth Whitman. New York: October House, 1972.

——— . "Without Jews." Trans. Nathan Halpern. In *A Treasury of Yiddish Poetry.* Ed. Irving Howe and Eliezer Greenberg. New York: Schocken Books, 1976.

Glatstein, Jacob; Knox, Israel; Margoshes, Samuel, ed. *Anthology of Holocaust Literature.* New York: Atheneum, 1973.

Glik, Hirsh. *Lider un Poemes* (Songs and Poems). Ed. Nachman Mayzel. New York: YIKUF, 1953.

Grynberg, Henryk. "The Holocaust in Polish Literature." *Notre Dame English Journal*, vol. 11, no. 2 (April 1979).

Gurdus, Luba Krugman. *Painful Echos . . . : Poems of the Holocaust from the Diary of Luba Krugman Gurdus.* Illustrated, bilingual edition. New York: Holocaust Library, 1985.

Halperin, Irving. *Messengers from the Dead: Literature of the Holocaust.* Philadelphia: Westminster Press, 1970.

Hołuj, Tadeusz. *Wiersze obozowe* (Concentration Camp Poetry) Lodz: Spółdzielna wydawnicza—książka, 1946.

Howe, Irving. *The Critical Point: On Literature and Culture.* New York: Horizon, 1973.

Howe, Irving, and Greenberg, Eliezer. *A Treasury of Yiddish Poetry.* New York: Schocken Books, 1976.

Jastruń, Mieczysław. "Pogrzeb" (Funeral). In *Z Otchłani: Poezje ghetta z podziemia Żydowskiego w Polsce* (Out of the Abyss: Ghetto Poetry of the Jewish Underground in Poland). New York: Association of Friends of our Tribune, 1945.

———. "Tu takzé jak w Jeruzalem" (Here too as in Jerusalem). In *Z Otchłani.*

Kaczerginski, Shmerke. *Ikh Bin Geven a Partisan: di Grine Legende* (I Was a Partisan: the green legend). Buenos Aires: Muskat y Zaslavski, 1952.

———. "Introduction." *Lider Fun Ghettos un Lagern.* Ed. Shmerke Kaczerginski and H. Leivick. New York: Shoulson Press, 1948.

———. "Partizaner Marsh" (March of the Partisans). *Lider Fun Ghettos un Lagern.*

———. "Shtiler . . . Shtiler" (Hush, Hush). *Lider fun Ghettos un Lagern.*

Kaplan, Chaim. "Journal of the Warsaw Ghetto." In *Commentary*, November 1965.

———. *The Warsaw Diary of Chaim Kaplan.* Trans. Abraham Katsh. New York: Colliers, 1976.

Karmel, Henryka and Ilona. *Wiersze wybrane* (Selected Poems). Stockholm, 1947.

Katzenelson, Yitzhak. *Dos Lid Funem Oysgehargetn Yiddishn Folk* (The Song of the Murdered Jewish People). New York: YKUF, 1948.

———. *The Song of the Murdered Jewish People.* Trans. and annot. Noah H. Rosenbloom. Israel: Beit Lohamei Haghettaot-Ghetto Fighters' House, 1980.

————. *Vitell Diary.* Trans. Myer Cohen. Israel: Ghetto Fighters' House, 1972.

————. *Yiddishe Ghetto Ksovim fun Varshe, 1940–1943* (Yiddish Ghetto Writings from Warsaw, 1940–1943). Ed. Yechiel Szeintuch. Israel: Beit Lohamei Hagettaot and Kibbutz Hameuchad Publishing House, 1984.

Kermish, Joseph, ed. *To Live With Honor and Die with Honor: Selected Documents from the Warsaw Ghetto Underground Archives "O.S.".* (Oneg Shabbath). Jerusalem: Yad Vashem, 1986.

Korczak, Janusz. *Ghetto Diary.* Trans. Jerzy Barbach and Barbara Krzywicka. New York: Holocaust Library, 1979.

Kovner, Abba. *A Canopy in the Desert: Selected Poems by Abba Kovner.* Ed. Shirley Kaufman with Ruth Adler and Nurit Orchan. Pittsburgh: University of Pittsburgh Press, 1973.

Kovner, Abba, and Nelly Sachs. *Selected Poems: Abba Kovner and Nelly Sachs.* Intro. Stephen Spender. Harmondsworth: Penguin, 1971.

Kruk, Herman. "Diary of the Vilna Ghetto." *YIVO Annual,* 13 (1958): 9–78.

————. *Togbukh Fun Vilner Ghetto* (Diary of the Vilna Ghetto). Ed. Mordecai Bernstein. New York: YIVO, 1961.

Lam, Andrzej, ed. *Ze Struny na Strunę: Wiersze poetów Polski odrodzonej* (From Chord to Chord: poems of Poland Regenerated). Krakow: Wydawnictwo Literackie, 1980.

Langer, Lawrence, L. *The Holocaust and the Literary Imagination.* New Haven: Yale University Press, 1975.

Lazar, Chaim. *Muranowska 7: The Warsaw Ghetto Rising.* Trans. Yosef Shachter. Tel-Aviv: Massada, P.E.C. Press Ltd., 1966.

Leftwich, Joseph, ed. *The Golden Peacock: A Worldwide Treasury of Yiddish Poetry.* New York: Thomas Yoseloff, 1969.

————, ed. and trans. "Song of the Death Camps—A Selection with Commentary." *Commentary,* 12 (1951): 269–74.

Levi, Primo. *The Drowned and the Saved.* Trans. Raymond Rosenthal. New York: Summit Books, 1987.

————. *Shema: Collected Poems of Primo Levi.* Trans. Ruth Feldman and Brian Swann. London: Menard Press, 1976.

————. *Survival in Auschwitz*. Trans. Stuart Woolf. New York: Collier Macmillan Publishers, 1959.

Lifton, Robert. *Death in Life: Survivors of Hiroshima*. New York: Random House, 1967.

Lubetkin, Zivia. *In the Days of Destruction and Revolt*. Trans. Ishai Tubbin. Israel: Beit Lohamei Hagettaot, 1981.

Maciejewska, Irena. "Introduction." In Władysław Szlengel, *Co czytałem umarłym: Wiersze ghetta warszawskiego* (This I Read to the Dead: Poetry in the Warsaw Ghetto). Ed. Irena Maciejewska. Warsaw: Państwowy institut wydawniczy, 1979.

————. "Poezja polska wobec powstania w gecie warszawskim" (Polish Poetry About the Uprising in the Warsaw Ghetto). Paper presented at the University of Warsaw in April 1988, commemorating the 45th Anniversary of the Warsaw ghetto uprising.

Mark, Ber. *Di Umgekumene Shrayber Fun di Ghettos un Lagern un Zayere Verk* (The Perished Writers of the Ghettos and Camps and their Work). Warsaw: Yiddish Bukh, 1954.

————. *Uprising in the Warsaw Ghetto*. Trans. Gershon Freidlin. New York: Schocken Books, 1975.

————, ed. *Tsvishn Lebn un Toyt* (Between Life and Death). Warsaw: Yiddish-buch, 1955.

Miłosz, Czesław. "Campo Dei Fiori." *Collected Poems*. New York: Ecco Press, 1973.

————. "Campo Di Fiori." *Z Otchłani* (Out of the Abyss).

————. *Captive Mind*. Trans. Jane Zielenko. New York: Knopf, 1953.

————. *The History of Polish Literature*. London: Macmillan Company, 1969.

————. *Utwory poetyckie* (Poems). Ann Arbor: Michigan Slavic Publications, 1976.

————. *The Witness of Poetry*. Cambridge: Harvard University Press, 1983.

Mintz, Alan. *Hurban: Responses to Catastrophe in Hebrew Literature*. New York: Columbia University Press, 1984.

Molodowsky, Kadia. "God of Mercy." Trans. Irving Howe. In *A Treasury of Yiddish Poetry*. New York: Schocken Books, 1976.

————. *Lider fun Khurbn* (Songs from the Ruins). Tel-Aviv: I. L. Peretz, 1962.

Noversztern, Abraham. *Abraham Sutzkever Bibliografye* (Abraham Stuzkever Bibliography). Tel-Aviv: Israel-Book, 1976.

Noy, Dov. "The Model of the Yiddish Lullaby." *Studies in Yiddish Literature and Folklore.* Research Projects of YIVO, the Institute for Jewish Studies. Monograph Series 7. Jerusalem: Hebrew University, 1986.

Pagis, Dan. *Points of Departure.* Trans. Stephen Michael. Philadelphia: Jewish Publication Society, 1981.

Przyboś, Julian. "Jestem pracownikiem słowa" (I Am a Craftsman of Words). In *Pieśń ujdzie cało* (The Word Will Continue Unscathed).

Ringelblum, Emanuel. *Notitsn Fun Varshever Ghetto* (Notes from the Warsaw Ghetto). Warsaw: Yiddish-buch Verlag, 1963. pp. 189–93.

Rosenbloom, Noah. "The Threnodist and the Threnody of the Holocaust." In Yitzhak Katzenelson. *The Song of the Murdered Jewish People.* Israel: Beit Lohamei Hagetaot; Hakibbutz Hameuchad Publishing House, 1980.

Rosenfeld, Alvin. *A Double Dying: Reflections on Holocaust Literature.* Bloomington: Indiana University Press, 1980.

Roskies, David, G. *Against the Apocalypse: Responses to Catastrophe in Modern Jewish Literature.* Cambridge, Mass., and London, England: Harvard University Press, 1984.

————. "The Holocaust According to the Literary Critics." *Prooftexts,* 1 (May 1981): 209–16.

————. *The Literature of Destruction: Jewish Responses to Catastrophe.* Philadelphia, New York, Jerusalem: The Jewish Publication Society: 5748/1988.

————. "The Pogrom Poem and the Literature of Destruction." *Notre Dame English Journal,* vol. 11, no. 2, 1979.

————. "Yiddish Writing in the Nazi Ghettos and the Art of the Incommensurate." *Modern Language Studies,* vol. 16, no. 1 (Winter 1986): 29–36.

————. *Night Words: A Midrash on the Holocaust.* Washington, D.C.: B'nai Brith Hillel Foundation, 1971.

Różewicz, Tadeusz. *The Survivor and Other Poems.* Trans. Magnus J. Krynski and Robert McGuire. Princeton: Princeton University Press, 1976.

Rubinowicz, David. *The Diary of David Rubinowicz.* Trans. Derek Bowman. Washington: Creative Options, 1982.

Rudashewski, Yitzhok. *The Diary of the Vilna Ghetto.* Trans. Percy Matenko. Israel: Ghetto Fighters' House, 1973.

Rudnicki, Adolf. *Ascent to Heaven.* Trans. H. C. Stevens. London: Dennis Dobson, 1951.

——— . *Żywe i martwe morze* (The Living and the Dead Sea). Warsaw: S. W. Czytelnik, 1956.

——— , ed. *Lest We Forget.* Warsaw: Polonia Foreign Language Publishing House, 1955.

Sachs, Nelly. *O the Chimneys.* Trans. Michael Hamburger et al. New York: Farrar, Straus and Giroux, 1974.

Schenker, Alexander, M. "Introduction." In Czesław Miłosz, *Utwory poetyckie,* Ann Arbor: Michigan Slavic Publications, 1976.

Senesh, Hanna. *Hanna Senesh: Her Life and Diary.* Trans. Martha Kohn. New York: Schocken Books, 1973.

Shayevitsch, Sh. *Lekh-Lekho* (Go You Forth). Ed. Nachman Blumental. Łódz: Centralna Żydowska Komisja Historyczna, 1946.

Sherwin, Byron L., "Wiesel's Midrash: The Writings of Elie Wiesel and their Relationship to Jewish Tradition." Ed. Alvin Rosenfeld and Irving Greenberg, *Confronting the Holocaust: The Impact of Elie Wiesel.* Bloomington and London: Indiana University Press, 1979.

Spiegel, Isaiah. *Shtern Laykhtn in Tom* (Stars Light in the Abyss: Stories Written in the Ghetto). 2 vols. Tel-Aviv: Israel-Book, 1976.

——— . *Tsvishn Tov un Alef: Gezamelte Lider* (Between Z and A: Selected Poems). Tel-Aviv: Yiddish Bukh, 1978.

Steiner, George. *In Bluebeard's Castle: Some Notes Towards the Redefinition of Culture.* New Haven: Yale University Press, 1971.

——— . *Language and Silence: Essays on Language, Literature and the Inhuman.* New York: Atheneum, 1967.

Sutzkever, Abraham. *Burnt Pearls: Ghetto Poems.* Trans. Seymour Mayne. Introd. Ruth Wisse. Oakville, Ontario: Mosaic Press/Valley Editions, 1981.

——— . "Di Ershte Nakht in Ghetto" (The First Night in the Ghetto), *Di Ershte Nakht in Ghetto.* Israel: Di Goldene Keyt, 1979.

———. *Fun Vilner Ghetto.* Moscow: Emes, 1946.

———. *Geheymshtot* (Secret Town). Tel-Aviv: Ahdot, 1948.

———. *Lider fun Yam Hamoves* (Songs from the Dead Sea). Tel Aviv: World Federation of Bergen-Belsen Associations, 1968.

———. Poetishe Verk (Poetic Works). 2 vols. Tel-Aviv, 1963.

———. *Yiddishe Gas* (Jewish Street). New York: Ferlag Matones, 1948.

Szeintuch, Yechiel. "The Corpus of Yiddish and Hebrew Literature from Ghettos and Concentration Camps and its Relevance for Holocaust Studies." *Studies in Yiddish Literature and Folklore.* Research Project of YIVO, the Institute of Jewish Studies. Monograph 7: 186–207. Jerusalem: Hebrew University of Jerusalem, 1986.

———. "The Work of Yitzhak Katzenelson." *Jerusalem Quarterly*, no. 26 (Winter 1983).

———, ed. and intro. Yitzhak Katzenelson, *Yiddishe Ghetto Ksovim* (Yiddish Ghetto Writing). Israel: Ghetto Fighters House and Kibbutz Hameuchad, 1984.

Szlengel, Władysław. *Co czytałem umarłym* (This I Read to the Dead). Ed. Irena Maciejewska. Warsaw: Państwowy Instytut Wydawniczy, 1977.

Waxman, Meyer. *A History of Jewish Literature.* 5 vols. New York: Thomas Yoseloff, 1960.

Weliczker, Leo. *Brygada śmierci: pamietnik* (The Death Brigade: A Diary) Lodz: Centralna Żydowska Komisja Historyczna w Polsce, 1946.

Wells, Leon Weliczker. *The Death Brigade: The Janowska Road.* New York: Holocaust Library, 1978.

Whitman, Ruth, Ed. and Trans. *An Anthology of Modern Jewish Poetry.* New York: October House, 1966.

Wiesel, Elie. *Ani Maamin: A Song Lost and Foud Again.* Trans. Marion Wiesel. New York: Random House, 1973.

———. *A Jew Today.* Trans. Marion Wiesel. New York: Vintage Books, 1979.

———. *Legends of Our Time.* New York: Avon, 1968.

———. *One Generation After.* Trans. Lily Edelman and the author. London: Weidenfeld and Nicolson, 1970.

Wisse, Ruth. "The Ghetto Poems of Abraham Sutzkever." In *The Jewish Book Annual.* New York: Jewish Book Council, 1979.

―――. "Introduction: The Ghetto Poems of Abraham Sutzkever." In Abraham Sutzkever, *Burnt Pearls.* Trans. Seymour Mayne. Oakville, Ontario, Canada: Mosaic Press/Valley Edition, 1981.

Witlin, Jozef. "Pokłon poetom ghetta" (Greetings to the Ghetto Poets). *Z otchłani* (Out of the Abyss). New York: Association of Friends of our Tribune, 1945.

Wyshogrod, Michael. "Some Theological Reflections on the Holocaust." *Response,* 25 (Spring 1978).

Yanasowicz, Itzhak. *Abraham Sutzkever: Zayn Lid un Zayn Proze* (Abraham Sutzkever: His Verse and His Prose). Tel-Aviv: Israel Book, 1981.

Young, James E. "Interpreting Literary Testimony: A Preface to Rereading Holocaust Diaries and Memoirs." *New Literary History,* 18 (Winter 1987): 339–46.

―――. "Memory and Monument." *Bitburg in Moral and Political Perspective,* ed. Geoffrey Hartman, pp. 103–13. Bloomington: Indiana University Press, 1986.

―――. *Writing and Rewriting the Holocaust: Narrative and the Consequence of Interpretation.* Bloomington and Indianapolis: Indiana University Press, 1988.

Zuckerman, Itzhak. "The Creation and Development of Ż.O.B." *A Holocaust Reader.* Ed. Lucy Dawidowicz. New York: Berhman House, 1976.

Index

A

Aesthetics, 2, 29, 39, 99, 103
Acmeists, 152
Aktion, 47, 48, 103, 155
Anti-Fascist Block (Warsaw ghetto), 145
Anti-Semitism, 168
Apenszlak, Jakob, 173
A.R. (revolutionary artists), 73
Arendt, Hannah, 146
Armja Krajowa (A.K.; Home Army), 134, 162, 168
Armja Ludowa (A.L.; People's Army), 168
Art songs, 120
Aryan(s), 51, 57, 71, 175, 186
Auschwitz concentration camp, 145
Auto-da-fe, 143
Avant-Guard (theater; Lodz ghetto), 12

B

Baal Shem Tov, 9
Ballads, 57, 111
Bau, Józef
 "Camp Hospital" (*Szpital obo-zowy*) by, 58–64
 "Hunger" (*Głód*) by, 64–65
Bertenschlager, 210
Beygelson, Dov, 125
Bialik, Chaim Nachman, 27–28, 83
 influence on Sutzkever, 27, 144
 "In the City of Slaughter" by, 144–45
Białoszewski, Miron, 102
Biblical references in poetry
 Katzenelson's, 5–6
 Sutzkever's, 136, 141
Books, in Warsaw ghetto, 96
Borowski, Tadeusz, 102
Borwich, Michał, 13, 71–72, 83, 96
Broyde, Kasriel, 10
Bruno, Giordano, 181–82, 184
Buber, Martin, 82
Buchenwald concentration camp, 63*illus.*, 65*illus.*, 206

C

Cassirer, Ernest, 26
Catastrophists, 21
Causality, 50
Celan, Paul, 7, 8
CENTOS (organization in Warsaw ghetto), 100

Children
  Lullabies for, 119–30
  in Sutzkever's "The Teacher
    Mire," 106–117
Children's theater (in Warsaw
  ghetto), 201
Christianity, 182, 186–87
Częstochowa concentration camp,
  191, 204, 209
Czerniakow, Adam, 40

D

Dante, 34, 61
Dawidowicz Lucy, 96, 99, 133
Death imprint, 34
Dehumanization process, 154, 206,
  207
Deportations, 48, 145
  of children, 122
Despair, 104
Diaspora, 169–70
  in Sutzkever's poetry, 137–142
  in Szlengel's poetry, 50
Disaster complex, 28
Documentary poems, 14, 19, 21,
  40, 56
Donat, Alexander, 146, 153, 157
DP camps, 191, 199
DROR (Freedom; organization in
  Warsaw ghetto), 12, 95

E

Edelman, Marek, 157
Einkesselung (encircling; in War-
  saw ghetto), 47–48
Eiron, 154
Eitinger, L., 205
Eldorado (theater; in Warsaw
  ghetto), 12
Eliade, Mircea, 186
Ember image, 32, 39, 40
Enlightenment, 3

Ezrahi, Sidra DeKoven, 32–33

F

Fackenheim, Emil, 90
Famina (theater; Warsaw ghetto),
  12
Folk songs, 120
Frye, Northrop, 106

G

Gentile Polish poets
  Miłosz, Czesław, 174–79, 181–88
  Przyboś, Julian, 73–77
Ghetto lexicon and colloquialisms,
  39, 56
Glatstein, Jacob, 7, 90
Glik, Hirsh, 11
God, 6–7
  and the crisis of faith, 6–7,
    86–93
  German self-divinization, 155
  indifference of, 84
  in poets, 80–81
  in Sutzkever's "Chant of a Jew-
    ish Poet in 1943," 78–83
  in Sutzkever's, "The Heart's
    Voice," 135–37
  in Szlengel's "Counterattack,"
    156
  in Szlengel's "It's High Time,"
    86–93
Great Chain of Being, 39, 56, 153
Greenberg, Eliezer, 6
Gross-Rosen concentration camp,
  58
Grotesque, the
  in Bau's poetry, 62
  in Sutzkever's poetry, 34, 57,
    110, 114
  in Szlengel's poetry, 21, 49, 51, 92
Grynberg, Henryk, 1
Gurdus, Luba Krugman, 189

H

Halpern, Moyshe Leyb, 28
Hangings, 198
Hanukkah, 170
Hasidic(ism), 7–8, 87, 104
Haskalah, 3
Hitler, Adolf, 146
Home Army (AK; Armja Krajowa),
   162, 168
Howe, Irving, 6

I

Introspectivists (In Zich; poetic
   movement), 4
Irony, 2, 23, 98,
   in Jastruń's poetry, 182
   in Miłosz's poetry, 184
   in Sutzkever's poetry, 33–34,
     110, 113, 165
   in Szlengel's poetry, 21, 24, 50,
     56, 104, 105, 152, 155

J

Jastruń, Mieczysław, 5, 173
   "Here Too as in Jerusalem" (Tu
     także jak w Jerusalem), by
     174, 179–84
Jeremiah, 6, 8
Jerusalem (ancient), 5, 170, 182
Jewish Combat Forces (ŻOB; Ży-
   dowska organizacja bojowa),
   145, 168, 171
Jewish unity, 143
Job, 8
Judah (son of Jacob), 136, 141
Judah Maccabee, 170
Judenrat in Warsaw ghetto,
   40, 48

K

Kaczerginski, Shmerke, 5, 12, 83
   "Hush, Hush" ("Shtiler, Shtiler")
     by, 125–130
   "March of the Partisans" ("Par-
     tizaner Marsh") by, 159–62
Kafka, Franz, 186
Kaplan, Chaim
   The Warsaw Diary of Chaim
     Kaplan by, 9, 33–34, 50, 72
Kapo 59, 62, 197, 206, 209
Katzenelson, Itzhak, 5–6
   By the Waters of Babylon by, 5
   drama studio in Warsaw ghetto
     directed by, 12
   on existence of God, 93
   resistance in poetry of, 10–11
   The Song of the Murdered Jew-
     ish People by, 89, 119, 131,
     156–157
Khaliastre, Di ("The Gang"; liter-
   ary movement), 4
Kiddush ha-Hayym, 81
Kiddush ha-Shem, 137
Kinemann, 209
Kishinev pogrom, 144
Kleyner Shtot Zal, Der ("Small
   City Theater"; in Vilna Ghetto),
   12
Klimov, Major General, 162
Komplety (secret private schools in
   Warsaw ghetto), 100, 200, 201
Korczak, Janusz, 40, 192
   Ghetto Diary by, 2
Kott, Jan, 173
Kramsztyk, Roman, 46 illus.

L

Lagerschwester, 209
Lechoń, Jan, 23
Leivick, H., 127
Lekert, Hirsh, 117

Lifton, Robert, 26–27, 34
Linke, B., 91*illus.*
Lodz ghetto, 69
  Yiddish theater in, 12
Lubetkin Zivia, 95, 133, 157
Lullabies, 119–190
  Spiegel's, 120–130
  Kaczerginski's, 125–130

M

Maccabees, 163, 165, 170
Maciejewska, Irena, 20, 40, 102
Maidanek concentration camp,
  182, 193–98, 207–8
Maimonides, 88
Mark, Ber, 168
Martyrdom, 36, 40, 143
  Sutzkever on resistance to,
  136–37
Marxism, 161
Melody Palace (theater; Warsaw
  ghetto), 12
Midrash, 90, 92, 169
Miłosz, Czesław, 3, 13, 73, 76,
  102, 173
  Captive Mind by, 187
  "Campo dei Fiori" by, 174–79
  "Campo di Fiori" by, 181–84
  "A Poor Christian Looks at the
    Ghetto" by, 184–88
  Salvation (Ocalenie), by 184
Molodowsky, Kadia, 7
Music
  lullabies, 119–30
  poems set to, 11–12
  songs, 98–99
Mussulmen, 60, 62, 208

N

Naming process, 141
Na Piętrku (The Second Floor;
  theater; Warsaw ghetto), 12

Narotch forest, 27, 143, 145
National Jewish Committee (*Ży-
  dowski komitet narodowy*), 175
New Azazel (Nowy Azazel) (the-
  ater; Warsaw ghetto), 12
Noy, Dov, 119

O

Oberska, Irena, 201
Olomucki, Halina, 202*illus.*
Oneg Shabbat, (Joys of the Sab-
  bath; secret archives; Warsaw
  ghetto), 96
*Out of the Abyss (Z otchłani;
  Apenszlak, editor)*, 173, 175

P

Pacifism, 137, 190
Parody, 21, 23
  in Szlengel, 92, 104
Particularism, 162
People's Army (AL; *Armja
  Ludowa*), 168
Partisans, 134
  Kaczerginski's poem to, 159–62
  in Sutzkever's "Song at the De-
    parture to the Forest," 162–165
Peretz, I. L., 83, 117
Pharmaki, 154
Pieck, Henri, 63, *illus.*, 65
Płaszów concentration camp, 65
Poetry
  banality, jocularity, nostalgia in,
    10, 11, 21
  as a call to armed resistance
    in Kaczerginski's "March of
      the Partisans," 159–62
    in Sutzkever's "To the Anni-
      versary of the Ghetto The-
      ater," 141–44
    in Sutzkever's "The Heart's
      Voice," 135–37

in Sutzkever's "The Lead
Plates of the Rom Press,"
165–171
in Sutzkever's "Song at the
Departure to the Forest,"
162–65
in Szlengel's "Counterattack,"
146–57
as communal participation, 106
as consolation and solace, 125,
129
as documentary, 14, 19, 21, 40, 56
of fact, 102, 106
as lamentation, 5, 32, 35, 125
minimilism in, 13, 102
modernist trends in, 13, 19
as moral (spiritual) opposition,
10, 14, 27, 71, 95, 98, 104, 205
in Sutzkever's "Chant of a
Jewish Poet in 1943," 78–83,
in Sutzkever's "The Heart's
Voice," 135–37
in Sutzkever's "The First
Night in Ghetto," 27
in Sutzkever's "Teacher Mire,"
106–117
satiric, the, in 10
as narrative, 111
oral (in concentration camps), 12
of street singers, 96–98
surreal, the, in 35, 57
as testimony, 2, 14, 19, 58, 96
in Warsaw ghetto, 95–96
see also Polish poetry; political
poetry; Yiddish poetry
Pogroms, 28, 144, 191
Polish poetry
folk tradition, 71
gentile, 73–77
underground organizations and,
133
in Warsaw ghetto, 95–96
Political and resistance poetry,
133–34
Kaczerginski's "March of the
Partisans," 159–62

by Miłosz and Jastruń, 174–88
Sutzkever's "To the Anniversary
of the Ghetto Theater," 138–44
Sutzkever's "The Heart's Voice,"
135–37
Sutzkever's "The Lead Plates of
the Rom Press," 165–71
Sutzkever's "Song at the Depar-
ture to the Forest," 162–65
Szlengel's "Counterattack,"
146–57
Ponary, 126, 128, 142, 162
Przyboś, Julian, 73–77, 81, 103,
105, 152, 175
Psychic numbing, 26–27

R

Rape, 209–10
Ration cards, 98
Redemption, 32
Rosenbloom, Noah, 6
Resistance
armed in Auschwitz, Bialystok,
Bendzin, Czestochowa, Cracow,
Sobibor, Treblinka, Warsaw
passive, 210
in poetry, 11
role of poetry in 133–34
in the Warsaw ghetto, 53, 146, 203
Zelbshutz (Jewish self-defense
groups) for, 145
Ringelblum, Emanuel, 20, 40, 96,
133, 157, 191
Rosenfeld, Alvin, 190
Roskies, David G. 1–3, 21
on Sutzkever, 29, 169
Rousset, David, 8–9, 62
Rowecki, Stefan ("Grot"; General),
168
Różewicz, Tadeusz, 102–3, 152
Rubisztajn, 98
Rudashevski, Yitshak 111, 113
Rudnicka forest, 143, 145
Rumkowski, H., 125

S

Sachs, Nelly, 7–8
  "O the Chimneys" by, 8
Sartre, Jean-Paul, 80
Schenker, Alexander M., 175
Schools in ghettos, 100, 200
  Sutzkever's "The Teacher Mire"
    on, 106–117
Self-censorship by survivor-poets, 29
Shakespeare, William, 206–07
Shayevitsh, Symche-Bunem, 5
  Lekh-lekho by, 69
Shekhina imagery, 35–36, 80
Sherwin, Byron, 87
Sholem Aleichem, 21, 83
  in Sutzkever's "The Teacher
    Mire," 113, 116
Silence, 9, 128, 183
Skamander movement, 21, 152, 175
Skarżysko concentration camp,
  194–98, 204, 206, 207–10
Sonderkommandos, 206
Songs, 98–99
  lullabies, 119–30
Soviet Union, 162
Spiegel, Isiah, 5, 129
  "Close Your Precious Eyes"
    (Makh Tsu di Eygelekh) by,
    120–22
  "Neither Raisins nor Almonds"
    (Nit Keyn Rozhinkes un Nit
    Keyn Mandlen) by, 122–24
Steinr, George, 189–190
Stern, Jonas, 118illus.
Street singers, 96–98
Suhl, Yuri, 157
Suicides, 104
Surreal, the
  in Jastruń, 183
  in Miłosz, 184, 186
  in Sutzkever, 35, 57, 142, 156
Sutzkever, Abraham, 5–7, 39, 73
  "To the Anniversary of the
    Ghetto Theater" (Tsum Yortog
    Fun Ghetto Teater) by, 138–44

"A Cartload of Shoes" (A Vogn
  Shikh) by, 53–58
"Chant of a Jewish Poet in
  1943" (Gezang Fun Yiddishn
  Dikhter in 1943) by, 77–82
"The Circus" by, 29, 167
concert organized by, 83
"First Night in the Ghetto" (Di
  Ershte Nakht in Ghetto) by,
  27–37, 167
"Grains of Wheat" (Kerndlekh
  Veyts) by, 66–67
"The Heart's Voice" (A Shtim
  Fun Harts) by, 135–37
introspection in, 27, 82
"The Lead Plates of the Rom
  Press" (Di Blayene Platn Fun
  Roms Drukeray) by, 165–171
linguistic manipulations in, 27
lyricism in, 27, 82
Miłosz and, 175
mysticism in, 165
pantheism in, 27, 57
romanticism in, 27, 165
"Three Roses" by, 29
"Song at the Departure to the
  Forest" (Bagleytlid Baym
  Avekgeyn in Vald), by 159,
  160, 162–65
"The Teacher Mire" (Di Lererin
  Mire) by, 106–117
Szeintuch, Yechiel, 1, 9–10
Szlengel, Władysław, 5, 6, 10, 14,
  20–21, 39–41
  "Call in the Night" by, 17–18
  "Counterattack" (Kontratak) by
    146–57, 186
  "It's High Time" (Już czas) by,
    83–93
  Sutzkever compared with, 29
  Sztuka (Art; cabaret) and, 12
  "Telephone" (Telefon) by, 21–27
  "Things" (Rzeczy) by, 41–53,
    56, 110
  "This I Read to the Dead" (Co
    czytałem umarłym) by, 100–106

"Windows Facing the Other Side"
(Oknona tamtą stronę) by, 11
Sztuka (Art; Warsaw ghetto caba-
ret) and, 12, 20

T

Theaters, 12
children's, in Warsaw ghetto, 201
Sutzkever's poem to, 138–44
Treblinka, 48, 84, 88, 90–93, 156, 182
Tuwim, Julian, 41

U

Übermenschen, 153
Umschlagplatz, 197
United Partisans Organization
(FPO; Vilna ghetto), 145
Universalism, 159–160

V

Vilna Ghetto
children in, 125
concert (Yiddish literature read-
ing in), 83
destruction of, 161
resistance in, 134
secret culture of, 100
Sutzkever's "A Carload of
Shoes" on, 54
Sutzkever's "The First Night in
the Ghetto" on, 27–37
Sutzkever in, 27, 29, 83
Sutzkever's "To the Anniversary
of the Ghetto Theater" in,
138–44
Sutzkever's "The Teacher Mire"
as history of, 110
United Partisans Organization
(FPO) in, 145
Weapons in, 169

Wilcza Lapa Hospital and, 169
Yiddish Theater in, 12
Yung Vilna (literary movement)
in, 4
YIVO Institute for Jewish Re-
search in, 66

V

Volkovisky, Alek, 125

W

Wailing Wall
Jastruń's "Here Too as in Jerusa-
lem" on, 182–84
Wandering Jew image, 50
Warsaw ghetto, 46*illus.*, 202*illus.*
Aktion in, 47–48
bunkers in, 100–04, 203
cauldron in, 47, 49
children's theaters in, 201
deportations to Treblinka from, 48
destruction of, 161, 181, 183
Einkesselung in, 47
January insurrection in, 146,
153–156
Jewish self-defense cadres in, 145
Judenrat in, 40, 48
Kaplan on, 9, 33
literary cabarets, cafes, and the-
aters in, 12
not giving in to despair in, 104
poetry in, 95–96, 133–34
schools in, 100, 200–01
secret archives in, 97*illus.*
secret culture in, 100
slave factories in, 155
street singers in, 96–98
socialist organization in, 145
Szlengel in, 20–21
Szlengel's "Counterattack" on
resistance in, 146–57
Szlengel's "Things" on, 45, 51, 56
Umschagplatz in, 197
uprising in, 53, 161, 203

Warsaw ghetto (continued)
Zionist organizations in, 145
Weapons
of Soviet-backed partisans, 162
Sutzkever's "The Lead Plates of
the Rom Press" on, 165–71
Wiesel, Elie, 187, 189–90
Wiesse, Ruth R., 37, 106, 115, 137
Wittlin, Józef, 174–76

Y

Yanasowicz, Yitzhak, 28
Yiddish poetry
folk tradition in, 71
lullabies, 119–30
post-World War II, 6
set to music, 11–12
in Warsaw ghetto, 95–96
Di Khaliastre, Di Yunge, and *In
Zikh* movements in, 4

YIKOR (*Yiddishe Kultur Organi-
zatsye;* Yiddish Cultural Organi-
zation), 95–96
YIVO Institute for Jewish
Research, 12, 66, 96
Yunge, Di (poetic movement), 4
Yung Vilne (Young Vilna; literary
movement), 4, 27, 82

Z

Zelbshutz (Jewish self-defense
groups), 145
Zionist organizations, 3, 145
Zich, In (Introspectivists; literary
movement), 4
Znicz, Michał, 201
Z Otchłani (Out of the Abyss;
Apenszlak, editor), 173, 175
Zukerman, Itzhak, 168, 171
Żywy Dziennik (Living Daily;
journal), 20